How to Supercharge & Turbocharge GM LS-Series Engines

Revised Edition

Barry Kluczyk

CarTech®

CarTech®

CarTech®, Inc.
6118 Main Street
North Branch, MN 55056
Phone: 651-277-1200 or 800-551-4754
Fax: 651-277-1203
www.cartechbooks.com

Edit by Bob Wilson
Layout by Hailey Samples

ISBN 978-1-61325-490-5
Item No. SA180

Library of Congress Cataloging-in-Publication Data

Names: Kluczyk, Barry, author.
Title: How to supercharge & turbocharge GM LS-series engines / Barry Kluczyk.
Other titles: How to supercharge and turbocharge GM LS-series engines
Description: Revised edition. | Forest Lake, MN : CarTech, Inc., [2019]
Identifiers: LCCN 2019002045 | ISBN 9781613254905
Subjects: LCSH: General Motors automobiles–Motors–Superchargers. | General
  Motors automobiles–Motors–Turbochargers. | General Motors
  automobiles–Motors–Modification.
Classification: LCC TL215.G4 K58 2019 | DDC 629.25/040288–dc23
LC record available at https://lccn.loc.gov/2019002045

Written, edited, and designed in the U.S.A.
Printed in China
10 9 8 7 6 5

DISTRIBUTION BY:

Europe
PGUK
63 Hatton Garden
London EC1N 8LE, England
Phone: 020 7061 1980 • Fax: 020 7242 3725
www.pguk.co.uk

Australia
Renniks Publications Ltd.
3/37-39 Green Street
Banksmeadow, NSW 2109, Australia
Phone: 2 9695 7055 • Fax: 2 9695 7355
www.renniks.com

Canada
Login Canada
300 Saulteaux Crescent
Winnipeg, MB, R3J 3T2 Canada
Phone: 800 665 1148 • Fax: 800 665 0103
www.lb.ca

CONTENTS

DEDICATION

To Mary Kluczyk

ACKNOWLEDGMENTS

I wish to acknowledge and thank the following for their assistance and support during the creation of this book: Brian Thomson and the technicians at Thomson Automotive; Joe Borschke at Stenod Performance; Dan Millen and the technicians at Livernois Motorsports; and Shari McCullough-Arfons and Sunpro; and Aaron Schoen.

A longtime cliché of the automotive world is the phrase "they don't build 'em like they used to." When it comes to the performance capability of the General Motors Gen III/Gen IV engines (commonly known as "LS" engines), that old adage couldn't be truer—but not in the traditional sense.

The LS engines aren't built like the old small-blocks, and that's a good thing. They've proven to be very durable and, with their exceptional airflow capabilities, they are capable of tremendous power with comparatively little work. Add a supercharger or turbo system to one of these compact powerhouses and the dyno numbers go through the roof. In fact, the only factor that holds back an LS engine from making astronomical horsepower is the amount of boost that can be safely shoved through it.

I first encountered the LS engine when the rest of the performance public did in the late 1990s. I was shooting stories at a variety of tuning shops and was, frankly, suspicious of the chassis dyno numbers that were being generated by LS1-powered F-Body cars and Corvettes with bolt-on superchargers. Compared to what the previous GM LT1 engines produced and the amount of time and money the Mustang guys were spending to get power out of their 4.6-liter pony cars, the ease at which 500 rear-wheel horsepower was spitting out of the LS-powered vehicles raised more than a few eyebrows. But, as time progressed and GM increased the displacement and performance range of its well-engineered new engine family, big power has become the norm. In fact, street cars pushing 900 hp and more are not hard to find.

Of course, there's more than one key required to unlock such supercharged performance. The high-flow attributes of the cylinder heads are tailor-made for big power, but it wouldn't be possible without easily adjustable factory controllers that enable tuning that are the envy of the Mustang and Hemi camps. The controllers, however, are mostly limited to the fuel they can direct into the engine and, in most cases, that ceiling is around the 1,000-hp level. After that, special injector requirements typically mean a stand-alone aftermarket controller that can handle them. But even then, the engine can still be tuned for streetable, pump-gas drivability.

This book outlines the basics of supercharging and turbocharging, as they're applied to LS engines. It doesn't suggest either method of forced induction is better than the other but points out the performance differences, installation challenges, and cost implications between them. There are also great tips for building an engine to support higher-boost combinations.

Whether you're looking for a simple bolt-on blower kit on an otherwise-stock fifth-generation Camaro or a custom-fabricated twin-turbo system for a Corvette Z06, you'll find plenty of ideas to ponder within these pages. And you'll see everything from a $46,000 turbo-kit installation to a homemade turbo system built with cast-off and salvage-yard parts.

If you're new to the performance world or, more specifically, the corner of it that involves forced induction, do yourself a favor and start browsing the online message boards and forums for ideas, and ask around for recommendations on knowledgeable and reputable tuning shops. Before you spend what will minimally be several thousand dollars on a blower or turbo system for your vehicle(s), you'll want to know unequivocally that it's going to deliver the performance you're seeking.

There's another old automotive saying: "Speed costs money; how fast do you want to go?" I believe that can be rewritten for the LS engine this way: Horsepower requires boost; how much can you afford?

Whatever your answer, a little forethought and some careful planning will ensure you'll come away satisfied when that boost-gauge needle swings into positive manifold pressure territory.

A Note about GM "LT" Engines

Although architecturally similar to the LS family of engines, the GM Gen V "LT" engines are not covered in this book. At the time this updated edition was published, aftermarket forced-induction support was mostly limited to bolt-on supercharger kits for popular applications such as the Camaro, the Corvette, and full-size trucks. And while many of the same general theories apply to LT engines, tuning support for them was also somewhat limited at the time of this writing. For these reasons, the author's focus is strictly on the LS-series.

LS Engines and Forced Induction

In general terms, and assuming everything else is equal, an internal combustion engine with larger displacement flows more air than a smaller-displacement engine. The engine with the greater airflow makes more power.

Forcing more air into an engine than it naturally draws can substantially increase the output of a smaller engine and give it the power of a larger engine. The forced or ambient air is delivered to the intake manifold at a pressure greater than the outside. It is denser, delivering more oxygen to the combustion chamber. When mixed with the appropriate ratio of additional fuel, the result is a more powerful combustion. That's the essence of supercharging; whether through an engine-driven supercharger or exhaust-driven turbocharger.

The technology for forced induction supercharging and turbocharging internal combustion engines has been around since the early 20th century, with automotive manufacturers employing the power-boosting effects for more than 80 years. Both supercharging and turbocharging are currently used on dozens of

Forced induction has been used to boost the power of engines for decades. Hot rodders made it a common practice after World War II, and engine-driven supercharging became popular on street and drag racing cars.

regular production automobiles, and they have been staples of the high-performance world since the close of World War II.

One of the most popular performance engines of today is GM's "LS" family. As technology progresses, it continues to become an increasingly popular choice for forced induction. Since its introduction in the late 1990s, the GM Gen III/Gen IV engine family (commonly known as LS) has proven itself as a capable foundation for high-performance engines. By relying on a conventional, cam-in-block configuration

General Motors experimented with turbocharging in the early 1960s and perfected it in the mid-1980s by combining it with electronic fuel injection. The turbocharged and intercooled V-6 engine of the 1986–1987 Buick Grand National outperformed most V-8s when new.

with the benefit of exceptionally high-flowing cylinder heads, the LS engine delivers tremendous torque at low RPM and great power at the upper rev range.

Forced induction was attempted with early LS engines, often with mixed results. Early adopters of supercharging and turbocharging typically encountered tuning trouble when they tried to work around the factory engine-control system and crank-triggered ignition system. That, and the greater airflow capability of the LS heads, made it difficult to match a supercharger or

In the early 1990s, General Motors adopted supercharging for a number of V-6-powered midsize and large passenger cars, including the Pontiac Grand Prix. The automaker used a Roots-blown 3.8L engine with a supercharger supplied by Eaton. The engines proved exceptionally robust and powerful, spawning a cult of enthusiasts who continue to modify and race the vehicles.

GM's relationship with Eaton superchargers reached its zenith in 2009 with the introduction of the factory-blown Corvette ZR1. With its sixth-generation supercharger atop its 6.2L V-8, the ZR1 is rated at 638 hp. It is the most powerful production car ever produced by General Motors. (Photo Courtesy General Motors)

Along with the Corvette ZR1, General Motors launched another factory-supercharged car in 2009: the Cadillac CTS-V. Like the ZR1, it featured a sixth-generation Eaton supercharger on a 6.2L engine, but the supercharger was smaller, resulting in only 556 hp. (Photo Courtesy General Motors)

turbocharger to the engine. Often, the blowers ran out of breath.

But much has changed in the years since tuners first experimented with supercharging the LS engine. Properly sized superchargers and turbochargers, relatively easy tuning, and other elements have made supercharging or turbocharging an LS-powered vehicle a simple, yet highly effective, method of generating a dramatic increase in power.

Of course, General Motors itself has adopted supercharging as a regular production method of building big power. The C6 Corvette ZR1's LS9 engine and the Gen II Cadillac CTS-V's LSA engine used Roots-type superchargers to make 638 hp and 556 hp, respectively. The engines were also designed with specific components to support forced induction.

LS Family Tree

The engine family commonly called the LS series debuted in 1997. General Motors called it the Gen III Small-Block with the iron-block versions in trucks and the all-aluminum LS1 version introduced in the then-new C5 Corvette. A year later, the LS1 replaced the Gen II LT1 Small-Block in Camaros and Firebirds. The LS1 displaced 5.7 liters, similar to the previous-generation small-block, but the cubic-inch measurement differed slightly: 346 for the LS1 versus the traditional 350.

In 1999, the Gen III platform spawned the higher-performance LS6 that was standard in the Corvette Z06. In 2005, the Gen IV branch of the LS family was born, differing from

An LS1 5.7-liter Gen III is shown. (Photo Courtesy General Motors)

the Gen III with cast-in provisions for fuel-saving cylinder deactivation, larger displacements, and revised camshaft sensing. The performance versions of the Gen IV include the LS2, LS3, LS9 supercharged, and LS7.

This is an LS3 6.2-liter Gen IV. (Photo Courtesy General Motors)

GM has continued to refer to its modern V-8 engine family as Gen III and Gen IV, but to the enthusiasts who quickly grasped the tremendous performance potential of the engines, every engine based on the platform is nicknamed "LS." The range of production engines from the LS platform is wide. On the truck side, iron-block engines have included 4.8L and 5.3L versions, as well as all-aluminum 6.0L and 6.2L premium engines. Car engines include 5.3L, 5.7L, 6.0L, 6.2L, and 7.0L displacements, including some configured for front-wheel drive.

Gen III Versus Gen IV

Despite some significant differences between Gen III and Gen IV cylinder blocks, all LS engines share common traits that include:

- 4.400-inch bore centers (matching the original small-block)
- Six-bolt, cross-bolted main bearing caps
- Center main thrust bearing
- 9.240-inch deck height
- Four-bolts-per-cylinder head bolt pattern
- 0.842-inch lifter bores
- Distributorless, coil-near-plug ignition system

The most distinguishing differences between Gen III and Gen IV cylinder blocks are larger bores (on some engines), different camshaft position sensor locations (front timing cover area on Gen IV blocks and top-rear position on Gen III blocks), and on most Gen IV blocks, cast-in provisions for GM's Active Fuel Management cylinder deactivation system.

There is great interchangeability between all LS engines, including between Gen III and Gen IV versions. Cylinder heads, crankshafts, intake manifolds, and more can be mixed and matched, but the devil is in the details. Not every head matches every intake manifold and not every crankshaft works with every engine combination. Will Handzel's *How to Build High-Performance Chevy LS1/LS6 V-8s* is a great reference source that outlines the more specific differences and interchangeability among Gen III-based engines.

LS1/LS6

LS1 5.7L (346-ci) engines were produced between the 1997 and 2004 model years in the United States (Corvette, Camaro, Firebird, and GTO) and stretching into 2005 in other markets (primarily Australia). The LS6 was introduced in 2001 in the Corvette Z06 and was manufactured through 2005, where it also was found in the Cadillac CTS-V. The LS1 and LS6 share a 5.7L displacement, but the LS6 production engine uses a unique block casting with enhanced strength, greater bay-to-bay breathing capability, and other minor differences. The heads, intake manifolds, and camshaft also are unique LS6 parts.

LS2/L76/L77

In 2005, the LS2 6.0L (364-ci) engine and the Gen IV design changes debuted. In GM performance vehicles, it was offered in the Corvette, GTO, and even the heritage-styled SSR roadster. It was the standard engine in the Pontiac G8 GT (L76) and is now the V-8 offered in the Chevrolet Caprice Police Pursuit Vehicle (L77). This engine is one of the most adaptable in the LS family, as LS1, LS6, LS3, and L92/L94 cylinder heads work well on it.

LS3/L99

Introduced on the 2008 Corvette, the LS3 brought LS-based performance to an unprecedented level: 430 hp from 6.2L (376 ci). The LS3 block not only had larger bores than the LS2 but also a strengthened casting to support more powerful applications, including the LS9 supercharged engine of the Corvette ZR1. The LS3 was also the standard engine in the fifth-generation Camaro SS and was offered in the Pontiac G8 GXP. The L99 version was equipped with GM's fuel-saving Active Fuel Management cylinder deactivation system and was standard on fifth-generation Camaro SS models equipped with an automatic transmission. A unique version of the LS3 used in some C6 Corvette Grand Sport applications incorporated a dry-sump oiling system.

LS4

Perhaps the most unique application of the LS engine in a car, the LS4 was a 5.3L version used in the front-wheel-drive Chevrolet Impala SS and Pontiac Grand Prix GXP. The LS4 had an aluminum block and unique, low-profile front-end accessory system, including a "flattened" water pump, to accommodate the transverse mounting position within the Impala and Grand Prix. It was rated at 303 hp and 323 ft-lbs of torque.

LS7

A legend in its own time. The LS7 was the standard engine in the C6 Corvette Z06 and fifth-generation Camaro Z28. Its 7.0L displacement (427 ci) made it the largest LS engine offered in production vehicles. Unlike LS1/LS6, LS2, and LS3 engines, the LS7 uses a Siamese-bore cylinder block design, which was required for its big 4.125-inch bores. Competition-proven heads and light-weight components, such as titanium rods and intake valves, made the LS7 a street-tuned racing engine with 505 hp. Chevrolet Performance's crate engine reflects the Camaro Z28 version, which features a unique Tri-Y exhaust manifold design.

LS9

The LS9 was the 6.2L super-charged and charge-cooled engine of the C6 Corvette ZR1, rated at 638 hp. The LS9 used a strengthened 6.2L block with stronger roto-cast cylinder heads and a sixth-generation 2.3L Roots-type supercharger. Like the LS7, it used a dry-sump oiling system.

Pictured is an LSA 6.2-liter super-charged Gen IV. (Photo Courtesy General Motors)

LSA

This supercharged 6.2L engine powered the 2009–2015 Cadillac CTS-V series and the 2012–2015 Camaro ZL1. Although similar to the LS9 in design, it was built with several differences, including hypereutectic pistons versus the LS9's forged pistons and a smaller 1.9L supercharger. It also has an eight-bolt flywheel versus the LS9's nine-bolt pattern. The LSA has a unique charge-cooler design on top of the supercharger (with differences between the Cadillac and Camaro ZL1 applications). It was rated at 556 hp in the CTS-V and 580 hp in the Camaro ZL1. Chevrolet Performance's crate engine reflects the Camaro ZL1 application.

Gen III and Gen IV Vortec Truck Engines

Although performance car engines have typically carried "LS" designations, truck engines built on this platform have been dubbed "Vortec." They are generally distinguished by iron cylinder blocks and smaller displacements than car engines. Interestingly, a 5.7L Vortec "LS" engine has never been offered. Here's a quick rundown of production LS truck engines.

4.8L: The smallest-displacement LS engine (293 ci); it uses an iron block with 3.78-inch bores and aluminum heads.

5.3L: The most common LS truck engine, it uses the same iron block with 3.78-inch bores as the 4.8L, but with a larger, 3.62-inch stroke (327 ci). Later versions equipped for Active Fuel Management and 2010-and-newer versions feature variable valve timing (cam phasing). Manufactured with iron and aluminum cylinder blocks.

6.0L: Used primarily in 3/4-ton and 1-ton trucks, the 6.0L (364 ci) uses an iron block (LY6 or L96) or aluminum block (L76) and aluminum heads with provisions for Active Fuel Management; some are equipped with variable valve timing.

6.2L: Commonly referred to by its L92, L9H, or L94 engine codes, the 6.2L (376-ci) engine uses an aluminum block and heads and incorporates advanced technology, including variable valve timing. The L92 was used primarily as a high-performance engine for the Cadillac Escalade and GMC Yukon Denali.

More About the Vortec 5.3L

With more than 10 years in service in millions of Chevy and GMC trucks, vans, and SUVs, the Vortec 5.3L engine is poised to become the classic 350 small-block of the LS engine family. They are readily available and affordable on the used engine market. Most feature iron cylinder blocks, but some have an aluminum engine block that is about 80 pounds lighter.

Adapting a 5.3L to a hot rod project is easier with Chevrolet Performance's 5.3L controller kit (part number 19256514), which is tailored to retrofit installations by "turning off" some of the production features that are unnecessary for a vintage car, including the cylinder-deactivating Active Fuel Management. It covers 2007–2009 applications (non-cam-phased) with the following engine codes:

- LC9 (2007–2009)
- LMG (2007–2009)
- LY5 (2007–2009)
- LH8 (2008–2009)
- LMF (2008–2009)

An L94 Vortec 6.2L Gen IV is shown. (Photo Courtesy General Motors)

Chevrolet Performance LS and LSX High-Performance Crate Engines

Chevrolet Performance has offered a number of LS high-performance crate engines based on production LS engines or the racing-oriented LSX series of components, including the cast-iron LSX Bowtie Block. They include:

LS376/515: Based on the LS3, it features the "ASA Hot Cam" to help push output to 525 hp and 477 ft-lbs of torque. It is designed for a carburetor.

LS376/525: Similar to the LS376/515, this version also uses the ASA Hot Cam, along with an LS3-based induction system and port fuel injection.

LSX376-B8: An economical crate engine that uses the LSX block, LS3 rotating parts, and the LS3 cylinder heads. It is offered without an oil pan or induction system, so that it can be tailored for the project vehicle.

LSX376-B15: Designed to accommodate additional power adders, or boost up to 15 psi, includes forged pistons, forged crank, and six-bolt LSX-LS3 cylinder heads.

LSX454: The displacement of the classic big-block with an all-forged rotating assembly and LSX-LS7 six-bolt cylinder heads. It is rated at 627 hp with a carburetor and 580 with an LS7 fuel-injection system.

LSX454R: A high-compression (13.1:1) version of the LSX454 designed for drag racing, featuring a mechanical roller cam, high-rise intake, and more. It is capable of more than 750 hp.

Supercharging Versus Turbocharging

At their most basic, turbochargers and superchargers are air pumps but with different pumping characteristics. The turbocharger is an exhaust-driven pump that saps no engine power when not making boost. A supercharger is an engine-driven pump that is essentially another component on the accessory drive system and requires a modicum of power to drive, even when it's not producing much or any boost.

The thermal efficiency, also known as adiabatic efficiency (the amount of combustion energy that is converted to power), is generally greater with a turbocharger system than a supercharger because it recycles a significant amount of exhaust energy to spin the compressor. That exhaust energy is lost to the exhaust system in normally aspirated and supercharged engines. That said, centrifugal and Lysholm (screw-type) superchargers can be up to 85-percent efficient, for comparable efficiency with a turbocharger.

In general terms, superchargers deliver greater power and torque at low- and mid-range RPM levels with nearly full boost available immediately at wide open throttle (WOT). A supercharger's effectiveness tends to trail off at higher RPM, while turbochargers typically deliver their greatest power contribution at mid- to high-RPM levels, with boost building progressively in line with an increase of engine speed. Turbochargers are also very good at building mid-range torque, and when properly sized, can deliver excellent low-end power too.

There are a number of factors to consider before purchasing a bolt-on system. The performance requirements and engine demands for custom combinations and racing applications are different, but

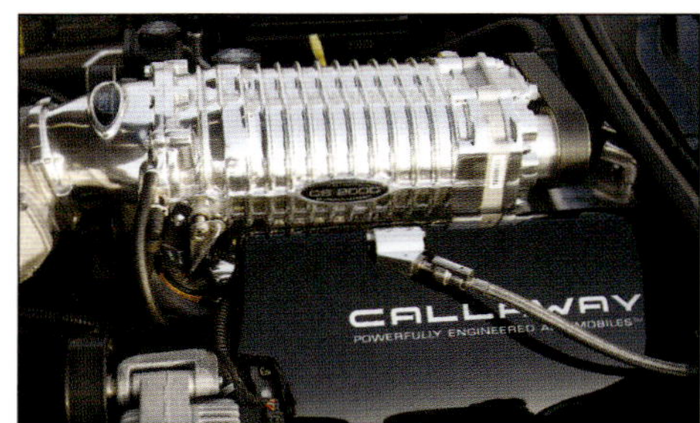

Superchargers (particularly Roots and screw-type blowers) are excellent at delivering low-RPM power, as they are always making at least a minimal amount of boost when the engine is running. That's because the supercharger is directly linked to the crankshaft via the drive belt. That connection also requires a small amount of horsepower to simply turn the supercharger.

Excellent airflow characteristics of the basic LS cylinder head design greatly exploit the benefits of forced induction, as air is easily and quickly moved through the engine. Because of this, a higher-capacity supercharger or larger turbo is often used, when compared to older, previous-generation Chevy small-block designs, to fulfill the airflow capability of a free-flowing LS engine.

for the enthusiast seeking to add a forced-induction system to his or her vehicle, the following points are the most relevant.

Power Projections

Generally speaking, a supercharger will produce about 6 percent greater horsepower for every pound (0.07 bar) of boost, while a turbocharger will produce about 7 percent greater power for every pound. The turbo's advantage there is due to the parasitic loss of the supercharger's drive system. It simply costs some

Turbochargers require no engine power to drive and, therefore, are considerably more efficient than an engine-driven supercharger. However, boost only occurs when the engine RPM rises. At low speeds, particularly off idle, the turbocharger provides no horsepower increase.

power for the crankshaft to drive the blower. The exhaust-driven turbocharger doesn't have such a drag.

Apart from the capacity to change the drive pulley on some superchargers, the output of a blower is pretty much determined by the size of the compressor. With a turbo system, a number of elements are easily manipulated to increase power. In fact, the almost-infinite adjustability of turbo systems is one of their primary appeals.

Performance Range

As noted earlier, superchargers (particularly Roots/screw types) generally deliver gobs of low-end power and become less efficient at higher RPM. The opposite is generally true for turbochargers; they tend to deliver their greatest performance as maximum boost is delivered with higher engine speed.

Drivability

Because an engine-driven supercharger is always "on," it tends to give a street-driven vehicle an abundance of off-the-line/low-speed pull; to the point where it is difficult to manage part-throttle driving in some instances, as tire spin becomes an issue. The higher-RPM power application of turbo systems typically makes

The advantage of turbocharging in a racing application is clearly illustrated in this partially constructed fourth-generation Firebird, as two very large turbochargers were adapted to an LS engine. Except for the older, "71"-series superchargers used in Top Fuel, Top Alcohol, and some Pro Mod–type drag racing classes, there aren't Roots and screw-type superchargers that deliver the airflow of a pair of extra-large turbos. Even large centrifugal blowers are limited to only one per engine. With a pair of turbos, each driven by half of the cylinders, the only real limit is keeping the engine itself together under maximum boost.

Modern Roots and screw-type superchargers make excellent choices for street-driven performance vehicles, as they deliver instant power at low speeds. They're also quieter and offer greater drivability than ever before. And when compared to custom or bolt-on turbo kits, they are very cost effective.

them more tractable at low speeds. The enthusiast wishing for supremacy off the line at stoplights with the instant application of full boost will probably enjoy a supercharger; while the enthusiast seeking a wider performance range will likely find a turbo system more rewarding.

Noise

Generally speaking, the compressors of most supercharger and turbocharger systems are very quiet these days. Turbos are essentially silent until they start spinning at high RPM, and the same is true for most Roots/screw-type blowers. Centrifugal superchargers are much quieter than they used to be, but at idle, they're not as quiet as turbos or Roots/screw-type superchargers.

Tuning

There's no real advantage between tuning a supercharged or turbocharged engine, as the need to maintain an adequate air/fuel ratio and optimal spark to avoid detonation is paramount with both methods. Both types of systems have unique needs for delivering safe, optimal performance, but the basic approach to tuning is similar. There's no clear advantage to either system.

Maintenance and Reliability

When installed and used properly, supercharger and turbocharger kits are very reliable with the compressors for both lubricated with engine oil, although some Roots/screw-type blowers feature self-contained lubrication systems. Over time, the drive belt for a supercharger must be inspected just like the engine's standard accessory belt, and after a few years, the compressor may require an inspection to ensure the tolerances and clearances are within specification limits for the rotors. Turbochargers are very susceptible to heat, and even with adequate lubrication, the internal seals and turbine can wear and allow oil blowby. This requires the turbo to be rebuilt.

System Cost

Because of a myriad of extra equipment (from the wastegate to the exhaust manifolds), turbocharger bolt-on kits generally cost two to three times more than supercharger kits. Additionally, turbocharger systems generally take longer to install than supercharger kits. This adds up when outsourcing the project to a professional shop.

Installation Impact on the Vehicle

Assuming all turbocharger and supercharger systems employ an intercooler, the Roots/screw-type supercharger systems generally require the fewest compromises and/or fabrication modifications during installation. Because they install in place of the intake manifold, few changes are required at the front of the engine or in the engine compartment. Consequently, they offer the most integrated, factory-looking appearance under the hood. Centrifugal superchargers require a mounting bracket on the front of the engine that can require moderate modification, removal, or relocation of factory components.

With bolt-on turbocharger systems, the installation of the exhaust manifolds, turbochargers, and associated plumbing typically require considerably more fabrication, modification, and relocation of stock parts than supercharger systems. An intercooled turbo system can also take up more real estate under the hood, particularly when using larger turbochargers. That can induce a number of fitment challenges that require additional fabrication to overcome.

A couple of the biggest advantages of a supercharger for a primarily street-driven vehicle is comparatively easy installation and a lower labor investment. Bolt-on kits (particularly Roots/screw-type systems that essentially swap out the original intake manifold) can be installed relatively quickly with little impact on the rest of the vehicle's components or systems. The quicker the installation, the lower the labor cost at a professional shop.

Installation Cost

Again, because of the extra equipment associated with them, turbocharger kits are generally more time consuming to install, and therefore, there are more labor costs.

So, while a turbo kit offers greater performance potential, the cost involved with this investment may steer some toward a supercharger. In fact, there are other factors to consider before ordering a system for your car.

For one, the tight confines of the engine compartments in Corvettes, Camaros/Firebirds, and GTOs/Monaros make packaging and installing a turbo kit very difficult. This not only makes the installation a painstaking and difficult procedure but can make future servicing all but impossible without an extensive teardown of the vehicle's front end.

There is more room in the engine compartments of full-size trucks, SUVs, and TrailBlazer SSs; but stuffing a turbo system can be a challenge in a regular street car.

My opinion is that turbocharging is great for vehicles destined to spend equal time on the street and strip; but for typical, street-driven vehicles, a supercharger system is the easier and more economical method to build power. Many tuners and manufacturers that fall on the turbo side of the argument will undoubtedly disagree; but when it comes to bolt-on, forced-induction kits, superchargers are easier and cheaper to implement with less maintenance.

Understanding Boost (Including PSI Versus Bar)

Whether it is a supercharger or a turbocharger system, the measure of pressurized air fed into the engine is referred to as "boost." It is the difference between the ambient air pressure and the increased air pressure that the boost-producing device generates at the intake manifold. Boost is the opposite of vacuum, which is what a nonboosted engine makes during normal operation.

When an engine isn't running, it generates no vacuum or boost (negative pressure), meaning the pressure in the intake manifold is the same as the ambient air pressure: about 14.7 pounds per square inch (psi). At idle and low-throttle conditions, an engine generates vacuum, indicating the pressure in the intake manifold is lower than the ambient pressure.

In a supercharged or a turbocharged engine, boost is created as more throttle is applied and the boost-generating device forces air into the intake manifold at a higher pressure than ambient (positive) pressure. The air pressure at the intake manifold swings from negative to positive; that's why high-performance boost gauges indicate both vacuum and boost measurements.

Boost is generated when the supercharger or the turbocharger creates air pressure greater than ambient when it is introduced to the engine (at the throttle body). Supercharged engines generate a small amount of boost whenever the engine is running, even at idle. Turbocharged engines require higher RPM to generate boost.

In North America, boost is generally measured in PSI, while bar is more common in other countries. When measuring in psi, the ambient air pressure is regarded as the base, or 0 pounds of boost. The positive pressure builds on that base with 1 pound of boost indicating 1 psi greater than ambient pressure.

With bar measurements, bar is roughly the equivalent of ambient air pressure. Technically, 1 bar is equivalent to 14.7 psi, not 14.5 psi, but many enthusiasts equate it to the normal atmospheric pressure, so a 0.5-bar pressure reading is roughly 7.25 pounds of boost. A full, 1-bar reading would indicate 14.5 pounds of boost.

Drag Racing

Turbochargers are common among Outlaw-type drag racing classes, where the virtually unlimited boost potential from increasingly larger turbos has enabled tremendous power levels. Simply put, superchargers haven't matched turbos for boost capability. That is changing with a new generation of larger, higher-flow superchargers, led primarily by ProCharger.

With the weight breaks offered to supercharged cars in many classes, the boost capability of the latest blowers puts racers on par with turbocharged competitors. Racer Tom Kempf, who has driven a turbocharged 10.5 Outlaw Firebird for more than a decade, is ready for the change.

"I've had a lot of success with turbochargers, but that has come with a number of compromises," Kempf says. "First and foremost is these big, powerful turbo engines are very hard on transmissions, when it comes to staging and building boost at the starting line. That's not an issue with a supercharger."

Supercharger systems are much less complex than turbo systems with far less plumbing. That reduces fabrication time during the vehicle's build and makes it easier to do between-round maintenance. The bottom line is turbochargers are still the power adder of choice for most racers, but the tide is turning.

"Turbo cars may still be running the quickest times," says Kempf. "But it seems that, more and more, the blower cars are winning the races. If we can get the boost we need from a blower, I'm ready for the change."

A new generation of centrifugal superchargers is challenging the boost capability of turbochargers that have long ruled Outlaw-type drag racing, offering comparable boost capability with less plumbing complexity and reduced stress on the transmission, particularly when staging.

LS Performance Potential

Simply put, the performance potential of a boosted LS engine is almost unlimited. Whether simply adding a bolt-on kit to an otherwise unmodified engine or building an engine from the ground up to support a larger horsepower goal, the parts are available to do it all, including dedicated performance cylinder blocks designed to withstand nearly 30 psi of turbocharged boost and more than 2,000 hp.

Realistically, most enthusiasts and builders are aiming for something more modest in a street-driven or street/strip car. But the already high power levels of stock LS-powered vehicles (from the 305 hp of the 1998–2002 LS1-powered F-Body cars to the 505 hp of the LS7-powered Corvette Z06) means the return on a supercharger or turbocharger investment will be impressive.

In most cases, a standard street-based bolt-on supercharger or turbocharger kit adds approximately 100 to 125 hp. Bolt-on twin-turbo systems can approach or exceed 200-hp gains, but extreme care must be taken with tuning on an engine with a stock rotating assembly, as factory-installed cast pistons and rods don't stand up long if detonation occurs, or even if there is excessive heat from a slightly lean air/fuel mixture.

In fact, when a forced-induction system is planned to exceed the stock engine's output by more than about 150 hp, the builder should consider fortifying the engine with forged rotating parts and lower compression pistons.

Cast Rotating Parts: Pushing the Factory Parts' Envelope

Production LS engines (except the C6 ZR1's LS9, the Gen V Camaro ZL1, and the Cadillac CTS-V's LSA) weren't designed for supercharging. And while the basic engine design has proven to be remarkably durable, the cylinder pressure generated by a supercharger or a turbocharger takes its toll on the engine's internal components.

The only LS engine from the factory to come with forged pistons was the LS9. All of the rest (the LS7 and LSA included) use hypereutectic (cast) aluminum pistons. Powdered metal rods and a mix of cast and forged crankshafts are used as well, but the bottom line is the basic rotating assembly was *not* designed for the rigors of forced induction.

That's not to say the factory parts don't withstand forced induction. In fact, typical bolt-on blower and turbo kits survive very well with otherwise-stock engines. Generally speaking, however, bolt-on kits deliver less than 15 pounds of boost and vehicles that are primarily street driven don't see extended use at wide open throttle.

When tuned properly, stock engines survive admirably. It's when the boost level is turned up and the vehicle's use sees increased racing duty that the longevity of the factory internal components is reduced. (See chapters 8 and 9 for engine-building guidelines, including the use of forged rotating components.)

Compression Ratio and Recommended Boost Limits

Another performance limitation when using forced induction on an LS engine with stock internal components is the high compression ratio. The engines in most popular LS-powered performance vehicles, from the LS1-powered F-Bodies to

Perhaps the ultimate demonstration of forced-induction LS power is the twin-turbocharged 1996 Impala SS built by GM Performance Parts. Its 400-ci LSX iron-block engine produces more than 2,000 hp with help from a pair of 88-mm turbos.

When building a forced-induction combination that's planned to exceed the performance level of a bolt-on kit with relatively mild boost, the investment in stronger rotating parts must be made. Most LS production engines don't come with a forged crankshaft, rods, or pistons. They're must-have items to ensure engine strength and durability.

the LS7-powered Corvette Z06 have comparatively high compression ratios that range from 9.0 to 11.0:1.

A high compression ratio supports greater power output but increases the tendency for the engine-damaging conditions of detonation and preignition. Those conditions can be especially hard on the factory-installed cast pistons. As a result, the boost pressure on otherwise-stock engines should be limited to prevent damage and ensure performance longevity.

Most intercooled/charge-cooled, street-intended bolt-on supercharger and turbo kits deliver between 5 and 8 pounds of boost, and that's sufficient for stock-engine vehicles. Some kits push toward 10 pounds (with turbo kits easily tuned to deliver much more), but anything more than about 12 pounds is pushing the boundary of engine safety. Enthusiasts and builders seeking more than about 12 pounds of boost from an LS engine should consider rebuilding it with forged rotating parts and a lower compression ratio of approximately 9.0 to 9.5:1.

Production Engine Compression Ratios	
GEN III Engines	
LS1 5.7L	10.1:1
LS6 5.7L	10.5:1
Vortec 5.3L (early trucks, including SSR)	9.5:1
Vortec 5.3L (later trucks)	9.9:1
Vortec 4.8L (truck applications)	9.1:1
GEN IV Engines	
LS2 6.0L	10.9:1
LS3 6.2L	10.7:1
L99 6.2L (2010+ Camaro SS with Active Fuel Management)	10.4:1
LS4 (front-drive application)	10.1:1
LS7 7.0L	11.0:1
LS9 6.2L	9.1:1
LSA 6.2L	9.0:1
L92/L94/L9H 6.2L	10.5:1
Vortec 6.0L (various truck applications)	9.4, 9.6, and 10.8:1

Crankcase Ventilation

LS engines have a tendency toward blowby, where combustion gases and engine oil slip past the piston rings. The condition is exacerbated with forced induction, which can push a considerable amount of oil out the engine in a relatively short period; and the factory positive crankcase ventilation (PCV) system may not accommodate the additional pressure introduced by a turbocharger or a supercharger.

Some turbo and supercharger kits include replacement valve cover breathers, but they may not be sufficient in some cases. Installing larger breathers and possibly a catch can for oil may be required. In racing applications, the engine may benefit from a vacuum pump. However, the bottom line for builders is: be prepared for blowby.

Importance of Tuning and Avoiding Detonation

The previous sections that described boost levels, compression ratios, and forged engine components are all tied together by the importance of proper tuning of a forced-induction engine. Without it, even the strongest engine parts don't last long under pressure if the air/fuel ratio is too lean or the engine is prone to detonation.

Detonation is the uncontrolled combustion that is typically caused by excessive heat in the cylinders, whether through a too-lean air/fuel mixture or other factors. The added heat generated by a blower or a turbo system makes forced-induction engines extremely susceptible to detonation, particularly under high load and higher boost levels.

A high compression ratio can also contribute to detonation, making it important that an otherwise-stock engine (especially an LS engine with

Because production LS engines have relatively high compression ratios, extreme care must be taken to avoid detonation with superchargers and turbo systems. Bolt-on kits can be tuned to minimize the risk, but lower-compression pistons should be used when building an engine for greater power and higher boost levels.

Enhanced crankcase ventilation is essential in a boosted LS engine to quell crankcase blowby. In some cases, a catch can for oil may be required in addition to conventional breathers.

---

its comparatively high compression ratio) is tuned properly to prevent detonation at all costs. Many builders are adept at installing the hardware of a turbocharger or supercharger system but don't have the knowledge to upload the proper software when it comes to the engine controller. Anyone who isn't proficient at tuning should leave it to someone who is (see chapter 7 for more tuning details).

Charge Cooling/Intercooling

To put it simply, compressing air, as superchargers and turbochargers do, generates heat. In the engine, that means an increase in the inlet air's (the boosted air that enters the engine) temperature of up to 200°F at 8 pounds of boost.

Hotter inlet air significantly reduces the effectiveness of the boosted air charge because it is less dense than cooler air. It also makes the engine more susceptible to detonation. A charge-cooling system, commonly called an intercooler, combats the effects of a hotter cooling system by forcing the air charge through a radiator-like device to reduce its temperature before it enters the engine at the throttle body. Because of the concern for detonation on LS engines with their relatively high compression ratios, almost all bolt-on super-

charger and turbocharger kits include a charge cooler.

There are two basic types of charge coolers: air-to-air and liquid-to-air (also known as water-to-air). With an air-to-air intercooler, the boosted air charge simply blows through a "radiator," where air rushing over the fins provides the cooling effect. A liquid-to-air system is more like a conventional radiator and includes a dedicated circuit of coolant (typically a 50-50 mix of antifreeze and water, just as in the engine's radiator).

Generally speaking, a liquid-to-air charge-cooling system is more effective on higher-powered, street-engine combinations and racing combinations. It requires a separate cooling circuit, a coolant reservoir, and an electric-driven water pump.

Auxiliary Instruments

Keeping tabs on a force-inducted engine usually requires instruments that aren't found in a vehicle's standard gauge cluster. That means adding auxiliary gauges, and it's a process that's been done as long as hot rodders have been experimenting with power adders (since the 1940s and 1950s).

A quick scan of any performance parts catalog or website reveals dozens of different instruments, all

seemingly vital to monitoring engine performance. But when it comes down to it, there are four gauges that are more important than the rest when used with supercharged and turbocharged engines.

Boost Gauge: A simple instrument to install by tapping into a vacuum source on the engine (usually by inserting a T-fitting where a vacuum hose is located on the intake manifold), it delivers a reading of positive manifold pressure when the supercharger or the turbocharger is generating boost. For most bolt-on supercharger and turbo systems, a gauge with a maximum range of 15 to 20 pounds of boost is adequate. Higher-boost gauges are available in 30- and 60-pound ranges.

Fuel Pressure Gauge: More important than the boost gauge is the fuel pressure gauge, which can provide a glimpse of inadequate fuel pressure and give the driver the opportunity to shut off the engine before a lean-out condition causes engine damage. An electric gauge is preferred for the higher fuel pressure of the electronically controlled injection systems found on LS engines. Because of the obvious safety concerns of tapping into the fuel system to draw the pressure reading, high-quality fittings and lines (including braided steel) must be used. Typically, the fuel sys-

A charge-cooling system not only helps deliver more power through a denser intake charge but it is especially important on street-driven cars to stave off the engine-damaging effects of detonation with the high compression ratio of internally stock engines.

Auxiliary gauges complement the forced-induction system, keeping tabs on the boost, fuel pressure, and more.

tem is tapped at the Schrader valve on the fuel rail or the fuel pressure regulator.

Air/Fuel Ratio Gauge: Like the fuel pressure gauge, an air/fuel ratio (AFR) gauge can indicate a potentially damaging lean condition, but it is also helpful for monitoring the mixture to optimize tuning across the RPM band. Installation is fairly simple. It simply connects to the wiring of the oxygen sensors, whether factory-style narrowband or wideband sensors. It is possible to split the connection so at the flick of a switch, the AFR from each cylinder bank is read separately. Or for the ultimate in engine minding, a pair of AFR gauges can be used to simultaneously monitor each cylinder bank.

Pyrometer (exhaust-gas temperature gauge): The pyrometer is more useful with turbocharged engines, where the exhaust temperatures can be extremely high. Excessively high exhaust temperature can indicate a lean fuel condition, restricted engine air supply, or a damaged turbocharger. Installation involves connecting the gauge to a thermocouple that is mounted on the exhaust manifold ahead of the turbocharger. Pyrometers are typically offered with maximum ranges of 1,200 to 2,400°F. Lower-range gauges should suffice for most low- and moderate-boost turbo engines.

Forced-Induction Terms

Throughout this book, a number of terms are used to describe or support specific characteristics, components, and performance related to forced induction. Reviewing them through the definitions below will enhance your comprehension of the following chapters.

Adiabatic Efficiency: The amount of heat generated when air is compressed by the supercharger or turbocharger in relation to the amount of the air compressed. Superchargers and turbochargers typically have adiabatic efficiency ratings of 50 to 75 percent. A 100-percent efficiency rate equals no heat generated during compression.

Air Compressor: With either a supercharger or a turbocharger, it is the fanlike device that blows pressurized air into the engine's air inlet.

Air Density Ratio: The difference between the denser air under boost and the outside air.

Air/Fuel Ratio (AFR): The mass difference between air and fuel during the combustion process. For gasoline engines, the optimal (see Stoichiometric) AFR is 14.7:1, or 14.7 times the mass in air to fuel. A higher number indicates a leaner mix (lower fuel content in the mix). A lower AFR number indicates a richer mix (one with greater fuel content). A lean mixture (one with a higher air/fuel ratio) can lead to detonation.

Blow-off Valve: A vacuum-actuated valve that releases excess boost pressure in the intake system of a supercharged or a turbocharged engine when the throttle is lifted or closed. The excess air pressure is released to the atmosphere.

Boost: The pressure of compressed air at the intake manifold that is generated by the supercharger or turbocharger. It is generally measured in pounds per square inch (psi) or bar. A 1-bar measure is equal to 14.7 psi.

Boost Controller: A device used to limit the air pressure that acts upon a turbocharger's wastegate actuator to control the maximum boost at the engine. It can be a mechanically or electronically controlled device.

Bypass Valve: Similar to a blow-off valve, it is a vacuum-actuated valve designed to release excess boost pressure in the intake system of a turbocharged car when the throttle is lifted or closed. The air pressure is recirculated back into the nonpressurized end of the intake (before the turbo) but after the mass airflow sensor.

Charge Cooler: A radiator-like device that is used to dissipate or reduce some of the heat generated by the compression of the boosted air charge, enabling greater power and/or helping reduce or eliminate the tendency for detonation.

Detonation: Abnormal and uncontrolled flame activity in the combustion chamber that can cause engine damage, typically due to excessive heat. In a forced-induction engine, detonation is generally caused by a lean fuel mixture, too-high compression, improper tuning, or a combination of all three.

Heat Exchanger: The radiator-like part of a charge-cooling system.

Intercooler: See Charge Cooler.

Preignition: Similar to detonation, preignition is a potentially catastrophic condition whereby heat retained in the cylinder causes the spark plug to act like a diesel engine's glow plug, igniting the incoming fuel charge before the piston reaches the top of its stroke. A cooler air charge can reduce the chance of preignition.

Stoichiometric Combustion: The ideal combustion process that completely burns the air/fuel mixture. Generally speaking, an AFR of 14.7:1 in a gasoline engine delivers stoichiometric combustion (see Air/Fuel Ratio).

Turbine: The part of a turbocharger that is acted upon by the engine's exhaust gases. Hot exhaust gases flow into the turbine, spinning it. In turn, the turbine spins the corresponding air compressor that blows fresh air into the engine.

Turbo Lag: The time difference between the application of the throttle and the power boost delivered by the turbocharger.

Wastegate: A boost-pressure-activated valve that allows excessive exhaust gas to bypass the turbocharger's turbine. It is used to control boost pressure.

Real-World Project: Larry Dye's 1,300-hp Gen V Camaro SS

"Small" isn't part of a Texan's vocabulary, so it should come as no surprise that when Gen V Camaro enthusiast Larry Dye wanted to hit the street and strip with something that would make a big impression, he didn't bother messing around with the stock 6.2L LS3 for very long. He went with a force-fed LS-based 427 engine boosted by a couple of turbos and a 200-shot of nitrous waiting in the wings for that final push over the edge.

"It makes about 1,300 horsepower to the tires," says Dye. "That may seem like overkill for a street/strip car, but it actually is drivable. You can drive it on the street comfortably or drive it to the track, change the tires and rip off a few 9-second ETs."

What's even more intriguing is the deceptive appearance and street-driving demeanor of the car. Apart from the roll bar inside, the interior is pretty much stock; at least, it's not a gutted, tin-covered race car cabin. The same goes for the exterior. There are no wings, extraneous scoops, or other race car accoutrements.

"The understated appearance wasn't necessarily intentional, because I didn't set out to build a dedicated race car at first. I just wanted a fast street car," says Dye. "The car evolved from a 650-horsepower supercharged combination with the original LS3 to a twin-turbo system on the LS3, which wasn't up to the power and punched a rod through the aluminum block. It was then that I doubled down with a new builder with a built-for-bear LSX engine, but we found the limits of that block before it was recently improved. Now, we're using a Dart LS Next block for the foundation."

Along with the Dart block, there's a Callies Magnum forged-steel crankshaft (4.000-inch stroke), a set of Wiseco pistons (4.125-inch bores), and 6.125-inch-long Callies Ultra H-beam connecting rods. There's also a custom-grind COMP Cams camshaft. Atop the rotating assembly sits a pair of LSX-LS7 six-bolt, high-flow ported cylinder heads delivering 410 cfm worth of airflow on the intake side and 275 cfm on the exhaust side (at 0.600-inch lift). The heads feature Del West 2.20-inch titanium intake valves and Manley Inconel exhaust valves measuring 1.61 inches, all complemented by Manley 0.700-inch-lift dual-coil valve springs and COMP Cams tool steel retainers. They are secured to the block via ARP 2000 head studs.

It's a solid, durable long-block that absorbs 23 pounds of boost generated by a pair of Precision Turbo & Engine hybrid 62/66-mm ball-bearing turbochargers. They blow into a Precision Metal Craft sheet metal intake manifold, where the pressurized air charge is mixed with fuel delivered via 140-lbs/hr injectors mounted in Aeromotive LS7 fuel rails. There are a couple of TiAL Q-series blow-off valves, too, to relieve pressure, along with an HKS EVC-V boost controller. The injectors are fed by a Weldon fuel pump in addition to the output from the OEM fuel pump.

The car makes this power on a street-friendly 93-octane tune, though they do use just a hint of water/methanol injection (from a custom-fabricated tank in the trunk) as a safety factor to help keep the charge temps down in the blistering Houston summer heat.

It's a combination that has proven durable on the street and strip, proving there's virtually no limit to boosted LS performance.

Larry Dye's twin-turbocharged street/strip Camaro SS runs low-9-second ETs.

With 23 pounds of boost feeding the engine in Larry Dye's Camaro, a sheet metal intake is used for safety instead of a factory-style plastic intake that could crack or shatter. The engine makes 1,300 hp with a pair of Precision Turbo & Engine ball-bearing turbos.

SUPERCHARGER TYPES AND SELECTION

Superchargers come in many different shapes and sizes, but they are related by a common attribute: they generate boost pressure via an engine-driven mechanism. Typically, superchargers are driven by a belt connected to the crankshaft.

When it comes to the commercially available superchargers for LS engines, there are two basic types: positive displacement and centrifugal. Positive displacement superchargers are "draw-through" designs, where the air charge is compressed *after* the throttle opening. Conversely, centrifugal superchargers, like turbochargers, are a "blow-through" design, where the air is compressed *prior* to entering the engine through the throttle opening.

Positive-Displacement Superchargers

Positive-displacement superchargers are those that spin a pair of multilobed rotors that mesh tightly to squeeze air through an outlet under high pressure. The displacement is derived from the amount of air delivered with each revolution of the supercharger. Typically, the

Most enthusiasts and hot rodders were introduced to street supercharging with the "Jimmy"-style Roots superchargers that originated on large truck and bus engines but were adapted to automotive engines. Although impressive looking and sounding, these blowers are pretty inefficient, but they're guaranteed to draw a crowd on cruise night.

larger the rotors, the more air the supercharger displaces.

Within the spectrum of positive-displacement superchargers are Roots types and Lysholm types. Following are design details and operational differences of the various supercharger types.

Roots-Type Supercharger

The Roots-type supercharger is an engine-driven air pump that contains a pair of long rotors that are twisted somewhat like pretzel sticks. As they spin around each other, incoming air is squeezed between the rotors and pushed under pressure into the engine, forcing more air into the engine than it could draw under "natural" aspiration. The rotors are driven by a pulley and belt that are connected to the engine's accessory drive system.

With a Roots blower, a discharge hole is located at one end of the supercharger case. As the rotors mesh and squeeze air, it is forced at high pressure through the discharge hole. It is relatively efficient, particularly in the later designs refined by OEM supplier Eaton.

The Roots blower was used on a variety of high-end automobiles in the early 20th century, including Cords, Bentleys, and Mercedes, but it really made its mark on the

---

aftermarket performance world when it was used on GMC-built transit buses of the 1930s and later. The buses used large superchargers to pump up the horsepower of their diesel engines. By the 1950s, enterprising drag racers began attaching GMC (also known as "Jimmy") blowers to automotive gasoline engines, and the rest is history.

The 71-series GMC blowers were adapted to street cars too. Those are the iconic superchargers seen reaching through the hoods of so many vintage street machines and Pro Street hot rods.

To the generation of late-model performance enthusiasts, Roots blowers are synonymous with Eaton superchargers. That company pioneered the use of smaller-displacement, low-profile Roots blowers on everything from Jaguars to the Pontiac Grand Prix GTP. The Corvette ZR1 uses an Eaton supercharger too.

Although Blower Drive Service offers manifolds to adapt the classic, tall 71-style blower to LS engines, those considering a Roots-type supercharger system for their vehicle are selecting one with an Eaton compressor.

Refinements to Eaton superchargers' rotor design over the years have made them quieter and more capable of greater airflow and boost; the packaging size and rotor speed is the biggest restriction to making tremendous power with them. Look around at professional and semiprofessional drag racers who rely on superchargers or turbochargers for power adders and you see virtually none use an Eaton-type blower. They just don't generate the boost necessary to support a very large displacement or the high-RPM power needs.

That said, Eaton blowers are exceptionally durable, dependable, and on the street make reasonably good power at lower RPM, especially when compared with centrifugal superchargers and turbochargers. The OEM quality of Eaton systems makes them nearly bulletproof and delivers exceptional drivability. They're not loud at low RPM and don't have on/off performance characteristics; the power comes on smoothly and firmly.

And while the hardware (including a custom intake manifold) can make Eaton-based kits somewhat expensive, their installation is clean, unobtrusive, and as close to a factory-style installation as can be found in aftermarket kits. Generally, most Eaton-based bolt-on kits are offered through California-based Magnuson, which developed a number of very popular kits for many LS-powered vehicles. Indeed, many of Magnuson's kits represent the easiest-to-install systems and have earned a reputation for excellent reliability.

Eaton's TVS

The Twin Vortices System (TVS) represents the sixth generation of Eaton's ubiquitous Roots supercharger design. It blends elements of a twin-screw compressor, including a four-lobe, high-helix (160-degree twist angle) rotor design. Previous Eaton superchargers featured a conventional three-lobe design.

As with the twin-screw design, the TVS supercharger was developed to expand the efficiency range of the supercharger to deliver more power at lower RPM and sustain boost at higher RPM while requiring less engine power to drive. And when compared with previous three-rotor designs, the TVS represents a night-and-day difference in overall performance. Wherever possible, the use of the TVS compressor is recommended. It is currently manufactured in 1.9-liter (MP1900) and 2.3-liter (MP2300) displacements. The design also features an internal bypass valve.

The TVS blower was designed primarily for OEM applications. In fact, it was driven by GM's performance and efficiency requirements for the LS9/LSA engines, which represent the first production applications for this new compressor (see "GM Factory-Supercharged LS9 and LSA Engines" later in this chapter).

Since appearing under the hood of the C6 Corvette ZR1 and the Cadillac CTS-V models, the TVS supercharger has grown into the

The C6 Corvette ZR1 introduced supercharging from the factory, relying on an Eaton TVS-based blower to push the 6.2L engine's output to 638 hp. It was the most powerful production engine ever from Chevrolet, and it was eclipsed only by the supercharged LT engines that came later in the C7 Corvette Z06 and ZR1 models. (Photo Courtesy General Motors)

Earlier Eaton-based supercharger systems, such as those found on the 3800 V-6 and larger V-8-size compressor, make excellent, usable power and absolutely help lower a vehicle's elapsed time at the drag strip. However, a comparatively limited power range and a tendency for the compressor to soak up engine heat make them better suited to vehicles used primarily on the street and occasionally at the track. Also, they feature drive pulleys that are pressed onto the drive gear. Swapping them to adjust boost pressure is very difficult and almost impossible to do with the supercharger installed on the engine and in the vehicle. Only specialized pulling tools designed for the job should be used; even then, there's no guarantee damage won't occur to the supercharger's nose section.

aftermarket. Eaton's Magnuson outlet offers a number of bolt-on kits for engines that have either cathedral- or rectangular-port heads. Additionally, Australia-based Harrop Engineering offers TVS-based kits (1.9L and 2.3L versions) for the 6.0L Pontiac GTO/G8 GT, as well as the VE-series Holden Commodore; and Edelbrock offers TVS-based "E-Force" supercharger kits for most popular LS production vehicles.

The newest edition to the Eaton lineup is the TVS 2650, a larger, 2.65L compressor that was introduced on the 6.2L LT5 engine that powered the C7 Corvette ZR1. Aftermarket versions of the blower have been introduced by companies including Harrop, as this larger supercharger promises to elevate the capability and output of LS engines. Besides offering a larger displacement with greater boost capability, the angle or "pitch" of the rotors is greater: 170 degrees versus the previous 160 degrees, contributing to greater overall airflow efficiency.

Lysholm/Twin-Screw Types

The Lysholm-type or twin-screw supercharger is similar in design and function to the Roots type, including squeezing air through a discharge hole in the case to deliver boosted air pressure to the engine.

For those who are building an LS engine for a street rod, a muscle car, or another older vehicle and appreciate the look of the old-school 71-style Jimmy blowers, Blower Drive Service offers supercharger kits for engines that use LS cathedral-port heads. This example was built by Martin Motorsports to be installed in a vintage Chevy II. Note the custom, marine-style intercooler sandwiched between the blower case and the intake manifold. It was the best solution to maintain the vintage drag racing look of the engine with its classic "bug catcher" intake.

Displacing 2.65 liters, the Eaton TVS 2650 produces 14 pounds (0.9 bar) of boost in the C7 Corvette ZR1's LT5 engine. That's about 4.5 psi more than the LT4 engine, but it is achieved with a slower 15,860-rpm maximum rotor speed, which helps keep down the pressurized air charge's temperature. Compared to the rotors in the LT4's supercharger, the LT5s are larger in diameter and have a unique, 170-degree pitch for the four-lobe design versus the previous TVS 160-degree pitch. The higher-pitch angle enhances the blower's efficiency at high RPM, helping it sustain max boost through the top of the RPM band. (Photo Courtesy General Motors)

The Gen V Camaro ZL1's LSA engine used a smaller, 1.7L TVS supercharger compared to the C6 ZR1's larger 2.3L blower. The result was 580 factory-blown horsepower. (Photo Courtesy General Motors)

This photo shows the unique, four-lobe rotors of the Eaton TVS blower. The quartet of lobes combined with the high helix (rotor angle) design gives the blower a quasi-twin-screw look. That's intentional because, similar to a twin-screw design, the TVS delivers greater performance at low and high RPM. (Photo Courtesy General Motors)

The large displacement of the 2.3L TVS compressor helps generate truly impressive performance. In the application seen here, a Harrop-supplied TVS blower was used on a 7.0L LS engine to make nearly 900 daily drivable horsepower on readily available pump gas. The engine was then stuffed into a Pontiac Solstice roadster by Thomson Automotive.

The Eaton compressor-based Magnuson bolt-on kits are very popular for C5/C6 Corvettes, Pontiac G8s, fifth-generation Camaros, and trucks/SUVs, and for good reason. They are relatively easy to install, deliver an excellent return on investment when it comes to horsepower, and have proven to be very durable. However, Corvette applications have underhood clearance problems, and an aftermarket or modified stock hood is typically required.

Edelbrock's supercharger kits use Eaton's four-rotor, 2.3L TVS compressor at their cores. Like the factory LSA and LS9 engines, the E-Force systems feature air-to-water intercooling systems with dual-brick-style heat exchangers mounted on top of the supercharger assembly. Design features of the E-Force system include a front-driven compressor and long, 12-inch intake runners that optimize low-RPM torque. For C6 Corvette owners, the advantage of the E-Force kit is that it mounts under the stock hood.

Based on the technology introduced on the C7 Corvette ZR1's LT5 engine, Eaton-based 2650 (2.65L) compressors are the largest-displacement TVS-style superchargers available. The 2650's rotors are larger in diameter than previous TVS rotors, which raises the overall height of the blower. That can present underhood clearance problems for some vehicles. The kit shown is from Harrop.

Rather than using the intermeshing lobes of the Roots type, the Lysholm uses a pair of worm screw-type rotors that squeeze air together to generate boost. It also generates internal compression, meaning it develops pressure progressively as the air is continually squeezed by the screws on its way to the discharge hole. This can help build more low-end power and deliver more boost at lower RPM. The relative efficiency of twin-screw superchargers is greater than a conventional Roots type. They also enable generally higher boost levels than Roots or centrifugal superchargers, providing 20 pounds or more with some compressors.

Sweden-based Lysholm Technologies AB (a company that has undergone several corporate changes in recent years) is the name behind the technology, and it manufactures many sizes of twin-screw compressors, ranging from 1.2 to 3.3 liters in displacement. Rather than offering retail systems, the company licenses its product to other manufacturers, including OEM companies such as Ford, which used a Lysholm supercharger on the 2003–2006 GT sports car (through a licensing agreement with Eaton that essentially made them Eaton superchargers).

In the performance aftermarket, Whipple Industries is just about the most recognizable name in twin-screw technology. Its Lysholm-type blowers derived from industrial air compressors were adapted to automotive use. For years, Whipple relied on the twin-screw compressors from the company currently known as Lysholm Technologies AB, but since 2005, it has used a twin-screw compressor of its own design. Whipple offers kits for Gen V Camaros, C6 Corvettes, LS-powered trucks, and the Chevrolet SS sedan.

In 2009, Vortech joined the twin-screw blower fray with the addition of a Lysholm-based supercharger of its own. Rather than manufacturing its own blowers, Vortech licensed the compressors from Lysholm Technologies AB and developed its own installation kits. Vortech offers 2.3- and 3.3-liter superchargers. Currently, the only dedicated twin-screw kit for LS engines from Vortech is for 5.3L truck engines. The company also offers "tuner" kits that can be adapted to a variety of LS engines, as long as a suitable manifold is available to match the ports on the cylinder heads.

Another player in the twin-screw market is Kenne Bell. At the time of publication, the company offered several twin-screw supercharger kits for the Gen V Camaro with compressors displacing 2.8, 3.6, 4.2, and 4.7 liters.

The principle of the twin-screw design is a pair of screw-shaped rotors that intermesh much like the rotors of a Roots blower, but the rotors' shapes create internal compression that helps boost low-end power. Whipple designed its own compressor in 2005. It features self-contained lubrication, a large bypass valve, and the capability of up to 30 pounds of boost. It is manufactured in a variety of sizes with many of them larger than the largest-displacement Eaton TVS compressor.

A Vortech supercharger system is installed on a fifth-generation Camaro SS.

This Lysholm twin-screw supercharger system is installed on a fifth-generation Camaro SS.

Vortech's Lysholm-supplied twin-screw supercharger system for 5.3L LS-powered GM trucks includes an integral bypass valve within the supercharger housing. The kit also includes a charge-cooler/intake manifold assembly (with fuel rail mounts), higher-rate fuel injectors, a pump system for the intercooler, and a cold-air-style air intake system. Tuning calibration is provided via a DiabloSport Predator programmer. Similar systems are expected for a variety of other LS-powered vehicles.

Centrifugal Superchargers

Although engine-driven and not exhaust-driven, a centrifugal supercharger generates boost much like a turbocharger. It uses an impeller (similar to a turbine) that spins upward of 40,000 rpm to draw air into the compressor and blow pressurized air into the engine.

The impeller is the engine-driven part of the supercharger, as it is linked via a pulley and belt to the crankshaft. After the impeller draws air into the compressor head unit, it is squeezed and forced into the supercharger's scroll (a chamber within the head unit that funnels the compressed-air charge out of a discharge tube and toward the engine's throttle body). The scroll has a progressive shape that gets larger the farther it is from the center of the head unit. That design feature reduces airflow while simultaneously increasing the air charge's pressure.

Air is compressed in the head unit when it leaves the impeller and is forced into the scroll. A venturi-like outlet, through which the air is forced, creates boost pressure, so the greater the impeller speed and the faster the air moves through the venturi, the higher the boost pressure.

A centrifugal supercharger is comparatively efficient, requiring relatively little engine power to drive, but its downside is the need for very high impeller speed to make horsepower-building boost. That's why centrifugal blowers are known mostly as mid- and higher-range power adders; the impeller speed at lower RPM doesn't make sufficient boost, and once the maximum impeller speed is achieved (usually around the peak horsepower mark), boost levels trail off at higher RPM.

A change to a smaller-diameter drive pulley can add a few extra pounds of boost, but matching a properly sized compressor head unit with the displacement and airflow capabilities of the engine is the key to sustaining power throughout the middle and upper ranges of the RPM band.

The two main players in the centrifugal supercharger business are Vortech Superchargers and Pro-Charger. Another centrifugal blower manufacturer is Rotrex, but currently, there were no direct applications for LS engines. The following is a closer look at the offerings from Vortech and ProCharger.

Vortech Superchargers

Vortech centrifugal superchargers have been mainstays of both the street and racing worlds. Typically, Vortech blowers are known for their relatively quiet performance and engine-oil-fed lubrication system (except for the V-3 compressor). Vortech has also been at the forefront of developing bolt-on kits, which are available for most popular LS-powered vehicles, including the fifth-generation Camaro. Several aftermarket companies, such as A&A Corvette, use Vortech compressors as the basis for tailored supercharger systems (see chapter 5 for details on installation).

Vortech offers a number of different compressors designed for a wide variety of performance requirements. They're also subdivided among "trim" types: X trim, F trim, SCi trim, etc. Here's a quick rundown on them.

V-1 Series: A high-performance compressor with high-speed ball bearings that makes it compatible for high-boost, cog-belt racing applications. Depending on the trim, a V-1 is capable of up to 26 pounds of boost and 1,200 cfm of airflow.

V-2 Series: Lower maximum boost (17 to 22 pounds, depending on the trim) and slightly lower maximum airflow than the V-1, but designed as a direct replacement. V-2 SQ trim is known for exceptionally quiet operation.

V-3 Series: The only internally lubricated compressor in Vortech's portfolio. A V-3 compressor fills the mounting brackets for V-1, V-2, V-4, V-5, and V-7 compressors. Maximum boost and airflow is similar to V-2 compressor trims.

V-4 Series: A racing-intended compressor that Vortech claims is twice as efficient as a Roots blower at 12 pounds of boost. Depending on the trim, a V-4 can produce up to 32 pounds of boost and flow 2,000 cfm.

V-5 Series: Designed for smaller-displacement engines, typically 4- and 6-cylinders, the V-5 is not well-suited to the airflow capabilities of LS V-8 engines.

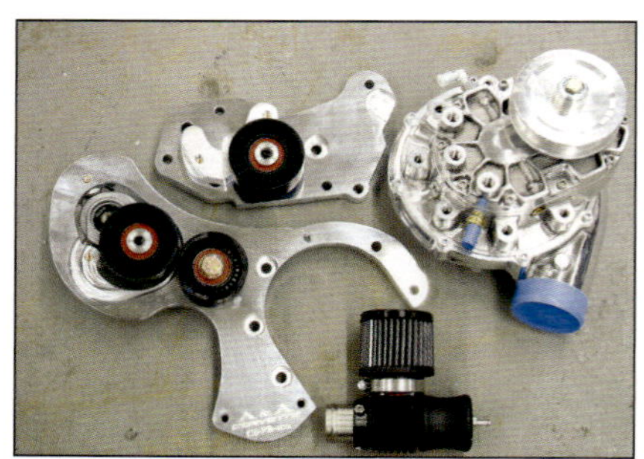

Vortech centrifugal superchargers typically make 6 to 8 pounds of boost in most bolt-on kits, but a range of higher-performing, racing-oriented compressors can supply more than 30 pounds of boost. Most of Vortech's compressors are interchangeable with the company's brackets, allowing you to swap compressors to better suit your engine combination. (See chapter 5 for installation details on a Vortech-based bolt-on system.)

V-7 Series: A high-flow, racing-intended compressor designed for modified engines built to accommodate high boost levels. Depending on the trim, a V-7 can flow more than 1,400 cfm and generate 30 pounds of boost.

V-9 Series: This more compact compressor is designed for engine compartments with little room, such as the fourth-generation F-Bodies. They're also designed for smaller-displacement V-8s (smaller than 400 ci). Maximum boost is about 14 pounds and maximum airflow is 750 cfm.

V-30 Series: Replacing the V-20 series, the V-30 is designed for racing applications and can push enough air to support 1,000 hp with about 35 pounds of boost.

An excellent reference chart of Vortech's various compressors, trims, and boost/airflow capacities is available at vortechsuperchargers.com.

ProCharger

Unlike Vortech blowers, most ProCharger compressors have a self-contained lubrication system, meaning there's no need to tap the oil pan for the oil feed source. Some of the ProCharger compressors are relatively loud, especially at idle, but their street-based blowers have become admirably quiet in recent years. The company offers bolt-on kits for most LS-powered production models, including C5 and C6 Corvettes, fourth-generation F-Bodies, Gen V Camaros, Pontiac GTOs and G8s, and more.

Like Vortech, there are numerous compressors in the ProCharger portfolio with several designed specifically for racing applications. In fact, ProCharger offers the largest centrifugal superchargers, with some capable (including the colossal F-3X-143

ProCharger Compressor Comparison Chart		
Compressor	Maximum Airflow (cfm)	Maximum Boost
P600B	1,200	24
P-1SC	1,200	30
P-1SC-1	1,200	32
P-1SC-2	1,200	30
D-1	1,400	32
D-1SC	1,400	32
F-1	1,525	38
F-1A	1,650	38
F-1C	1,850	38
D-1R	2,000	32
F-1R	2,000	38
F-2M	2,250	40
F-2	2,700	38
F-2R	2,750	38
F-3A-117	2,800	40
F-3A-123	3,100	40
F-3R-131	3,600	45
F-3R-139	4,000	45

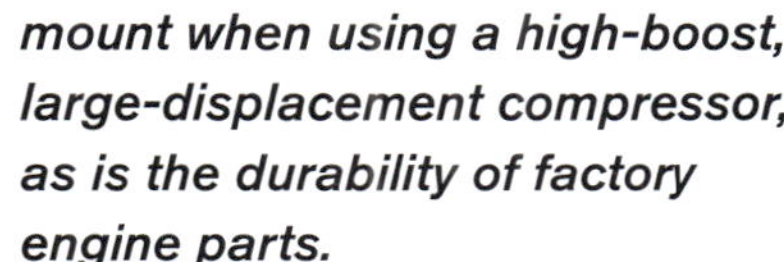

Here's a typical bolt-on ProCharger system on a fifth-generation Camaro SS. As with Vortech superchargers, ProCharger's larger compressors are mostly interchangeable with the bracketry, allowing custom combinations. Proper tuning is paramount when using a high-boost, large-displacement compressor, as is the durability of factory engine parts.

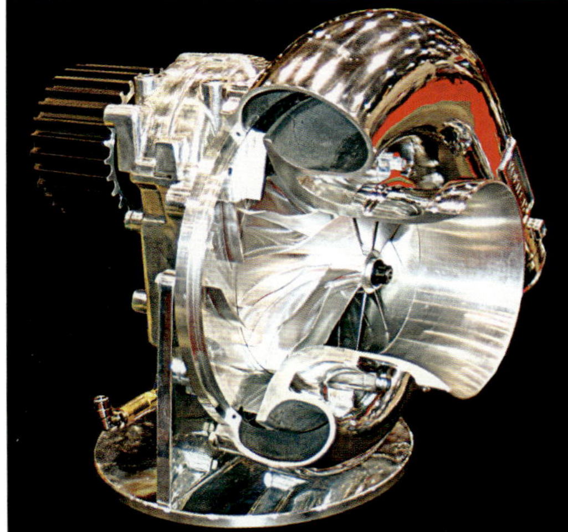

ProCharger's large compressors and cog-style belt-drive systems are designed for racing applications, and several compressors are capable of 40 pounds of boost or more. It is these big blowers that are giving some turbo systems a run for their money in drag racing. This is ProCharger's F3R compressor.

compressor) of producing up to 60 pounds of boost and flowing 4,500 cfm. And with less-complex tubing routing than high-boost turbo systems, ProCharger offers a viable alternative for the street and drag strip.

It is worth reviewing the complete compressor lineups from Vortech and ProCharger before investing in a bolt-on kit or a stand-alone setup for a custom engine project. Take the time to compare their respective performance traits and match them to the goals of your project.

Kit and Cost Considerations

Unlike turbocharger systems, there are a great number of bolt-on blower kits designed to work on stock LS engines. The number of kits changes constantly as new vehicle models are introduced and supercharger manufacturers and other aftermarket companies develop kits for them. For Roots-type systems, Magnuson's kits cover most popular LS-powered vehicles. When it comes to twin-screw systems, there are few choices for vehicles with rectangular-port heads; most are designed for earlier, cathedral-port engines (LS1, LS2, and LS6). Vortech's new twin-screw blower is offered in kit form for the rectangular-port LS3 engine of the Camaro and G8 GXP with more applications expected.

To ensure pump-gas compatibility and to lower the risk of detonation, bolt-on kits typically make less than 10 pounds of boost and deliver around 80 to 125 additional horsepower with preprogrammed tuning. Greater performance is attainable with custom tuning, smaller-diameter pulleys, and the like, but such changes increase the risk of detonation on stock engines with high compression ratios and cast rotating parts.

Of course, cost is an important factor for any enthusiast selecting a supercharger kit. One of the important factors in the centrifugal supercharger's favor is generally a lower purchase cost in kit form when compared with Roots/screw kits. That's because the ability to mount the compressor head unit almost anywhere allows manufacturers to bundle most of the kits with universal components. Typically, only relatively inexpensive mounting brackets and other related components separate, say, a 2006 GTO kit from a 2002 Camaro Z28 system.

The Roots/screw-type systems generally require a dedicated intake manifold that must be matched to the heads, and casting an entire intake manifold is a lot more expensive than laser cutting a steel mounting bracket for a centrifugal blower.

Where Roots/screw blowers can narrow the price gap with centrifugal kits is in the installation labor charge. Typically, it takes less time to install a Roots/screw-type system on most vehicles, as centrifugal blowers typically require more extensive modification of the accessory drive system.

Supercharger Comparison Chart

Manufacturer/ Retailer	Compressor	Cathedral Port Kits	Rectangular Port Kits	Notes
A&A Corvette	Centrifugal	N/A	N/A	Uses Vortech compressors
ATI ProCharger	Centrifugal	N/A	N/A	Systems not dependent on cylinder head design
Blower Drive Service	Roots	Yes	No	Old-school, 6-71-type blower case does not fit under the hood
Edelbrock	Roots	Yes	Yes	Uses Eaton TVS compressor; kits for fifth-generation Camaro, LS2-powered C6 Corvette, and LS3-powered C6 Corvette
Harrop	Roots (Eaton TVS)	Yes	Yes	Kits limited to GTO/Monaro and G8 GT/Commodore; and 2010+ Camaros
Kenne Bell	Twin-screw	Yes	No	Kits for 1997–2004 Corvettes only
Magna Charger	Roots (Eaton, including TVS)	Yes	Yes	Kits for most popular LS vehicles; easy and quick bolt-on installation
Rotrex	Centrifugal	No	No	No LS applications at press time, but they've been long-promised
Vortech	Centrifugal	N/A	N/A	Systems not dependent on cylinder head design
Vortech	Twin-screw	Yes	No	Systems not dependent on cylinder head design
Whipple Industries	Twin-screw	Yes	Yes	Various truck kits and bolt-on kit for the 2010+ Camaro SS

The relative ease of installation and tuning, as well as the limited impact on other factory vehicle systems, makes a bolt-on supercharger an increasingly cost-effective alternative to a custom-built engine. That's exactly what Berger Chevrolet did with the latest versions of its limited-production Berger Camaros. On its earlier fourth-generation models, the dealership sourced custom, 500-hp, naturally aspirated engines that cost much more to build and install than the Magnuson kits used on its fifth-generation cars.

Unlike a Roots or twin-screw blower, which delivers maximum boost at relatively low RPM, a centrifugal (such as this ProCharger D1SC) increases its airflow with the RPM, much like a turbo. Maximum boost comes at the engine's maximum RPM.

Here's the 550-hp engine of the Berger Camaro. It uses nothing more than a Magnuson kit (non-TVS compressor) and the kit's supplied tuning upgrade. It is a simple upgrade that delivers a huge increase in performance.

Positive-Displacement Versus Centrifugal Blowers

When it comes to supercharged horsepower, positive-displacement superchargers and centrifugal blowers produce it differently. In simple terms, a centrifugal supercharger's boost increases exponentially with engine speed, while a positive-displacement supercharger's airflow is linear with maximum boost occurring very low in the RPM band. That means a Roots or twin-screw blower that delivers, for example, 500 cfm of air at 2,500 rpm pushes 1,000 cfm at 5,000 rpm.

With a centrifugal supercharger, boost builds in a nonlinear way, much like a turbocharger. As RPM increases, the airflow from the compressor increases at a faster rate. Because of that, maximum boost is not achieved until the engine's redline, or maximum RPM level.

The differences in airflow delivery create very different performance curves and driving experiences. In general terms, a positive-displacement supercharger has a flatter power curve with more low-RPM power. The centrifugal delivers a greater feeling of increasing power as the revs climb. On the street, and all other things being as equal as possible, a positive-displacement blower feels stronger on the low end, especially directly off idle. A Roots or twin-screw blower makes a small amount of boost whenever the engine is running. The centrifugal, on the other hand, "rolls" into its boost and is generally easier to launch, with a stronger feel through the mid- and upper-range RPM levels.

The nonlinear airflow delivery also makes the centrifugal supercharger better suited for drag racing, because the graduated boost application enables an easier launch, with greater power coming on as the RPM increases. Of course, with peak boost not occurring until redline, the blower's effectiveness is not fully realized at lower RPM.

In general terms, a street vehicle with a positive-displacement blower feels the effects of the blower immediately and at all low-RPM levels, while a centrifugally blown car feels more like stock until around the 3,000-rpm level. There is also a more pronounced application of the power with a centrifugal blower, but not the "on/off" feeling of a turbocharger.

How Much "Blower" Do You Need?

Unless you are adapting a GMC 71-series-style Roots blower, which is offered in tremendous size increments for drag racing, there is a limit to the effectiveness of many bolt-on, underhood-type superchargers. If the supercharger (be it a positive displacement or centrifugal) can't flow enough air to support the engine's high-RPM requirements, horsepower falls off and the effectiveness of the supercharger is greatly diminished. Increasing the boost pressure increases the effectiveness to a certain degree, but in the end a supercharger with a larger compressor is the best way to optimize the blower's performance across the RPM band.

The great airflow capability of LS engines and the larger displacements offered in production and aftermarket versions of the engine make sizing a supercharger particularly important, as the smaller-displacement superchargers that were common on a street car only a few years ago simply don't flow enough to support later and larger-displacement LS combinations.

At the time of publication, the 4.7L Lysholm twin-screw supercharger from Kenne Bell was the largest positive-displacement supercharger offered in bolt-on kits, although the Eaton TVS 2650 blower topped the Roots-type offerings. Whipple offers 3.3-, 4.0-, and 5.0-liter compressors, but none had been adapted to LS engines in bolt-on kits.

When it comes to centrifugal superchargers, both Vortech and ProCharger offer a number of large compressors to suit high-powered street engines and dedicated racing combinations.

matched with a commensurately sized compressor.

Getting the most from a supercharger, regardless of the compressor design, is dependent on flowing enough air to satisfy the airflow capability of the engine. A blower's maximum boost will not be realized on a large-displacement engine that isn't

Positive-Displacement Blowers: Calculating Boost and Increased Boost with a Pulley Change

Changing the supercharger drive and/or the crankshaft pulley/damper is the common method for increasing the boost output of the blower. Generally speaking, reducing the size (diameter) of the supercharger drive pulley will spin the rotors faster to produce more boost. Increased temperature in the boosted air charge is an inevitable byproduct as well. Depending on the engine combination, there can be a point of diminishing return with such a change, but it's the most effective way to increase the output of the supercharger.

Determining the approximate amount of boost a positive-displacement blower such as an Eaton TVS or Whipple will produce, as well as how much more it will produce with a pulley change, is determined with a few simple calculations. First, start with the theoretical max boost of the combination. It's determined with this formula:

$$PR \times 14.7 \times SV / EV \, (\tfrac{1}{2}) - 14.7 = \text{max boost (psi)}$$

Air flowing through the heat exchangers of an intercooling system will reduce the maximum pressure of the boosted air charge before it enters the engine. This cutaway shows the integrated charge-cooling brick on an Edelbrock E-Force supercharger with Eaton TVS 2650 rotors.

PR is the pulley ratio, which is the size of the crankshaft pulley divided by the supercharger pulley. For example: An 8.2-inch-diameter (208-mm) crankshaft pulley and a 3.1-inch supercharger pulley (78 mm) delivers a pulley ratio of 2.64 (8.2 / 3.1 = 2.64).

14.7 is the normal air pressure: 14.7 psi (1 bar).

SV is the supercharger volume in liters. For an Eaton 2300 TVS-type blower, that would be 2.3 liters.

EV is half of the engine volume.

The total engine volume is divided in two because one rotation on a four-cycle engine is only half of a complete cycle. For an LS3 6.2L engine, the engine volume number for the equation would be 3.1L.

14.7, again, is atmospheric pressure.

Putting it all together for an LS3 with a 2300 supercharger and a 2.64 pulley ratio lands at 14.09 pounds of max boost: 2.64 (PR) x 14.7 x 2.3 (SV) / 3.1 (EV ½) – 14.7 = 14.09 pounds of boost (0.97 bar).

Changing the pulley sizes changes the pulley ratio, thereby affecting the maximum boost capability of the compressor. With the example above, changing only the blower drive pulley from 3.1 inches to 2.8 inches (approximately a 10-percent reduction) changes the pulley ratio to 2.93. When plugged into the boost calculation formula, the maximum boost increases to 17.25 psi (1.2 bar).

The comparatively minor change in pulley size makes a significant change in the speed of the supercharger and its output. The caveat here is that a significant increase in boost comes with a significant increase in heat that can lead to detonation.

It is also important to note that the boost calculation formula does not take into account a couple of important factors that will reduce the maximum boost pressure that actually enters the engine. The first is the overlap factor. All engines, even those with blower-friendly camshafts, have a measure of valve overlap, where the intake valve opens before the exhaust valve closes. The amount of overlap determines how much boost is siphoned off; there is approximately 5-percent loss for every 10 degrees of overlap. On a combination with 8 pounds of calculated boost (0.55 bar) and 10 degrees of overlap, the loss is 0.4 psi (0.27 bar), for a total of 7.6 pounds of boost (0.52 bar).

The other factor is the intercooling system and other airflow restrictions. The boosted air charge will lose some of its maximum pressure as it travels through the intercooling circuit's heat exchangers. The bottom line is the maximum theoretical boost will not be the pressure of the air that enters the engine. The formulas given, however, provide guidelines for determining the output of a blower and the expected results of pulley changes.

Centrifugal Superchargers: Calculating Maximum Boost

The airflow output of a centrifugal supercharger increases with the square of its impeller speed. That generally means it makes very low boost at low engine speeds and increases with engine speed.

Calculating max boost for a centrifugal blower, at a given RPM level, starts with determining the engine airflow requirement:

$$D \times RPM / 3{,}456 \times 0.9$$

D is the engine displacement in cubic inches.

RPM is the engine speed.

3,456 is a calculation factor.

0.9 is the estimated volumetric efficiency of the engine without boost.

Let's assume the calculation is for an LS3 engine, which has a displacement of 376 ci, and we're calculating for the engine's performance at 6,000 rpm. The formula works out like this: 376 (D) x 6,000 (RPM) / 3,456 x 0.9 = 587.5. That means the airflow requirement for the engine is 587.5 cfm at 6,000 rpm.

Maximum supercharger boost depends on the airflow capability of the compressor and the displacement of the engine. Because it takes more air to fill the cylinders, the same compressor will produce less boost on a larger-displacement engine.

Next, the max airflow of the supercharger (let's say 1,000 cfm) is divided by the engine's airflow requirement, multiplied by 14.7 (atmospheric pressure) and, finally, one "atmosphere" (14.7) is subtracted from the total to arrive at the theoretical max boost for the given engine speed. It looks like this: 1,000 / 587.5 x 14.7 – 14.7 = 10.32 pounds of max boost (0.71 bar) at 6,000 rpm.

Increasing the supercharger's airflow, moving up from the 1,000-cfm ProCharger C-2 compressor to the 1,500 P-1SC, for example, increases boost at 6,000 rpm to 22.83 pounds of boost (1.57 bar), a 220-percent increase in boost for a 50-percent increase in supercharger airflow.

As with positive-displacement superchargers, the max boost of a centrifugal system is affected by valve overlap and the restriction of the charge-cooling system, as well as other factors, such as ambient air temperature. Similarly, more boost brings more heat, which can lead to detonation without proper tuning considerations.

Music to the Ears?

For many contemplating a supercharger, the sound, or lack thereof, is an important consideration. Whether it's the *whir* of a centrifugal's impeller or the meshing of a set of rotors, superchargers generate sound during operation. Some think it's noise, while others think it's music to their ears.

Generally speaking, centrifugal superchargers are noisier. At least, they make more sound than Roots and screw-type blowers at idle and low RPM. The Roots/screw-type compressors are, for the most part, silent at idle.

Companies, such as Vortech, have worked hard to reduce the low-speed sound of their centrifugal units, while others, like Powerdyne, use quieter, belt-driven impellers rather than gear-driven ones. But for the most part, the sound hasn't been eliminated. If a subtler, stealthier approach is desired, the Roots/screw blower is the way to go. For those who don't mind rolling up to a stoplight and having all eyes focus on the hood area of their vehicle, a centrifugal does the trick.

The Importance of a Charge Cooler

Almost every supercharger and turbocharger kit for LS-powered vehicles includes some type of charge cooler or intercooler to reduce the inlet temperature of the boosted air before it enters the engine through the throttle body. It's necessary to ward off the engine-damaging effects of detonation and/or preignition (conditions LS engines are particularly susceptible to because of their high compression ratios).

In general terms, forced-induction engines are safer with compression ratios in the neighborhood of 8.5 to 9.5:1, but LS engines have much greater "squeeze" from the pistons. The LS7 engine of the Corvette Z06 has 11:1 compression, the LS3 is at 10.7:1, and even the original LS1 engine had a 10.25:1 compression ratio. By comparison, the factory-supercharged C6 Corvette ZR1's LS9 engine was equipped with a blower-friendly 9.1:1 compression ratio.

So, routing the boosted air charge through the cooler reduces the maximum boost level, but it typically enhances horsepower because the cooler air charge is denser than a heat-soaked charge. And it's the only option on vehicles with an otherwise-stock engine assembly.

Surge Protection

Regardless of whether it's a Roots/screw-type or centrifugal supercharger, compressor surge occurs when the blower is making boost, but the throttle suddenly closes, such as when the driver pulls his or her foot off the gas pedal. When this occurs, the blower keeps pushing air into the closed throttle body. When the pressure inside the throttle body is higher than the pressure being generated by the supercharger, air blows back toward the compressor.

In low-boost applications, this isn't a big problem, but with higher boost (more than 10 pounds or so) the comparatively great pressure can cause damage to the engine, supercharger, or both. Venting the excess pressure that builds when the throttle snaps closed is the cure, and that can be done with either a blow-off valve (which vents excess air back into the atmosphere) or a bypass valve (which vents the air back into the compressor).

Pulley Size and Performance

Sometimes not even the installation of an entire supercharger system suits some enthusiasts. They look to extract every pound of boost possible from the blower, and that usually leads to swapping the factory-installed drive pulley for a smaller-diameter pulley.

The smaller pulley typically generates more boost because it forces the rotors to spin faster. You should

Experimentation with supercharger pulley sizes must be done carefully to prevent detonation. Even comparatively small changes in pulley size can have a dramatic effect on increasing boost and, consequently, the chances of detonation.

Adequate belt engagement is a challenge for high-boost supercharged engines that use the factory accessory drive system, as belt slippage can not only affect overall performance but also quickly ruin the drive belt. A dedicated drive system for the supercharger itself is an option but typically not offered in most bolt-on kits.

explore all the performance ramifications of the swap before performing it because the gain may be negligible or lead to a number of other issues that must be addressed, including the following:

- The pulleys on Eaton-based Roots superchargers, such as those sold through Magnuson and Harrop, typically have pressed-on pulleys that require special tools for removal. In fact, the procedure typically requires the removal of the supercharger if it has already been installed on the engine; so, if a pulley swap is considered, have it performed before the supercharger is installed on the vehicle.
- The greater boost of a smaller pulley can push against the engine's threshold for detonation (or exceed it), requiring revised tuning and possibly the use of higher-octane fuel.
- In many cases, the smaller pulley also requires the investment in a slightly smaller drive belt. During the swap, the tensioner and/or other idler pulleys should be inspected for wear.

Another method to increase the boost from the supercharger is a larger-diameter crankshaft pulley/balancer, which spins all of the accessories (including the supercharger) faster. The flip side to this method is that the faster rate is not necessarily healthy for the other accessories. It could affect the performance or shorten the life of the water pump, alternator, and more.

Building boost by changing the blower pulley is not without consequence. Spinning the supercharger faster creates more heat that must be dealt with through the charge-cooling system to stave off detonation. The higher boost and consequentially higher power output of the engine can also lead to belt slippage problems.

Belt Wrap and Belt Size

The drive system of a supercharger puts a tremendous amount of additional load on the belt-driven accessory system of an engine. At high RPM and under maximum boost, a supercharger belt with a production-style, cogless design can slip, robbing horsepower and possibly causing engine damage. Most blower kit manufacturers design the belt drive with a lot of belt-to-pulley contact. This higher degree of "belt wrap" helps mitigate slippage.

For bolt-on blower kits making up to about 12 pounds of boost, inserting the supercharger into the stock, six-rib accessory-drive system generally doesn't cause a problem, especially if the belt routing ensures good belt wrap. When building for a higher boost application, however, a separate, wider belt system should be considered between the blower and crankshaft pulley.

Chevrolet used a wide, 10-rib belt system for the supercharged LS9 engine; and a number of aftermarket companies also offer 10-rib conversion kits for systems aimed at generating more than 12 pounds of boost. The progression of technology, as well as continually larger compressors such as the Eaton TVS 2650, has pushed the limits of what's available for adequate belt coverage. The supercharged LT5 in the C7 Corvette ZR1, for example, uses an 11-rib belt drive to support the engine's 755 hp.

Builders pushing beyond 800 hp on a street-based combination that is intended to include the other engine accessories will be challenged to accommodate the belt size and wrap needs for dependable, slip-free performance. A custom drive system is always an option, but it is a costly one in terms of price and its impact on the other accessories.

GM Factory-Supercharged LS9 and LSA Engines

Launched in 2008, the C6 Corvette ZR1 and Cadillac CTS-V were the first LS production engines from General Motors to use forced induction. Each features an Eaton-developed Roots-type supercharger blowing via a charge cooler into a 6.2L engine.

The ZR1's LS9 engine is rated at 638 hp and 604 ft-lbs of torque, while the CTS-V's LSA engine is rated at 556 hp and 551 ft-lbs of torque. Despite both engines using a similar supercharger design and 6.2-liter displacement, the LSA is not simply a detuned version of the LS9. The engines are built with a number of different components.

The Corvette ZR1 LS9 6.2-liter is shown. (Photo Courtesy General Motors)

Pictured is the Cadillac CTS-V LSA 6.2-liter. (Photo Courtesy General Motors)

Among the most notable differences between the engines are the superchargers. The LS9 uses a 2.3-liter compressor, while the LSA uses a smaller 1.9-liter blower. Both superchargers are based on Eaton's sixth-generation Roots design that features four-lobe rotors for greater efficiency. The comparatively large displacement of superchargers (particularly on the LS9) helps the engines overcome two of supercharging's biggest hurdles: low-end torque and high-end horsepower.

The LS9, for example, makes big power at lower RPM and carries it in a wide arc to 6,600 rpm. GM testing has shown the engine makes approximately 300 hp at 3,000 rpm and nearly 320 ft-lbs of torque at only 1,000 rpm. Torque tops 585 ft-lbs at about the 4,000-rpm mark, while horsepower peaks at 6,500 rpm. The engine produces 90 percent of peak torque from 2,600 to 6,000 rpm.

Both engines are offered through Chevrolet Performance as complete crate-engine assemblies, offering enthusiasts a ready-to-go alternative to building a supercharged engine from scratch. The part number for the LS9 engine is 19201990; the part number for the LSA is 19211708. Supplies, however, are dwindling and supporting components, such as the front-end accessory drive systems, are also in short supply, at the time this book was published.

What follows is a look at the components and processes that comprise these unique powerplants.

Cylinder Block and Rotating Assembly

Both engines feature an aluminum cylinder block with the LS-standard six-bolt main bearing caps. The LS9 uses steel main caps and the LSA uses nodular-iron caps. The block also features enlarged vent windows in the second and third bulkheads for enhanced bay-to-bay breathing. Cast-iron cylinder liners, measuring 4.06 inches in bore diameter, are inserted in the aluminum block, and they are finish-bored and honed with a deck plate installed. The deck plate simulates the pressure and slight dimensional variances applied to the block when the cylinder heads are installed, ensuring a higher degree of accuracy that promotes maximum cylinder head sealing, piston-ring fit, and overall engine performance.

A forged-steel crankshaft delivers the engines' 3.62-inch stroke. On the LS9, it features a nine-bolt flange (the outer face of the crankshaft on which the flywheel is mounted) that provides more clamping strength. The LSA uses an eight-bolt flange. Other (non-supercharged) LS engines have a six-bolt flange. A torsional damper mounted to the front of the crankshaft features a keyway and friction washer, which is designed to support the engine's high loads.

With the LS9, a set of titanium connecting rods and forged-aluminum pistons are used. The LSA uses powdered-metal rods and hypereutectic (cast) aluminum pistons. Both engines have a 9.1:1 compression ratio.

The LS9 is built with forged-aluminum pistons; the LSA comes from the factory with hypereutectic aluminum pistons. (Photo Courtesy General Motors)

The supercharger cases of the LS9 and LSA incorporate dual brick-style heat exchangers for their respective intercooling systems. Here, the top section of the LSA's intercooler cover is removed, showing the triangular discharge port from the compressor. (Photo Courtesy General Motors)

Cylinder Heads

The basic cylinder head design of the LS9 and LSA is similar to the L92-type head found on GM's LS3 V-8, but it is cast with a premium A356T6 alloy that is better at handling the heat generated by the supercharged engine, particularly in the bridge area of the cylinder head between the intake and exhaust valves.

In addition to the special aluminum alloy, each head is created with a roto-cast method. Also known as spin casting, the process involves pouring the molten alloy into a rotating mold. This makes for more even distribution of the material and virtually eliminates porosity (air bubbles or pockets trapped in the casting) for a stronger finished product.

Although the heads are based on the L92 design, they feature swirl-inducing wings that are cast into the intake ports. This improves the mixture motion of the pressurized air/fuel charge. Both engines feature 2.16-inch-diameter intake valves and 1.59-inch-diameter exhaust valves, but the LS9 uses more exotic titanium intake and hollow-stem, sodium-filled exhaust valves.

Camshaft and Valvetrain

The broad power band enabled by the LS9's large, 2.3-liter supercharger allowed GM engineers to specify a camshaft with a relatively low lift of 0.555 inch for both the intake and exhaust valves. It is a low-overlap cam with lower lift and slower valve-closing speeds than the Z06's 505-hp LS7, giving the LS9 very smooth idle and drivability qualities.

Similarly, the LSA's camshaft delivers a relatively low 0.480-inch lift on the intake and exhaust sides. The valvetrains of both engines feature many parts-bin components from the production LS3 engine, including the lifters, rocker arms, and valve springs. However, the LS9 uses the valve-spring retainers from the LS7 engine.

Supercharger and Charge Cooler

Both engines use a sixth-generation supercharger from Eaton. Its primary improvement is a four-lobe rotor design that promotes quieter and more efficient performance. The LS9's R2300 supercharger features a case that is specific to the Corvette ZR1. Its maximum boost pressure is 10.5 psi. The LSA uses the 1.9-liter R1900 compressor and delivers up to 9 psi of boost.

Both engines employ a liquid-to-air charge-cooling system to reduce inlet-air temperature after it exits the supercharger, reducing the inlet-air temperature by up to 140°F. Each charge-cooling system includes a dedicated coolant circuit with a remote-mounted pump and reservoir.

The charge-cooler design differs for each engine because of the production packaging within the cars. The LS9 uses a "dual brick" system with a pair of low-profile heat exchangers mounted longitudinally on either side of the supercharger. The LSA's charge cooler is mounted atop the supercharger, owing to the Cadillac's greater hood clearance. Coupled with the supercharger itself, this integrated design mounts to the intake.

Oiling System

The LS9 uses a dry-sump oiling system that is similar in design to the LS7's system but features a higher-capacity pump to ensure adequate oil pressure at the higher cornering loads the ZR1 is capable of achieving. An oil pan-mounted cooler is also integrated, along with piston-cooling oil squirters located in the cylinder block.

The LSA engine uses a conventional, wet-sump oiling system, but also includes oil squirters in the cylinder block.

Water Pump

To compensate for the heavier load generated by the supercharger drive system, an LS9-specific water pump with increased bearing capacity is used.

Accessory Drive System

To package the accessory drive system in the Corvette's engine compartment, the supercharger drive was integrated into the main drive system. This required a wider, 11-rib accessory drive system to be used with the LS9 to support the load delivered by the supercharger.

Fuel System

Both engines use fuel injectors with center-feed fuel lines. The center-feed system ensures even fuel flow between the cylinders with less noise. To ensure fuel system performance during low-speed operation and under the extreme performance requirements of WOT, a dual-pressure fuel system was developed. This system operates at 36 psi (250 kPa) at idle and low speed and ratchets up to 87 psi (600 kPa) at higher-speed and WOT conditions. The LS9 uses 48-lbs/hr injectors.

Throttle Body

An 87-mm, single-bore throttle body is used to draw air into the LSA; an 89-mm throttle body is on the LS9. Both are electronically controlled.

TURBOCHARGER TYPES AND SELECTION

Swiss engineer Dr. Alfred Büchi is credited with developing the first exhaust-driven turbocharger sometime around 1912. By 1915, he published a proposal for employing a turbocharger on a diesel engine, but the idea was mostly ignored for the next few years. The first real-world applications were in aviation, where turbochargers helped aircraft engines build power in the thin air of higher altitudes.

Turbocharged aircraft engines became more prevalent during World War II but were far from common. General Electric was the big supplier of turbochargers to American aircraft during the war, and that's when J. C. "Cliff" Garrett entered the picture. His company supplied after-cooling systems that were used with GE's turbochargers on B-17 bombers.

After the war, Garrett continued manufacturing gas-turbine engines and experimenting with turbocharging. That led to the formation of a spin-off division of his company called AiResearch Industrial Division. It would later be renamed Garrett Automotive. Proving Dr. Büchi was onto something, but simply a few decades ahead of his time, early automotive-industry uses were targeted at diesel-powered over-the-road trucks, as well as similarly powered industrial engines.

Interestingly, engine-driven supercharging had been used successfully in automobiles since the 1920s, even if it wasn't a widespread technology. Nonetheless, turbocharging didn't arrive on the North American automotive market until the early 1960s, when several import-fighting, rear-engine compacts were released by General Motors. They included the Chevrolet Corvair and Oldsmobile Jetfire, but while performance was adequate, durability and reliability were not.

Turbocharging mostly disappeared for the next 15 years or so, when its use became more widespread in large

Turbocharged and intercooled 1986–1987 Buick Grand Nationals also featured electronically controlled fuel injection, ushering in the modern era of turbocharged performance for a new generation of enthusiasts.

trucks and racing. The technology was also revisited by mainstream auto manufacturers after the fuel crisis of the 1970s as a way to balance performance and fuel economy.

Buick, Ford, and Chrysler developed turbocharged powertrains in the late 1970s, but it wasn't until the advent of modern-style electronic engine-control systems, electronically controlled fuel injection, and intercooling systems that turbocharging became a viable, reliable, and consistent method of building horsepower. Volkswagen and Mercedes-Benz also offered turbocharged models at that time.

The intercooled turbo engine of the 1986–1987 Buick Grand National was a landmark design, not only in factory force-fed GM vehicles but in the advancement of mainstream turbocharging. At a time when many V-8 "performance" cars struggled to offer 200 hp, the intercooled Grand National's 3.8L V-6 was offered with 235 hp (rising to 245 hp in 1987). And while Ford's 2.3L turbocharged engine was offered as a performance engine in the 1980s, the Grand National was the first turbocharged production model that offered a distinct advantage over V-8-powered competitors.

The Grand National shares nothing with the modern LS engine, but the basics of its intercooled turbo system are essentially the same as the aftermarket systems employed today.

A pair of intercooled turbos was adapted to the classic Chevy small-block V-8 to power the Callaway Twin Turbo Corvette. The system was well integrated, and the base 5.7L engine was upgraded with lower-compression pistons and heavy-duty rotating components to support the load of the turbochargers. It was a combination that increased horsepower about 50 percent over the stock Corvette's rating.

This photo illustrates the complexities of designing and/ or installing a custom turbo system, where the requirements for the system's plumbing and the mounting for large turbochargers present problems. For systems intended primarily for racing, concessions can be made by modifying the chassis, but systems for street-driven vehicles can present greater packaging challenges, which adds time and cost, compared to bolt-on supercharger systems.

Here's another F-Body with a turbo system adapted to it. Rather than squeezing a kit around the necessary factory chassis components of a street car, this drag racer is essentially built around the turbo system. This design simplifies many of the installation procedures for the turbo system, but (as is clear from the photo) the car won't be suitable for the street or street legal when completed.

LS-Powered Production Vehicles

A number of turbo kits are available for production LS-powered vehicles and knowledgeable tuning shops can custom build them with the necessary components and good tube-bending skills.

With nearly unlimited performance potential, good low- and moderate-speed driving characteristics and the undeniable aura of exoticness, there's much to like about the prospect of turbocharging a Corvette, Pontiac G8, or TrailBlazer SS. That doesn't mean, however, that it's the most practical solution to building a high-powered street car.

As mentioned in chapter 1, the investment in kit cost and installation labor makes a turbo system typically more expensive when compared with a typical bolt-on supercharger system. There is usually more fabrication required to install a turbo system. I followed the installation of several supercharger and turbocharger systems and found a large gap in the time and special fabrication required between them, ranging from approximately 8 hours for the installation of an intercooled supercharger kit on a Pontiac G8 GT (see chapter 5) to more than 40 hours for a turbo kit installed on a fourth-generation Trans Am.

At shop labor rates of up to $100 per hour, the installation time becomes an important and expensive consideration. On the low end of the labor rate scale, the additional time of the Trans Am's kit versus the G8's would add up to about $2,000.

With the tuning capability and driveline component strength (transmission, axle, etc.) comparatively equal between supercharged and

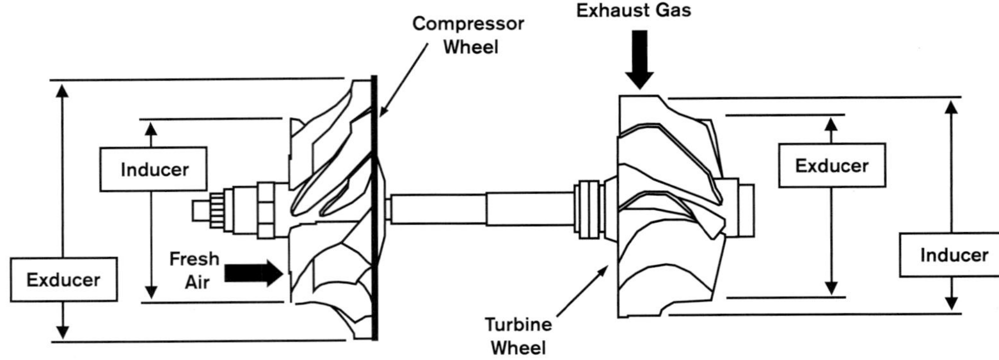

This illustration shows the internal elements of a turbocharger. When the exhaust gas spins the turbine, it simultaneously spins the compressor that is drawing in the fresh air that is forced into the engine. Exhaust gas is not fed into the engine.

turbocharged production vehicles, there's no clear advantage of one over the other. The performance potential with a turbo system is undeniably greater, and for the enthusiast who envisions taking his or her car's performance to higher levels in the future, a basic turbo system is an excellent foundation. System complexity and consequential installation cost, however, should weigh heavily on the decision to invest in one.

Turbocharger Component Terms

As noted earlier, a turbocharger uses engine exhaust to spin the turbine, which is connected via the center hub shaft to the compressor side of the housing to generate boost. The basic components are defined in the following list.

Turbine: The exhaust-driven wheel.

Compressor/Impeller: The wheel spun by the action of the turbine that compresses air and generates boost.

Center Hub Rotating Assembly: The "floating" shaft that links the turbine and compressor/impeller wheels.

Inducer Wheel: The portion of the turbine or compressor wheel where airflow enters it; on a turbine wheel, it is the "major" diameter section, while on the compressor wheel, it is the "minor" diameter section.

Exducer Wheel: The portion of the turbine or compressor wheel where airflow exits it; on a turbine wheel, it is the "minor" diameter section, while on the compressor wheel, it is the "major" diameter section.

For most manufacturers, the general size of the turbocharger is measured in millimeters across either the turbine inducer or the compressor exducer. Racers who must comply with sanctioning rules regarding turbocharger size should check the rules carefully to determine whether the size of the turbo is measured at the impeller inducer or the compressor exducer.

At its very basic, the turbo system channels exhaust gas via an exhaust manifold to the turbine side of the turbocharger. When the turbocharger is mounted directly to or very near the exhaust manifold, the manifold must be sufficiently thick and strong to withstand not only the heat of the turbo system but also the reduction in temperature when the system is not under load or the engine is turned off. Thick cast-iron manifolds traditionally do the best job at this because they resist warping.

With this view of a basic turbocharger, it is easy to visualize its operation. Exhaust gas enters through the rectangular port on the left, which mounts on or near the exhaust manifold and spins the turbine. When the turbine spins, it acts on a shaft that simultaneously spins the compressor on the opposite side of the unit. The spinning compressor draws in fresh air, compresses it, and sends it as the boosted air charge into the engine.

Like the exhaust manifolds in a turbo system, the turbine side of a turbocharger is typically constructed of thick cast iron. The mounting flange (seen here) has a thick pad to resist warping.

The compressor side of the turbocharger is what sends fresh air under pressure into the engine. A common misperception about turbos is that exhaust gas is somehow part of the boosted air charge. It is not. Exhaust gas is only used to spin the turbo in order for the compressor to generate a pressurized charge of fresh air.

Logically, the larger the size of the turbocharger, the more air it can push. However, the larger the turbo, the greater the chance for lag (the delay between the time the throttle is opened and the turbo spools enough to generate boost). Regardless of the size of the turbo, heat is a byproduct that must be dealt with to optimize performance and prevent engine damage.

Operation Basics

Like a supercharger, the turbocharger helps increase engine power through increased volumetric efficiency. It does this by compressing the engine's intake air, making it denser, and forcing it into the engine at greater pressure than normal. When combined with the correct amount of additional fuel to match the denser air charge's correspondingly greater oxygen content, it is a safe and reliable method for increasing the amount of air the engine can pump at a given RPM level.

The additional air delivered by the turbocharger comes from exhaust gas that exits the engine and blows into a turbine. The turbine spins an air compressor that blows fresh air into the engine's intake tract. The turbine and air compressor portions of the turbochargers are separate housings bolted together and linked by an interconnecting turbine shaft.

Generally speaking, the size of the turbocharger determines the volume of air it can generate, or the amount of boost it's capable of blowing into the engine (i.e., the larger the turbo, the greater the boost). That's a simplification of the theory of building horsepower with a turbocharger, but it's suitable for this portion of the discussion.

The boost level is carefully tailored in production vehicles to deliver a balance of on-demand performance and fuel efficiency, along with smoothness and quietness that is acceptable to the 99.9 percent of the car-buying public that isn't interested in running 9-second quarter-mile ETs. In these factory applications, the size of the turbocharger is carefully selected, along with matched turbine and air-compressor sizes.

Whether a tailored factory system or high-performance aftermarket system for an LS engine, all turbocharger systems are affected by factors that influence overall performance and efficiency, including:

Heat: Turbochargers generate tremendous heat that is radiated through the engine compartment. It can elevate the inlet air temperature, reducing boost and possibly promoting detonation or preignition.

Turbo Lag: The time difference between the application of the throttle and corresponding response in boost-induced power. This is typically due to the "spool-up" time it takes for the turbine to get up to sufficient speed to generate boost with the air compressor. Turbo lag has been a longtime detriment to turbocharging with its tendency generally increased along with the size of the turbo.

Turbo Size: A larger turbocharger typically makes more power, but it can also induce greater turbo lag, as it takes a larger turbine more time to spool up. Conversely, a smaller turbocharger may spool up quicker but not deliver the desired power gain or at the desired RPM level.

There is more to turbocharging than can possibly be described and explained in this single chapter. I recommend Jay K. Miller's book *Turbo: Real World High-Performance Turbocharger Systems*. It offers a wealth of more-in-depth information on the theory, design, and application of turbo systems (go to cartechbooks .com for more information).

Dealing with the Heat

The heat generated by a turbo system is part of the price to pay for performance. It uses the already-hot exhaust gases and, rather than immediately expelling them all through the exhaust system, retains a portion to spool the turbine. The heat radiated by the turbocharger can quickly build up in closed or tightly packed engine compartments, such as the fourth-generation Camaro and Firebird or the C5/C6 Corvettes. That heat is generally absorbed by the air intake system, heating the air charge and reducing its density.

Combating engine-compartment heat can be done with a variety of thermal wraps and thermal barriers placed on or around the affected components; a lower mounting position of the turbo(s) also helps. The innovative system designs from Utah-based Squires Turbo Systems (STS) approaches the problem by locating

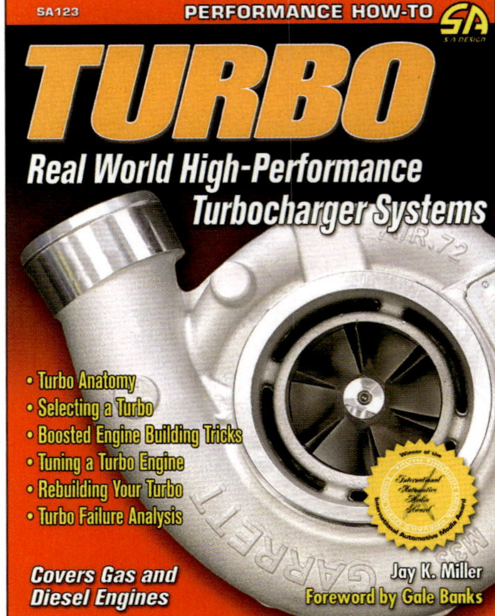

There is more to turbocharging than can possibly be described and explained in this single chapter. I recommend Jay K. Miller's book Turbo: Real World High-Performance Turbocharger Systems *for information on the theory, design, and application of turbo systems.*

Turbo systems generate a lot of heat under the hood that can damage parts and promote detonation. This twin-turbo setup uses a number of thermal barriers and wraps on the exhaust system, fuel lines, and more. Such measures are relatively cheap insurance and help ensure engine longevity.

The heat of a turbo system is easily absorbed by the intake system, which saps power and promotes detonation. That makes an intercooler all the more important. Its heat exchanger should be mounted in an area that receives direct, fresh air, typically in front of the radiator.

the turbocharger near the rear axle and removing it (and the heat it generates) from the engine compartment. (See chapter 6 for installation details.)

Fighting Turbo Lag

As for turbo lag, it has always been an issue with turbocharger systems and is generally more prevalent on larger turbochargers, as more inertia is required to spool up the larger, heavier turbine when compared with a smaller turbo. Ceramic roller thrust bearings are used in some lightweight turbochargers to reduce inertia, while the aspect ratio of the turbo's exhaust housing influences lag through the affect its aspect ratio has on spool-up time.

One of the more effective ways to combat turbo lag is with a high-flow exhaust system. Some backpressure is required to help the turbine spool, but a freer-flowing exhaust system minimizes the time required for it to generate boost. On engines where quick spool-up and more low-RPM power are desired, the use of a pair of

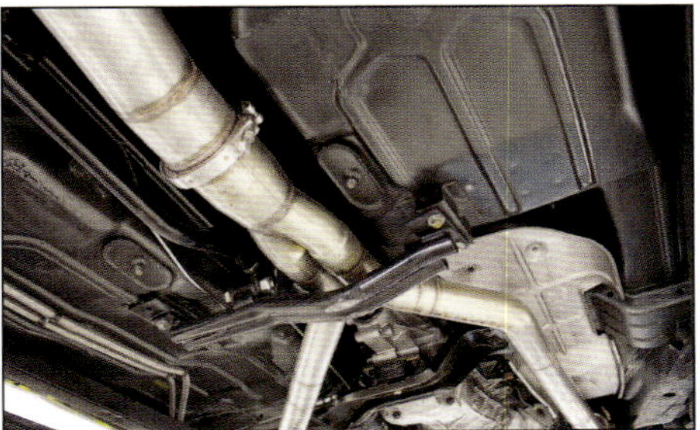

A high-flow, restriction-free exhaust system can reduce turbo lag, although street enthusiasts have to balance low restriction with legal sound compliance. Fortunately, turbo systems can mute some of the loudness of an engine, so there's more room to play when it comes to implementing a free-flow exhaust system that won't draw the ire of neighbors or the ticket books of police officers.

smaller turbochargers rather than a larger, single unit can help.

Ball-Bearing Turbos

The standard, conventional "floating" bearing in a turbocharger is what the turbine wheel rotates on during spool-up. Minimizing friction as the turbine spins on the bearing reduces inertia for quicker spool-up and enables greater maximum turbine speed.

High-performance turbo systems also undergo tremendous thrust load; the greater the boost pressure, the greater the load on the turbo's internal components. In the quest for greater turbocharger efficiency and durability, the ball-bearing-type turbo was developed by Garrett (currently a division of Honeywell). As its name suggests, the ball-bearing turbo's center section (also known as the cartridge) on which the turbine shift spins features low-friction ball bearings. The lower friction significantly reduces inertia, delivering a more immediate spool-up of the turbine. The bearings are surrounded by a film of oil that not only lubricates but also acts as a vibration damper.

On the heels of the ball-bearing turbo came the ceramic roller thrust bearing that was pioneered by Turbonetics. It is commonly known as the ceramic ball-bearing turbo, as the bearing is made of a silicone-nitride ceramic material. With this design, the lightweight, heat-resistant ceramic ball bearing is used on the air-compressor side of the turbocharger, while the turbine side uses a conventional floating bearing.

The Garrett-style turbo uses a pair of ball bearings, while the Turbonetics design uses a single bearing. Both enable quicker spool-up through reduced friction (Turbonet-

ics claims only half the exhaust energy is required to drive the turbine), but just as importantly, they have the capability to withstand substantially greater thrust load. In fact, Turbonetics claims up to 600-percent-greater thrust capacity than a conventional turbo bearing. Turbonetics also claims the builder can step up to a larger turbo size without compromising drivability on the street thanks to the reduced turbo lag and more immediate delivery of power.

While the quicker spool-up of these low-friction turbochargers is immediately noticeable when compared with a turbo using a conventional floating bearing, the advantage is more useful with vehicles where boost is desired during driving conditions, such as primarily street driving or road racing. On a vehicle designed primarily for drag racing, the difference in spool-up on the starting line doesn't affect performance when launching under boost, but the greater thrust load capability ultimately means longer turbo life. This is due to the great load on the turbo that comes during staging, as the turbocharger is brought up to high speed to launch under boost. The sustained high RPM of the turbo on the starting line generates tremendous heat and load, so a ball-bearing turbo pays off with performance longevity.

But, along with greater performance, ball-bearing turbochargers (whether the Garrett-style or Turbonetics design) bring a significant price premium, perhaps up to double the cost of a conventional-bearing turbocharger. However, the performance and strength virtues of ball-bearing turbochargers are well established; if your budget allows,

On a racing engine, a turbo can almost never be too large (rules permitting), but for street vehicles, there is a sweet spot between small and large that delivers effective horsepower without lag. The minimum requirement for an engine is tied to its airflow at the maximum engine speed.

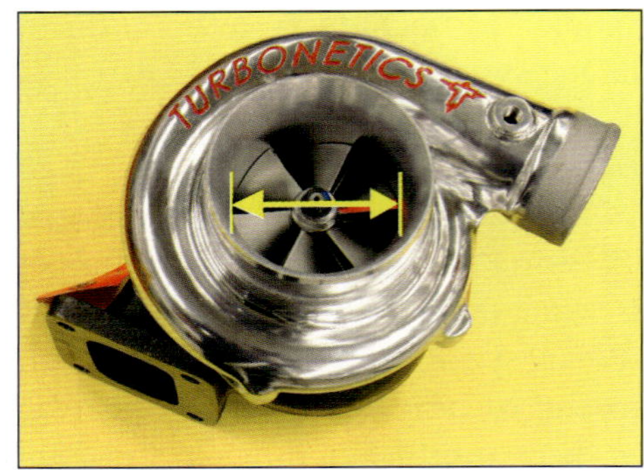

The size of a turbocharger is typically defined by the diameter of the inducer section of the compressor wheel (i.e., 76, 88, 91 mm, etc.). The inducer portion of the wheel is the section visible in the housing (shown here). It can also be described with the size of the turbine wheel, such as "77/85," which indicates a 77-mm inducer compressor and an 85-mm turbine wheel.

the ball-bearing turbo is the way to go.

Understanding Turbocharger Sizes

Turbocharger sizes are commonly referred to in a single millimeter dimension, such as "88-mm" or "76-mm." Such references indicate the inducer diameter of the compressor wheel, the turbine-driven wheel that forces air into the intake system. The compressor and turbine wheels feature inducer and exducer profiles, so the inducer diameter is not the full diameter of the wheel. It is essentially the portion of the wheel that's exposed from the housing.

Additional references will include the size of the turbine wheel, which is larger than the inducer compressor measurement (i.e., "76-91"). In other words, it's a turbocharger with a 76-mm inducer compressor wheel and a 91-mm turbine wheel. Turbo manufacturers have varied methods of identifying their products, but most incorporate either the inducer compressor size or the compressor and turbine sizes in their product names. For example, Precision Turbo

& Engine's PT88 turbo features an 88-mm inducer compressor wheel while the PT7285 turbocharger features a 72-mm inducer compressor and an 85-mm turbine. If the model includes only a single number, such as the PT88, it will be the inducer compressor size.

And, yes, larger-sized turbochargers offer greater airflow capability than smaller turbos, but unless the application is a dedicated drag racing combination, bigger is not always better for optimal performance. Proper sizing is the key to strong power on demand without lag or other dead spots in the power curve.

Selecting the Right-Size Turbocharger

Determining the optimal turbocharger size starts with a target engine output level and the engine's airflow requirements. Let's use a 6.0L LS2 engine as an example, with the goal of producing 800 hp.

First, the minimum airflow for the engine is required, assuming it will make peak power at 6,000 rpm. That's achieved by multiplying the engine displacement (364 ci for the LS2), by the max RPM (6,000) and volumetric efficiency, which is typically 85 percent for a naturally aspirated engine, and dividing the product by 3,456. The equation looks like this:

Displacement x RPM x 0.85 / 3,456 = Minimum CFM (Cubic Feet per Minute)

Or:

364 x 6,000 x 0.85 / 3,456 = 537.152 cfm

That means the LS2 must have a minimum airflow rating of at least 537.152 cfm in a naturally aspirated combination. That figure is used in the next calculation to help determine the turbocharged airflow rate required to help achieve the 800-hp target. First, the pressure ratio is required. It assumes the maximum pressure delivered by the turbocharger—let's assume 20 psi (1.4 bar)—and adds it to atmospheric pressure (14.7 psi / 0 bar at sea level) and divides the sum by atmospheric pressure: 14.7 + 20 / 14.7 = 2.36.

Next, the turbocharged airflow rate is determined by multiplying the engine's airflow requirement (cfm) with the turbocharger's pressure ratio: 537.152 x 2.36 = 1,267 cfm. That is the minimum airflow at peak RPM the turbocharger system needs to provide to achieve the targeted power level.

From there, the pressure ratio and turbocharged airflow rate are plotted on a manufacturer's compressor map, which outlines a turbo's airflow efficiency at various pressure ratios, to determine the optimally sized turbocharger. There's more math involved, too, because most manufacturers use a mass airflow measurement (pounds per minute) rather than cubic feet per minute. So, the 1,267 cfm airflow rating is multiplied by 0.076 to achieve the mass airflow requirement: 1,267 x 0.076 = 96.3. In other words, the turbocharged airflow rate is 96.3 pounds per minute.

With the converted airflow rate, the pressure ratio (2.36) plotted on one axis and the turbocharged airflow rate (96.3) is plotted on another for a given turbocharger, an "88-mm" turbo, for example. Where they meet on the map should be as close to 80-percent efficiency as possible. If the efficiency rate is significantly below 80, a larger turbocharger should be selected and the numbers replotted on its compressor map.

It is important to note that turbo manufacturer websites and catalogs don't always provide airflow ratings or compressor maps for their various turbochargers. In the absence of those references, determining the airflow requirements for the engine and then discussing them with a manufacturer's technical support is the best option.

As boost pressure can vary with a variety of conditions and degrade as air flows through an intercooling system, it's a good idea to upsize the turbocharger to the next larger size if the calculations land on the maximum output for a given turbo size.

One more thing: The corrected turbocharged airflow rating can be used to estimate the engine's horsepower under max boost because 1 pound of airflow per minute equals about 10 hp. So, the corrected airflow rating of 96.3 is simply multiplied by 10 to offer a projected horsepower rat-

ing of 952 at 6,000 rpm. That's plenty more than the 800-hp target, offering some flexibility in achieving the performance goal. In fact, a smaller turbo that spools faster (less lag) could be considered to achieve the 800-hp goal.

Turbocharger Aspect Ratio

Another important element to turbocharger design, size, and selection is the aspect ratio, which is the ratio of the area of the housing's cone to radius from the turbine or air compressor's center. Aspect ratios are measured on both the exhaust side and the air compressor side. On either side, the ratio is determined by dividing the cross section of the turbo by the distance from the center of that section to the center of the turbine wheel.

The aspect ratio should be constant throughout the housing because the spiral-shaped housing reduces in size the closer it is to the center. The spiral shape is known as the volute; it directs airflow to the turbine. Comparing similar-size turbochargers with different aspect ratios, a greater ratio (identified by a larger number) enhances upper-RPM performance with greater airflow but requires longer turbine spool-up time. A turbo with a smaller aspect ratio has quicker spool-up, but less upper-RPM airflow.

For turbocharged engines used primarily on the street and for road racing, a smaller aspect ratio on the exhaust side of the turbo delivers the best performance, as it promotes quicker spool-up and, consequently, more immediate power delivery. For drag racing, a larger aspect ratio helps build power at higher RPM, where it is more effective.

The size of the turbo and other factors ultimately determine the

Measuring A/R Ratio

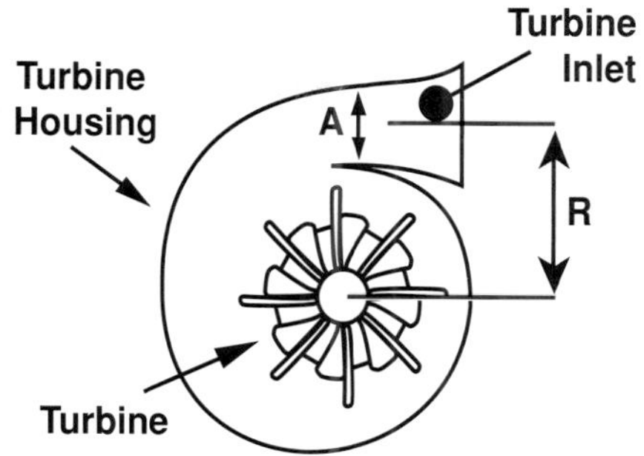

This diagram illustrates how the aspect ratio on a turbocharger is measured.

maximum airflow capability, but knowing how the aspect ratio affects performance should influence the decision when selecting similarly sized turbochargers.

Pitfalls of Mixing Turbines and Compressors

The turbine and compressor sections of a turbocharger must complement one another in order to produce strong, effective performance. Generally, turbocharger manufacturers and retailers match the exhaust-driven-turbine half of the turbo housing with an appropriate air-compressor half to generate optimal volumetric efficiency.

But in the quest to squeeze more boost from the system and generate more power, some builders experiment with different-size components, such as installing a larger turbine in the exhaust housing or bolting a larger air compressor to a smaller turbine. The changes drastically affect the turbocharger's performance and should be attempted only if you have extensive knowledge and experience with turbocharging systems. It is very easy to kill the performance advantage of a turbo system with mismatched components that

A conventional twin-turbo kit is shown with two turbos and two cast-iron exhaust manifolds.

Wastegates can be integrated on the turbo or external, but most new turbochargers feature integral wastegates. They are easily adjusted or modified to change the maximum boost pressure, increasing it for more power and decreasing it to dial it down.

generate heat and noise but little in the way of effective boost.

If you are experimenting with a custom turbo system for the first time, consult turbo manufacturers and experienced builders prior to purchasing or bolting on a new turbocharger. A defined horsepower goal or application, such as street and/or drag racing, helps the experts size a turbocharger that is the most appropriate for the project.

The complementing engine combination must also be considered in the role of volumetric efficiency, as the cylinder head–airflow characteristics, camshaft specifications, and even the intake manifold can affect performance under boost. In other words, it's not necessary to experiment with internal turbo modifications if a camshaft swap would be a more logical and effective alternative.

Only after the as-delivered turbo has been tested and its performance parameters thoroughly understood and explored should you consider experimenting with its turbine and air-compressor components. Optimal volumetric efficiency is the goal and messing with the manufacturer's balanced turbo assembly is a good way to adversely affect it.

This is an external wastegate from TiAL with a 41-mm valve seat. Different-size wastegates have different-sized valves. Larger wastegates should be used with systems that generate greater airflow. External wastegates can be modified via their springs, which alter the resistance against boost pressure required to open them.

Elements of a Turbo System

Of course, a turbocharging system is comprised of more than the turbocharger itself. A number of supporting components go into it, each affecting performance and durability in important ways. They include the following.

Turbo Exhaust Manifolds: They replace the conventional exhaust manifolds and mount the turbochargers, positioning the turbine side within the flow stream of the exhaust.

Turbocharger(s): The exhaust-trim air compressor that generates boost to increase horsepower.

Down Pipe: The exhaust pipe located immediately after the turbocharger, which receives the exhaust after it spins the turbine, as well as the exhaust from the wastegate.

Wastegate: It is essentially a bypass valve for the turbine, whereby a portion of the exhaust gas is diverted around, instead blowing off into the turbine. It is used to tune or limit boost pressure by limiting the maximum exhaust flow to the turbine. When the maximum boost level is reached, the wastegate opens to bleed off exhaust pressure and prevent the turbo boost level from increasing.

Blow-off Valve (BOV): A device mounted on the air-intake pipe, between the turbo and the throttle body, that bleeds off excessive boost, which builds after the throttle is quickly closed—a condition known as compressor surge.

Bypass Valve: Similar to a blow-off valve, the bypass valve vents excessive

That unmistakable "whoosh" heard with turbo systems comes when the blow-off valve opens to vent excessive air pressure. It is mounted between the intercooler and throttle body.

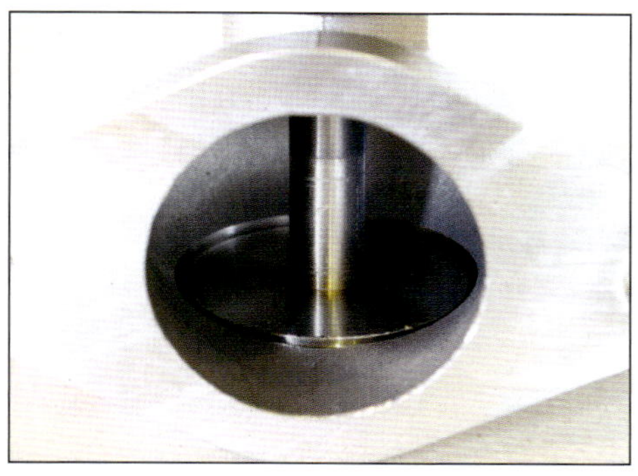

This inside view of a TiAL blow-off valve shows the vacuum-operated valve itself. As with wastegates, blow-off valves can be tuned, but their primary purpose is to prevent boost from forcing its way into the engine when the throttle closes.

Here's a boost controller integrated with an STS turbo system. It is a digital controller, but other electronic controllers enable the driver to dial in the desired boost from a remote control. Manual boost controllers are adjustable, much like the valve settings on adjustable shock absorbers.

boost pressure; but rather than venting it to the atmosphere, as the BOV does, the bypass valve vents it back to the compressor inlet.

Intercooler: The air-charge-cooling device that reduces the inlet temperature of the boosted air charge, which serves to maximize power and reduce the chance for detonation.

Complementing the basic elements of the turbo system, of course, are the corresponding fuel and ignition system upgrades, such as the fuel injectors, fuel pump, spark plugs, etc.

Boost Controller and Turbo Timer

In addition to the basic system elements described above, a couple of accessories that optimize longevity and performance are the boost controller and turbo timer. Neither are required to enable a turbo system's operation, but they work to prevent damage and extend the operating range of the system.

The boost controller, as its name implies, is a device that controls the boost level of a turbo system, either limiting its maximum boost level or helping ensure a desired boost level at different RPM levels or throttle positions, as maximum boost can still be achieved with some systems without WOT. The boost controller works by bleeding off air pressure at the wastegate back into the intake system or venting it to the atmosphere.

Manual boost controllers are available and relatively simple to install and operate, but electronic boost controllers are better suited to an electronically controlled LS engine. They can be "dialed in" to deliver prescribed boost pressure at different RPM levels for finely tuned performance. You should check with the turbocharger manufacturer for recommendations of either the most appropriate boost controller or possible hardware changes suggested for the turbocharger itself. The spring in the wastegate, as well as other turbo system components, can be very sensitive and affected adversely with an aggressive controller.

A turbo timer is an electronically controlled device that keeps the engine running for a length of time to allow adequate cooling of the turbocharger after extended driving under high load. With it, the engine idles for a predetermined period, which allows the turbine to cool from extremely high exhaust temperature with oil continuing to circulate through the system. This is a more important feature for vehicles that are routinely raced, such as drag cars, which benefit from the cool-down period in the pit area. With a street-driven vehicle, the cool-down period can be performed simply by keeping the engine's RPM low and out of boost for several minutes before turning off the engine.

Single- Versus Twin-Turbo Systems

One of the methods of generating more turbocharged power is employing a pair of smaller, parallel turbochargers (one turbo for each bank of cylinders) rather than a single, larger turbo. This approach generally benefits chassis and engine compartments that are mostly stock and have limited room for a large single turbo, but

Packaging a twin-turbo system can be challenging, even with the relatively open space of a full-size truck's engine compartment (seen here). Also, the size of the turbochargers will determine the most effective mounting position. A pair of small turbos is comparatively easy to mount directly off the exhaust manifolds or slightly below them. Larger turbos (as seen here) need more room. This system was designed to accommodate a pair of larger turbos.

On a street-driven vehicle, a number of inescapable details affect the design and implementation of a custom turbo system. Here, routing of the large-diameter down tube from a remotely mounted turbocharger shows some obvious interference issues with the vehicle's brake master cylinder. A smaller-diameter tube or one with another bend in it will likely make enough room for the master cylinder but may cause a restriction that increases turbo lag.

This photo clearly illustrates the elements of the turbo system and their relationship with one another. At the bottom of the system, the exhaust tubes from the exhaust header can be seen merging into the collector that mounts on the turbine side of the turbocharger. At the left of the system, the large-diameter down tube carries exhaust away after it spins the turbine. Also visible is a TiAL wastegate. Note how it is integrated with the down tube, as that's where the excess pressure is vented. Finally, the compressor side of the turbo is visible on the right with the discharge end open. Tubing will be routing from it through an intercooler and on to the engine's throttle body.

When the turbochargers are too large to mount directly to the manifolds on the engine, they'll typically end up mounted in the engine compartment. That requires a completely custom-fitted exhaust system to feed the turbine and carry away the exhaust via the down tubes. Because the turbos are located away from the exhaust manifolds, the manifolds themselves don't need to be cast iron. Here, a custom turbo exhaust system is being tacked together from conventional exhaust tubing. Such work adds complexity and cost to a turbo system.

Here's the front view of the compressor side of the turbo seen in the previous photo. The taped-over section is where fresh air is drawn into the compressor. A filter-capped air intake tube will be attached to this section of the turbo.

Texas-based Fastlane Inc. offers a single-turbo bolt-on kit for the 2010+ Camaro SS. It includes a BorgWarner extended-tip turbocharger (with a large 71.5-mm compressor wheel). The company claims the system is tuned for about 7 pounds of boost, which delivers an increase of more than 100 hp on an otherwise-stock engine.

many builders use twin turbos for aesthetic reasons too.

A belief that a pair of smaller turbos spool faster and deliver more power at lower RPM isn't entirely true. Although small turbos typically spool quicker than large turbos, when they're used in a twin-turbo system, each is receiving only half the exhaust pressure as a single-turbo system. So in practical terms, the advantage of a twin-turbo system on a street car lies in the ability to package it within a tight engine compartment.

One of the most dramatic and effective examples of twin turbochargers is the Callaway Twin Turbo Corvette offered between 1987 and 1990. It used a pair of compact turbos to produce a little more than 12 pounds of boost and very little lag within the confines of the standard C4 Corvette engine compartment.

When it comes to racing engines, it is generally true that a pair of turbochargers enables more horsepower than a single-turbo system. However, the design and tuning of a twin-turbo racing engine is different from a single-turbo system to make direct comparisons not entirely accurate. Suffice it to say that, in a racing engine, more power can be had when more than one turbocharger is employed.

Bolt-On Turbo Kits and Tuner Systems

Time has proven that bolt-on turbo kits are tough to design, manufacture, and market successfully. The investment in development time, numerous special parts required for each vehicle model, and the razor-thin line those manufacturers must balance between recouping their costs and selling kits at a reasonable price often sinks them after only a few years. Consequently, the number of bolt-on kits is considerably fewer than supercharger systems.

When it comes to turbocharged LS vehicles, Australia-based APS Performance has emerged as the preeminent manufacturer. If offers kits for the C5 and C6 Corvettes, the Pontiac GTO and G8, the Holden Monaro and Commodore, and the 1998–2002 Camaro/Firebird. In North America, the kits are available through a number of affiliated dealers. APS Performance's kits have proven to be very well engineered. The inclusive kits are packed with all the hardware required to install them, as well as detailed instruction manuals.

Similarly, additional manufacturers offer vehicle-specific kits for popular LS-powered vehicles. The following list highlights the more-established manufacturers and their available systems:

Turbo Technology
- Fourth-generation F-Body single-turbo system
- C5 Corvette (including Z06) twin-turbo system
- C6 Corvette (including Z06) twin-turbo system

Turbonetics
- Gen V Camaro twin-turbo system

AGP Turbo
- Gen V Camaro single-turbo system

UPP Turbo Systems
- Gen V Camaro SS twin-turbo system
- C5 Corvette twin-turbo system
- C6 Corvette (including Z06) twin-turbo system
- Pontiac GTO/Holden Monaro twin-turbo system
- Pontiac G8/Holden Commodore twin-turbo system

Armageddon Turbo Systems
- 2014–2018 Chevrolet Tahoe/Suburban and GMC Yukon/Yukon XL twin-turbo system

On 3 Performance
- Fourth-generation F-Body single-turbo system
- Gen V Camaro SS single-turbo system
- C6 Corvette (including Z06) twin-turbo system
- 1999–2006 Full-size truck twin-turbo system
- 2007–2013 Full-size truck twin-turbo system
- 2014–2018 Full-size truck twin-turbo system

Although the systems mentioned are designed specifically for various vehicles and include precut tubing

Elements of a 10.5 Street Outlaw Turbo Engine

Tom Kempf has spent the better part of a decade with turbocharged power in his Firebird Firehawk-bodied race car, running low-4-second eighth-mile ETs in 10.5 Street Outlaw and similar classes. It's a competitive combination that exemplifies the state of the art in modern, LS-based racing.

The combination has also proven exceptionally durable, requiring only essential maintenance and requisite inspections. In more than four years of running the twin-turbo engine highlighted here, it has never suffered an internal failure or a head gasket failure. And he hasn't had to change out the aluminum rods.

The 454-ci (7.4L) engine was built by Billy Briggs Racing, whose namesake has built a reputation for high-boost racing LS engines. Briggs and Kempf originally collaborated on a single-turbo engine before upgrading to the twin-turbo design. When pushing 60 pounds of boost (4.1 bar), the engine produces approximately 3,500 hp. Typically, Kempf runs about 45 pounds of boost (3.1 bar) for around 3,000 hp. The following are the primary components that generate that power reliably.

Block: The cylinder block is an early version of Dart's LS Next design with 4.125-inch bores, which modifies the basic LS architecture by eliminating the Y-block-type skirts that extend below the crankshaft centerline. Doing so drastically reduces the windage from the skirted block's separated crankcase bays.

Crankshaft: Callies Ultra Billet (Timken 4330 alloy steel) with a 4.250-inch stroke.

Connecting rods: GRP CNC-machined billet aluminum; 6.125 inches in length.

Pistons: Gibtec billet aluminum.

Compression ratio: 11.0:1

Oiling: Six-stage dry sump with Dailey oil pump and catch can.

Camshaft: 60 mm with custom grind from COMP Cams used with needle roller bearings.

Cam drive: Jesel belt drive.

Cylinder heads: Mast Motorsports billet aluminum Mozez canted-valve with 2.250-inch exhaust valves and 1.600-inch Inconel exhaust valves; machined for double O-ring sealing.

Valvetrain: Jesel shaft-mount roller rockers with XXX dual-coil valve springs.

Ignition: Front-drive distributor with MSD Pro Mag 44 magneto and ignition box.

Drag racer Tom Kempf's twin-turbocharged F-Body is rooted in a 454-ci engine using a Dart LS Next block and Mast Motorsports billet aluminum Mozez canted-valve cylinder heads.

Up to 60 pounds of boost is delivered by a pair of Precision Turbo & Engine PT91 turbos with ceramic ball-bearing center hubs. The 91-mm inducer compressors are matched with 102-mm turbines.

Turbochargers: Two Precision *Turbo & Engine* ceramic ball-bearing Gen I PT91 turbos (91-mm inducer compressor) with Gen II turbines (103-mm). Max boost is approximately 60 psi (4.1 bar).

Turbo system plumbing: Has 2-inch exhaust headers that

flow into 3-inch collectors that feed the "hot" side of the turbochargers; the intake tubes are 3.5-inch diameter and merge ahead of the throttle body. The exhaust tubing is 5 inches in diameter.

Wastegates and blow-off valves: The system incorporates a pair of Turbo Smart 60-mm wastegates and Turbo Smart blow-off valves.

Throttle body and intake manifold: A Wilson Manifolds 105-mm cable-operated throttle body is mounted on a homemade aluminum intake manifold.

Fuel system: The engine runs on methanol, delivered via a Waterman Racing fuel pump to 16 Precision Turbo & Engine Injectors: eight 550 lbs/hr primary injectors and eight 225 lbs/hr supporting injectors. The base fuel pressure is about 95 psi (6.5 bar), and the system incorporates a pair of Kinsler bypass valves.

Electronics: The engine's ECU is a Big Stuff 3 controller; and the system also incorporates an AMS 2000 boost controller and Race Pak data logger. ◼

After drawing air through a 105-mm throttle body and into a custom-fabricated intake manifold, the boosted air charge is mixed with methanol supplied by 16 fuel injectors. Here, the injectors can be seen on the top and bottom sides of the intake runners.

and other mounting hardware, the term bolt-on is somewhat of a misnomer. Unlike, say, an Eaton-based supercharger kit for a Pontiac G8 that can be installed in a single working day at a tuning shop (see chapter 5), some of the turbo kits described here require up to four times the labor investment. Turbo system installation typically requires some measure of fabrication, even with bolt-on kits.

The tools (including a vehicle lift) and experience required to facilitate the typical installation of a bolt-on turbo kit makes professional help very advised. Assuming a professional shop handles the installation, the cost of the system increases by the number of hours the shop takes to do it. And with 20 to 40 hours of labor at typical shop rates, that could add $1,500 to $2,500, or more, to the final cost of the system.

Many turbo systems are designed and installed on an individual basis by performance tuning shops (see chapter 6). This is typically done on vehicles that can't take advantage of a pre-engineered, bolt-on kit from an aftermarket vendor. An experienced shop can engineer a low-to-moderate-boost single- or twin-turbo system that essentially bolts onto a stock engine.

Perhaps the most unique and, in many ways, the most innovative bolt-on turbo systems are those from Squires Turbo Systems (STS), which was acquired by Holley in 2018. The company has streamlined the installation process and removed the turbo-generated heat under the hood by moving the turbochargers to the rear of the vehicle chassis, near the rear axle.

Beneath the bumper of a late-model Pontiac GTO/Holden Monaro is a Squires Turbo Systems turbo kit. The remote-mounted turbo drastically reduces under-hood temperatures and eliminates the need for a costly set of new exhaust manifolds.

In a nutshell, an STS system takes exhaust from the stock manifolds and runs it beneath the vehicle (much like a conventional exhaust system), where it meets the turbo (very close to the exhaust outlet). The traditional turbo system blows into the turbo directly from the exhaust manifold. STS claims this lowers the overall temperature of the turbo system, reducing underhood heat, as well as lowering the intake-air charge temperature.

The use of the original exhaust manifolds helps lower the cost of STS kits, relative to other turbo systems. They're still more expensive than most bolt-on supercharger systems, but the comparatively quick installation and lower component content makes them much more competitive with a blower when installation labor is factored into the equation.

Previously, STS Turbo offered vehicle-specific kits for most pop-ular LS-powered vehicles, but that has changed to a range of universal kits developed for the general displacement range of the engine. They include single-turbo kits for engines from 4.0 to 5.0 liters of displacement, 5.0 to 6.0 liters, and 6.0 to 7.0 liters. Designed as universal systems that require additional fabrication of the air and exhaust tubes, the kits include the turbocharger, the wastegate, mounting flanges, an air filter, oiling system provisions, and a wiring harness. They do not include exhaust tubing, air intake tubing, a blow-off valve, higher-capacity fuel injectors, or a tuner.

There are also twin-turbo kits for LS3-powered C6 Corvettes, including a complete kit and a "tuner" kit that doesn't include higher-rate injectors and a few other items. Chapter 6 includes an installation overview of an STS Turbo system.

Long regarded for exemplary engineering and extreme performance results, Indiana-based Lingenfelter Performance Engineering takes turbo systems to a unique level for LS-powered vehicles. The company offers a number of turbocharging systems, but rather than bolt-on kits, the systems involve completely rebuilt engines engineered to support forced induction. Its 800-hp LS7 twin-turbo system for the Corvette Z06 is the ultimate example. It uses all-new rotating parts, modified cylinder heads, and a revised fuel system in conjunction with carefully tuned turbo components that include:

- Two Garrett oil-lubricated and liquid-cooled ball-bearing turbochargers
- Lingenfelter-designed turbo compressor housings and exhaust housings with integral wastegates
- Air-to-air charge-cooling system
- Lingenfelter-designed stainless steel exhaust manifolds/turbo outlets
- Belt-driven turbocharger scavenge pump and turbo oil-drain reservoir

Obviously, the Lingenfelter system is more than a bolt-on kit, and its cost reflects that. The base price for the system is more than $45,000, but that includes an essentially brand-new engine engineered for the heat and stress of a high-boost turbo system. It may not be the least-expensive option, but with a 3-year/36,000-mile warranty backing it, it should prove to be one of the most durable. Lingenfelter offers similar turbo packages for other LS-powered vehicles.

KIT PREINSTALLATION

This chapter discusses peripheral modifications that are commonly performed to support kits, including fuel system upgrades, spark plug selection, and the process known as "pinning" the crankshaft and balancer. For the most part, the factory cooling system on LS-powered vehicles is sufficient to support bolt-on power adders. In fact, at low speeds and part-throttle conditions, the cooling needs of the engine are no greater than normal.

Removing the front fascia or bumper cover to install the intercooling system's heat exchanger, plumbing, and hardware typically requires the removal of the front tires. This provides access to and adequate leverage on the fascia's fasteners.

Body and Chassis Component Removal

Systems that incorporate a charge-cooling system, typically a liquid-to-air or air-to-air system, require the installation of a radiator-style heat exchanger. It is generally mounted at the front of the vehicle to ingest air via the grille/fascia assembly, either straight through the grille or from beneath the fascia. In most cases, this requires removal of the fascia, bumper cover, grille, and sometimes even the headlamps.

Although the attachment of the body/chassis components may seem obvious, read the kit instructions carefully and proceed cautiously. The plastic body parts and fasteners that typically comprise the components to be removed aren't designed for repeated installation and removal; and the fasteners can be especially fragile.

A kit with good instructions points out all of the fasteners that require removal; and even after they're removed, there will likely be press-kit/snap-fit attachments, particularly with the bumper cover. When it's clear that all other fasteners are removed, a firm tug on the fascia usually pulls it free from the chassis.

There are inexpensive specialized tools that enable the removal of the factory fasteners quickly and without damaging them. Buying one is a wise investment before starting the installation project. Overpriced replacement clips/fasteners are always available at the dealer in case you damage one.

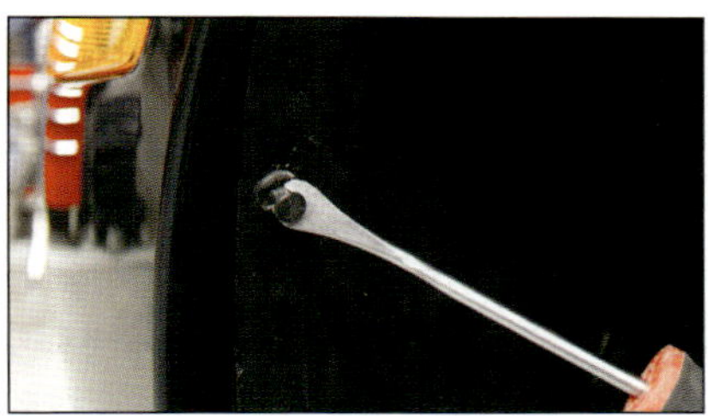

Most vehicles' fascia and other under-body plastic components are held in place with plastic pushpins. They can be pried out with a flat-blade screwdriver, but a more efficient method (and one that won't damage the pins) is to use a dedicated trim-removal tool.

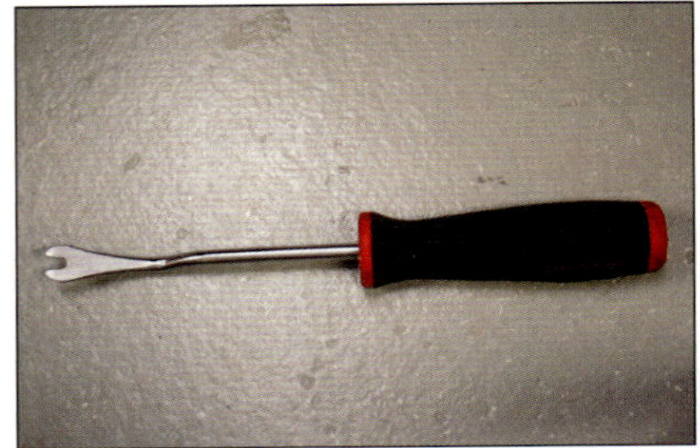

Trim-removal tools (such as this one) are available at most auto parts stores and most online tool sources. They're inexpensive and make a smart addition to any home toolbox.

Fuel-pressure relief is accomplished by accessing the Schrader valve located behind the black cap on the driver-side fuel rail. The cap simply unscrews similar to the air valve on a tire.

Engine Preparation

Before touching the engine or any of the vehicle's mechanical components, the power must be disconnected by removing the battery cable from the negative terminal. Most intercooled supercharger and turbocharger systems also require the draining of the engine coolant. The coolant can be reused if it is captured in a clean, contaminant-free receptacle.

Study the manufacturer's assembly manual prior to starting the project. This helps identify special tools or other necessities that need to be addressed, items that would incon-

Even after the pushpins and other fasteners are removed, the bumper cover/fascia may still be held in place with locking clips. Pulling the bumper cover firmly should unhook it, but it will likely be accompanied by the sound of cracking or breaking plastic. If done correctly, no harm is done and the part snaps back into place at the conclusion of the project.

If a blower or turbo kit's instructions call for draining the coolant, it may be easier to remove the radiator for added clearance when pinning the crankshaft. It's also a necessary step when performing a camshaft swap in a vehicle.

The tip of a flat-blade screwdriver is pressed on the Schrader valve to relieve pressure within the fuel lines. Care must be taken (including wearing eye protection) to prevent injury from the high-pressure spray of fuel that could occur. The procedure shouldn't be performed near heat sources or an open flame.

This photo shows the drilled and tapped oil-return hole at the front of the oil pan on a C6 Corvette, at the lower corner of the driver's side. Other LS vehicles requiring a return hole have them in essentially the same place. The fitting for the return line has also been installed, using a liquid sealer in addition to the torque specifications for the fitting in the pan.

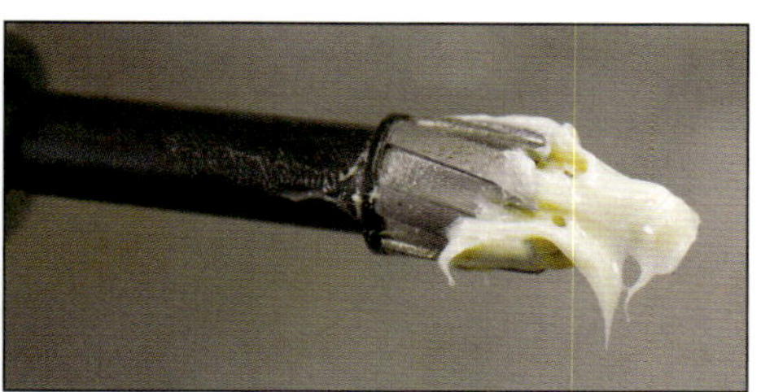

Some kits supply the necessary drill bit for modifying the oil pan. It is very important to use white lithium grease (or similar) on the end of the bit to capture material and shavings from the oil pan as they are removed. Needless to say, stray metal shavings should not enter the engine. Some builders drill the hole with oil still in the pan to help flush out the shavings immediately.

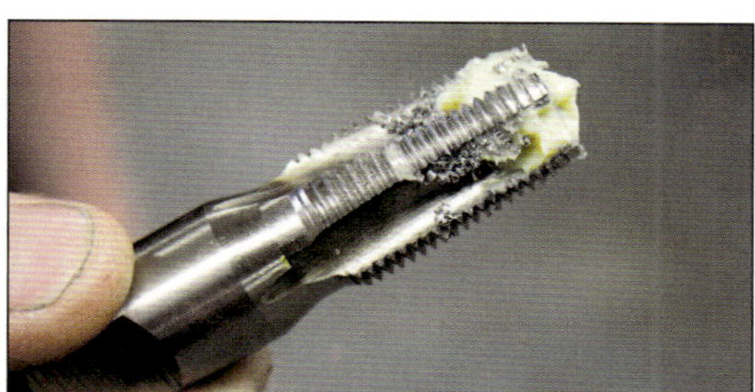

After the hole in the oil pan is drilled, it is chased with a tap to provide threads for the hose fitting. The shavings seen here in the grease on this tap illustrate the importance of protective measures, as those shavings would otherwise have fallen into the oil pan.

veniently interrupt the installation process because they're not in your toolbox. One of the more uncommon tools that may be required is a torque wrench with angle measures, as most of the factory fasteners on LS engines are torque-to-yield types that are final-torqued to a specific angle rather than a conventional ft-lbs measure (see page 110 for more information).

Fuel-Pressure Relief

The addition of a blower or turbo system most likely comes with higher-capacity fuel injectors, which requires removal of the fuel rail to swap the injectors. Before that can be accomplished, the pressure in the fuel rails must be relieved to prevent fuel spraying on the installer and the vehicle when the fuel line is disconnected.

If the vehicle has sat for a long period without starting, such as overnight, the pressure at the fuel rail shouldn't be great, but the relief procedure should still be followed for maximum safety (and it should be accomplished with eye protection). The procedure is simple. Follow these steps:

1. Make sure the engine is off, the ignition key is in the off position

or removed, and the negative battery cable is disconnected.

2. Remove the black cap from the front end of the driver-side fuel rail, exposing the Schrader valve that is also used as a fuel-pressure test port.

3. Place a rag under the port to capture and soak up any fuel that may leak or blow out.

4. With the tip of a flat-blade screwdriver, gently and quickly press on the valve just to gauge pressure in the fuel rails.

5. Hold the screwdriver tip against the valve as necessary (similar to releasing air from a tire valve) until the pressure is eliminated.

6. With the pressure relieved, the valve cap can be reinstalled and the fuel rail/injector assembly removed.

Oil Pan/Oil System Modifications

Some superchargers, such as centrifugals and Vortech blowers, have external lubrication systems, being lubricated with oil circulated from the engine. This requires feed and return lines between the compressor and the engine. The feed line is usually routed from an unused port on the cylinder block, but connecting the return line to the engine requires drilling and tapping a hole in the oil pan.

When performed correctly, the oil pan modification is a leak-free, maintenance-free change, but it permanently alters the oil pan (even if the supercharger is removed at a future time). For some enthusiasts, the thought of drilling into the oil pan is enough to dissuade them from a particular system. If that includes you, check with the retailer or blower-

kit manufacturer about the compressor's lubrication.

"Pinning" the Crankshaft

The crankshaft damper/pulley on almost all production LS engines is a press-fit type, meaning it is pressed onto the front hub of the crankshaft and does not have the complementing locking feature of a traditional keyway on the hub. A large, 24-mm bolt secures the damper to the crankshaft after it is pressed into place, but there are no fasteners between the rear face of the damper and front edge of the crankshaft.

Although in stock and even mildly modified combinations this isn't a problem, there is a chance the damper could slip or spin on the crankshaft in higher-power engines, particularly supercharged and turbocharged applications that see a quick spin-up of the engine speed. A slipping damper can cause a number of problems, including altered ignition timing.

A relatively simple method of guarding against unwanted slippage is "pinning" the damper to the crankshaft. It involves drilling a small hole through the face of the damper that interfaces with the crankshaft hub and a complementing hole into the end of the crank hub. This is performed carefully after the damper is pressed onto the crankshaft.

After the holes are drilled, one or two dowel-type pins are inserted, providing a slip-free link between the crank and damper. The standard damper bolt is fastened too. When this modification is performed correctly, the pinned crankshaft and damper are locked together, regardless of the amount of power (or boost) the engine produces.

Supercharger systems that require pinning the crankshaft should include a template tool similar to this one. The threaded section replaces the factory damper bolt, and the thick washer serves as the pin template with a hole or tool drilled through it. This tool has a single-pin template with only one hole.

The pinning procedure is easily accomplished in the vehicle, but depending on the model, it may be necessary to remove the cooling fan assembly and possibly the radiator to provide enough room to insert the drill at the proper angle. On C5 and C6 Corvettes, the process requires the removal of the steering rack for maximum clearance and an unobstructed angle (reinstallation of the rack requires suspension alignment after the project is completed).

It may be very difficult to initially break loose the 24-mm bolt, requiring the added leverage of a breaker bar or something similar. When attempting to remove the bolt, it is imperative to prevent the crankshaft from turning. On a manual-transmission vehicle, the transmission is placed in fourth gear to prevent movement, while an automatic-equipped vehicle needs a tool to positively hold the flexplate; specialized tools are available for this.

Pinning the Crankshaft

1 *The first step in the procedure is removal of the 24-mm bolt holding the damper against the crankshaft hub. It is a very tightly torqued bolt that typically requires the leverage of a breaker bar to break it loose; according to GM's engine assembly recommendations, the bolt should not be reused. Because it is a torque-to-yield fastener, it should be replaced with a new bolt after removal.*

4 *The pins are nothing more than small, lightweight dowels similar to what is used to locate cylinder heads on the cylinder block. They're all that's necessary to provide a positive lock between the crankshaft and the damper.*

7 *Inserting the pins requires nothing more than a few careful taps from a hammer to seat them. No sealer or other fasteners are required.*

2 *After the damper bolt is removed and the tool is installed, a drill is simply inserted through the template's hole(s) and driven into both the damper and the crank hub.*

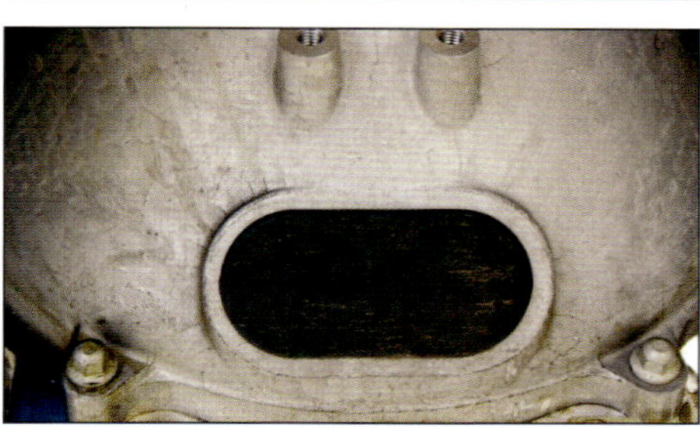

3 *Here's what a two-pin modification looks like after the holes have been drilled. Note how they straddle both the crank hub and the damper.*

5 *Here is the damper/hub assembly with the pins installed.*

6 *Another method of holding the damper in place is to insert a tool that holds the flywheel or flexplate. Access to the flexplate to hold it during the tightening of the damper bolt is available by removing this rubber plug at the bottom rear of the bellhousing.*

8 *With the pins in place, a new damper bolt should be installed, per GM's assembly manual specifications. The process involves tightening the original bolt to 240 ft-lbs to ensure the damper is correctly installed. Then, the new bolt is tightened to 37 ft-lbs and torqued to 140 degrees.*

Pinning the Crankshaft *(Continued)*

9 The final torque angle of the damper bolt is an extremely high torque spec (approximately the equivalent of 250 ft-lbs) and requires considerable leverage to hold the flywheel or flexplate to prevent the crankshaft from turning. Specialized tools are available for this job, but one of the most effective methods is to use a serpentine belt wrapped around the balancer and air-conditioning pulley, which holds the damper in place.

10 The placement of the steering rack on C5/C6 Corvettes generally requires its removal for the pinning procedure. It is easily unbolted and pulled out of the way, but extreme care must be taken to ensure the steering wheel is pointed straight ahead and held there during the removal process. This can be done by running masking tape (or another low-residue tape) between the top of the steering wheel and the dashboard. After the steering rack is unbolted, the individual spindles can be moved, but they must be returned to the original position when the rack is reinstalled. A sensor in the steering system detects whether the rack and wheel are aligned; if they are not, drivability may suffer and a trouble code is triggered on the driver information center. The steering wheel should not be touched while the steering rack is unbolted and/or removed.

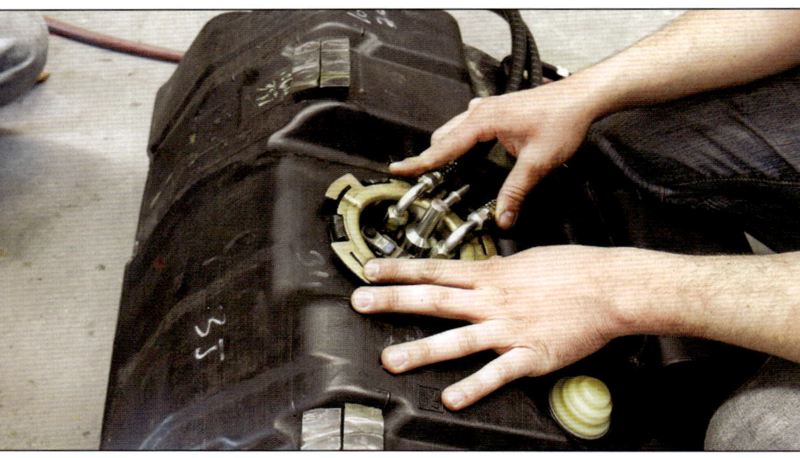

11 Replacing the in-tank fuel pump on most LS-powered vehicles requires the removal of the fuel tank, as the access hole is located on the top of the tank. Brass tools should be used when loosening or tightening the lock ring on the fastener to prevent accidental sparks near the gas fumes.

Fuel Pump

The additional air delivered by the blower or turbo must be accompanied by a corresponding increase of fuel to make power. And it's not just the quantity of the additional fuel that's important, it's the sustained pressure at which it's delivered.

For most LS-powered vehicles using a bolt-on power adder kit and no other internal engine modifications, higher-capacity fuel injectors may suffice; and they should be included with most kits. When larger injectors alone aren't enough, higher-capacity fuel pump(s) and/or a fuel-pump amplifier are required.

In most cases, swapping the fuel pump is a simple procedure that involves dropping the fuel tank to remove the stock pump and inserting the new one. While it's true that it's better to have more pump capacity than not enough, it's also possible to have too much. Generally speaking, most supercharged/turbocharged LS engines need a pump rated at a minimum of 190 liters per hour (lph), which is the equivalent of 50 gallons per hour (gph) or 301 pounds per hour (lbs/hr). This suits an engine up to approximately 600 flywheel horsepower.

If the horsepower is expected to be between 600 and about 850, a 255-lph (67-gph/404-lbs/hr) pump should be used. Beyond that, a custom system is likely required that can include an inline "helper" pump. Australia-based turbo kit manufacturer APS offers a dual-fuel pump kit that fits a variety of LS vehicles and is rated for more than 1,000 hp.

The Kenne Bell Boost-A-Pump

For many LS-powered vehicles (mostly 2003 and later), an alter-

Here is a typical Boost-A-Pump installation. Installation is fairly simple. It is wired into the existing power wire that leads to the fuel pump with additional wiring leading to the driver-adjustable control knob. On this Corvette, the driver-side rear wheel-well liner was removed to mount the unit. The reinstalled liner provides weather protection.

native to replacing the in-tank fuel pump (or complementing a replacement pump) is the addition of a Kenne Bell Boost-A-Pump. It works essentially like an amplifier for the electric in-tank pump, increasing the voltage by up to 17.5 volts when necessary. It also increases the voltage on demand, such as under boost conditions, and allows normal operation in low-speed, zero-boost conditions.

The principle of the Boost-A-Pump is quite simple: increase the voltage to the fuel pump to increase fuel flow. But along with increased fuel flow is the necessary requirement of sustained fuel pressure to ensure a safe air/fuel ratio. Because the electric, in-tank fuel pump is essentially an electric motor, the amount of voltage it receives determines its speed and output. The Boost-A-Pump's increased voltage sustains fuel pressure as long as necessary. Generally, it increases voltage to the pump when boost exceeds 4.5 pounds.

The on-demand operation of the Boost-A-Pump has several advantages, such as not overloading the fuel system during low-speed, no-boost conditions. The manufacturer claims it supports up to 1,000 hp when used in conjunction with the factory, in-tank fuel pump and can actually enhance the life of the stock pump. The system is adjusted with a control knob that enables between 1- and 50-percent increase in voltage on demand.

If a supercharger or a turbocharger kit does not include a Boost-A-Pump, you should consider adding one if fuel pressure fluctuates significantly at wide open throttle.

Fuel Injectors

Most bolt-on systems that require the stock fuel injectors to be replaced with higher-rate injectors include them with the kit or provide specific instructions for the size (flow rate) and injector type, if they must be obtained separately. If the injectors are replaced, it is extremely important

For most supercharger and turbocharger systems, higher-capacity fuel injectors are required. Typically, they're included with bolt-on kits. They must be installed prior to starting the engine with the blower or turbo kit, but the engine should never be started with new injectors until the engine controller is "told" about them through a new tune.

that the engine is never started until the engine-control computer has been flashed with new tuning data that includes the new injectors' specifications. Doing so almost immediately fouls the spark plugs and could lead to other problems or engine damage. Start the engine only after new injector data has been programmed into the controller.

The formula for selecting the appropriate-size injectors is referenced in chapter 9.

Spark Plugs

In almost every supercharger or turbocharger installation, the engine's spark plugs should be replaced with those of a "colder" range and a tighter electrode gap. In fact, many bolt-on kits include a set of new plugs as part of their standard equipment.

There are two primary reasons for the new plugs: heat range and proper gap. The colder heat range of the plugs helps ward off the preignition and detonation conditions that are crucial to maximum performance and trouble-free drivability. Forced induction generates greater cylinder pressure and therefore more heat, and stock spark plugs that get overheated can glow like the glow plugs of a diesel engine. This promotes preignition since the heat of a glowing plug tip lights off the incoming air/fuel charge before the piston reaches the top of its stroke.

The heat range is a rating of a spark plug's capability of absorbing/removing heat from the combustion chamber. It is determined by design elements such as the plug's center electrode material and insulator design, as well as the length of the ceramic center insulator nose. A longer insulator nose exposes more ceramic to the combustion gases to promote heat retention.

It's important to remember that the heat range has nothing to do with the energy output or voltage transfer of the plug. Heat ranges are indicated on plugs with a numeral, such as 5, 6, or 7; the lower numbers indicate hotter heat ranges. For example, a plug with a heat range of 5 is hotter than one with a heat range of 6.

Most LS production engines use plugs with a heat range of 5 or lower, as heat retention is desired to warm up the engine more quickly. In turn, that helps the catalytic converter heat up quicker, in order to reduce cold-start emissions.

A heat range of at least 6 should be used on supercharged and turbocharged engines.

As for the importance of a tighter-than-stock electrode gap, it's necessary to ensure a strong, consistent spark that won't get blown out by the increased cylinder pressure that comes with supercharger/turbocharger boost. Think of it as attempting to light a match outdoors when there's no wind (natural aspiration) versus when there's a stiff breeze (supercharged/turbocharged).

The gap of stock plugs may be sufficient for low-boost, bolt-on kits used with few other modifications. Since it's important to use replacement, colder-range plugs anyway, they should be gapped to suit the supercharger/turbocharger requirements. For most forced-induction applications, a gap of about 0.030 inch is optimal.

Colder-range spark plugs are a must on supercharged and turbocharged engines. Many engine builders and supercharger/turbocharger kit manufacturers prefer the NGK TR-6 spark plug in boosted LS engines. It has a heat range of 6 and the plug gap is close to spot-on out of the box.

To prevent galling or other problems when installing new spark plugs in aluminum cylinder heads, the plugs' threads should be coated with anti-seize compound.

Real-World Project: Camshaft and Valve Springs Swap

Bolt-on supercharger and turbo-charger kits can be complemented with a change to a camshaft that's tailored to the airflow and performance potential of the power adder (see chapter 9 for camshaft selection details). Because portions of the top and/or front of the engine require removal or disassembly to facilitate the blower/turbo kit installation, swapping the camshaft (and required stiffer, higher-rate valve springs) is a way of knocking off two birds with the same stone.

The unique details of the LS engine allow the cam and springs to be easily changed without having to remove the cylinder heads. This is because the lifters can be "locked" with a simple full rotation of the camshaft to prevent them from falling into the cylinder block when the cam is removed.

A few unique tools are required for the procedure, mostly to support the valve springs' removal and installation. They include a compressed-air hose with a threaded fitting on the end for the spark-plug holes in the cylinder heads, as well as a valve spring compressor/removal tool.

This project was performed at Detroit-area Stenod Performance on a TrailBlazer SS that was also receiving a Magnuson Roots-type blower system.

A valve spring removal tool (seen here) is required to squeeze the spring's coils to remove the valve keepers and retainers and to also reinsert the keepers and retainer during installation. This spring tool is from Performance Tool (part number W84001) and is available from Northern Tool and Equipment.

Camshaft and Valve Spring Swap

1 The project begins with swapping the valve springs. Access to them is gained by unbolting and removing the ignition coil assembly followed by the valve covers. When the valve covers are off, the rocker arms are the next to be removed. This is simple because they're mounted on a fixture that holds all of them. Once unbolted, the rocker arms come off as a single assembly. The pushrods should also be removed.

2 To hold the valves in place when the springs are removed, the cylinder combustion chamber must be pressurized with air (approximately 120 psi). There are specialized air hose fittings for this job, but a compression test gauge also works.

3 A stock LS2 valve spring (left) is shown with a heavy-duty, higher-rate spring from COMP Cams (right). The stock spring has a single coil and a slight beehive shape. Note the smaller-width top compared to the COMP Cams spring. The replacement spring has a pair of inner and outer coils for exceptional strength. The stronger spring is not only necessary for standing up to the higher valve lift delivered by the new camshaft but it better withstands the cylinder pressure created by the blower or turbo.

Camshaft and Valve Spring Swap *(Continued)*

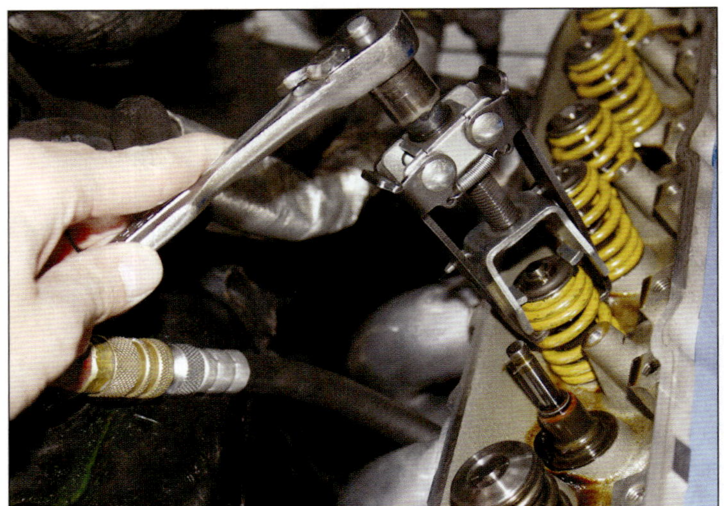

4 With the air line connected at the spark plug hole, lower the spring tool onto the top of the spring. Use a ratchet to compress the spring until the retainer and keepers can be removed, freeing the spring. Extreme care must be taken since the spring is under tremendous pressure and could cause an injury or even damage if it breaks loose from the tool.

5 New valve stem seals go with the replacement valve springs, so the originals must be removed with the springs. Gentle tugging with pliers is generally all that's needed to pull them off the valve stems.

6 Prior to the new spring's installation, the new valve stem seal is slipped on. It is a tight fit that generally requires assistance to seat it all the way down onto the cylinder head surface. In this case, a deep-well socket placed on top of the seal and a few gentle taps from a mallet or hammer does the trick.

7 In the reverse of the process for removal, the compressed valve spring is slipped over the valve stem and seal. Then, the keepers and retainer are installed and the spring compressor tool is backed off until the spring is held firmly in place.

8 *Replacement of the stock camshaft begins with the removal of the front cover. Like the valve covers, its seals don't require replacement if the removal/installation procedures don't damage them.*

9 *Here's one of the cylinder heads with its new set of springs. At this point, it's easier to hold off reinstalling the pushrods, rocker arms, and valve covers until the new camshaft has been installed. If the O-ring-style valve cover seals were not damaged during removal, they do not require replacement.*

10 *To remove the camshaft, you must first remove the oil pump and timing chain set. The oil pump is the first to go, as seen here. Note the large, single bolt on the camshaft timing gear on this LS2 engine. Earlier LS engines were equipped with smaller, three-bolt fastening setups for holding the gear to the camshaft, but later engines were equipped with the large, single-bolt fastener. It is imperative to match the new camshaft and the timing gear because they are not interchangeable.*

11 *The oil pump has fasteners on the bottom edge that are very difficult to reach. Removing them requires a very slim wrench or a ratcheting wrench. A rag placed beneath the pump helps prevent the bolts from falling into the engine if they were to slip from the wrench or your grasp.*

Camshaft and Valve Spring Swap *(Continued)*

12 Next, the crankshaft is rotated until indicator marks on the cam gear and crankshaft sprocket are aligned. The cam gear's "dot" goes to the bottom, and the crank sprocket's dot aligns at the top. This indicates cylinder number-1 is at top dead center.

14 The timing gear tensioner is the next component to be removed.

16 Before the stock camshaft is pulled out of the engine, it must be rotated a few times while still in its bore. Doing so pushes the lifters into a locked position that enables the camshaft to be removed without the lifters falling into the engine.

13 With the timing gear correctly aligned, the cam gear is unbolted and removed. The crankshaft sprocket remains installed on the engine.

15 After the tensioner is removed, the camshaft retaining plate is unbolted and can be removed too.

17 Once the camshaft has been rotated to lock the lifters in place, the camshaft can be removed. Care must be taken when pulling the cam out of the cylinder block to prevent damaging the cam bearings.

18 Selecting a camshaft with the lift, duration, and lobe-separation-angle specifications tailored to the supercharger or turbocharger kit can enhance the performance and drivability of the new power adder system. (See chapter 9 for information on choosing the right camshaft.)

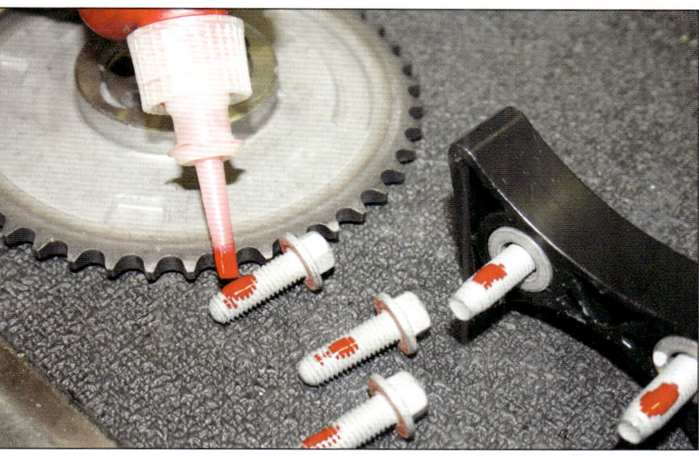

19 Red Loctite thread sealer (or similar) should be applied to the cam gear bolts, as well as to the timing chain guide bolts, prior to installation.

20 Next, the new camshaft is inserted into the engine. The roller design of the valvetrain, and the fact that the inside of the engine is already well lubricated from regular use, means the application of conventional camshaft lube on the cam lobes isn't necessary.

21 Finally, the timing chain guide, timing chain, and cam gear are reinstalled. The cam/cam gear must be lined up again with the dot on the crankshaft sprocket to ensure correct ignition timing at startup. If the engine has relatively few miles on it, the original timing chain can be reused. After this step, the remainder of the procedure simply involves reinstallation of the oil pump, front cover, and other engine accessories.

22 Because the replacement camshaft used here features the three-bolt cam gear fastening design of earlier LS engines, the stock single-bolt gear could not be reused. A three-bolt gear was obtained, along with a replacement timing gear guide that replaces the more cumbersome stock tensioner.

SUPERCHARGER INSTALLATION PROJECTS

This chapter offers in-depth looks at the two basic types of bolt-on supercharger systems: Roots/screw-type compressors that replace the intake manifold and centrifugal systems that mount to the engine's front accessory-drive system. Both systems are typical in that they are delivered with all of the components and hardware required for installation, including fuel-system upgrades such as fuel injectors. (See chapter 4 for general information on important details such as fascia removal, fuel-pressure relief, the importance of spark plug selection, and pinning the crankshaft).

It's important to note that while this chapter provides a detailed look at the typical procedures involved with the installations, not every step or process is outlined. In other words, it is no substitute for the manufacturer's assembly manual, which should be followed to the letter.

Project 1: Roots/Screw-Type Supercharger Kit

This project involves the installation of a Magna Charger kit on a 2008 Pontiac G8 GT (LS2 6.0L engine). The kit consists of an MP 1900 (1.9-liter displacement) compressor (see chapter 2) and liquid-to-air intercooling system. It includes almost every piece of hardware required for installation, including a plug-in flash tuner.

Although this project illustrates the installation on the Pontiac G8 GT, the procedures and methods are largely the same for all Magnuson kits for LS-powered vehicles; and they are very similar to the steps required to install a screw-type blower kit. In the broadest terms, the installation requires the following:

- Replacing the stock intake manifold with the supercharger compressor/manifold assembly
- Swapping the throttle body onto the supercharger system
- Mounting the intercooler's heat exchanger and routing its hoses and hardware
- Replacing the serpentine drive belt to accommodate the supercharger drive pulley
- Installing higher-capacity fuel injectors (and any other fuel system enhancements)

General Tools Required

- Metric wrenches and sockets (standard and deep)
- Metric Allen wrenches/sockets
- Torque wrench
- Phillips-head and flathead screwdrivers
- Fuel-line disconnection tool (may be included with the kit)
- Drill (possibly requiring angled head)
- Hose cutters and hose clamp pliers
- Trim removal tool ■

- Uploading a revised engine-calibration program to the engine controller

As is the case with most contemporary Roots/screw-type supercharger kits, the Magnuson system is delivered with the compressor pre-mounted to the intake manifold. This greatly enhances the speed and ease of the installation. It also reveals the only significant downside to the project: additional mass. The lightweight, composite factory intake manifold weighs next to nothing, but bolting on the Magnuson compressor/manifold assembly adds about 50 pounds over the front axle of the vehicle. Under boost, those extra pounds disappear, but it's not an inconsequential consideration, particularly on finely balanced cars like the Corvette.

Generally speaking, the quality and completeness of the Magnuson kit is exceptional. It is a bolt-on system in the very best sense of the term, requiring little fabrication and mostly common hand tools. In the case of this G8 project car, no additional fuel-system enhancements were required (apart from the supplied, higher-rate injectors and the self-contained lubrication system), which eliminates an entire procedure that some other kits may require. In fact, an experienced technician should be able to install the kit within a day with additional time required for proper tuning and evaluation. The same cannot be said for most bolt-on turbocharger systems, which require considerably longer labor time (see chapter 6).

The installation outlined here was performed at Dearborn Heights, Michigan-based Livernois Motorsports with tuning completed by Dan Millen, using the company's recently introduced X-Treme Cal Tuning software (see chapter 7). On Livernois' chassis dyno, the otherwise-stock Pontiac G8 GT recorded 423 hp and 401 ft-lbs of torque at the rear wheels with a peak of approximately 8 pounds of boost. That represents an increase of more than 35 percent in horsepower versus the stock 312-hp rating and about 20-percent more torque than the baseline 312-ft-lbs rating.

Millen indicated the G8 would have seen a greater response but the supercharged airflow was hampered at the back end by the stock exhaust system.

"At the very least, a cat-back-style system is needed when you add a supercharger," he said. "Headers and high-flow cats help greatly, too, to uncork the exhaust because supercharged engines don't need much backpressure to make the most power."

To prove his point, shortly after the installation was completed, Livernois Motorsports performed an identical installation on another G8 GT and Millen uploaded essentially the same tune but the second car was already equipped with a cat-back exhaust system. The comparison with the stock-exhaust car was dramatic: 438 hp and 445 ft-lbs of torque at the tires. That's a significant 15 hp and 44 ft-lbs difference. Without a doubt, a less-restrictive exhaust system benefits the greater airflow generated by the supercharger. Such an upgrade should be the standard operating procedure for an enthusiast wishing to maximize the performance benefit from the sizable investment made in the supercharger system.

The photos in this chapter should be referenced as the general steps used for all Roots/screw-type supercharger systems.

Using HP Tuners software, Dan Millen performed the tuning on the G8, dialing in the new 62-lbs/hr injectors and the blower system's other parameters. He was initially disappointed with the comparatively tame horsepower result. Millen attacked his keyboard and came up with 423 hp and 401 ft-lbs of torque at the tires, for more than 35-percent greater horsepower and about 20-percent more torque than the 312-hp/335-ft-lbs baseline figures.

When it comes to attaching a price tag to the supercharger's power increase, the Magnuson kit typically retails in the $6,500 to $7,000 neighborhood. If you're going to have it professionally installed and tuned, as was done with the project car here, you're probably looking at another $1,500 to $2,000 for labor, miscellaneous service parts, and tuning.

The Eaton-based Magnuson supercharger system is delivered ready to bolt on. In fact, the 1.9-liter supercharger was pre-mounted to the intake manifold (as seen here). The satin-black finish looks more OEM than the typical bare-metal finish of most blowers. The other primary components of the system include the heat exchanger, the electric pump, and the coolant reservoir for the charge-cooling system. It is a dedicated system, meaning it is separate from the engine's cooling system and maintains its own circuit of coolant (the same 50-50 mix of water and coolant used in engines).

Installing a Magna Charger Kit

1 The supercharger kit's charge cooler requires removal of the front fascia. That starts with removal of the front tires to provide access to the myriad of fasteners (most of them plastic pushpin types) on the inside of the wheel well. There are also seemingly endless fasteners on the bottom of the fascia. The car used in this project is wrapped with protective coverings to prevent damage to the body. (See chapter 4 for more information on fascia removal.)

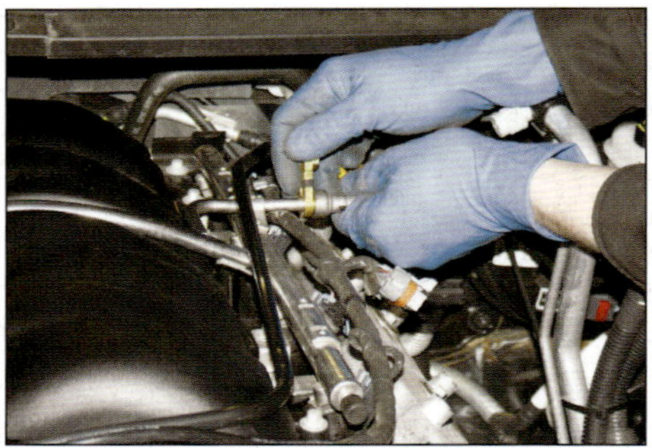

2 After the fascia's fasteners are removed, it pulls off as one big component, but it still requires some muscle to pull it free from the clips that hold it to the chassis. It sounds like the clips are breaking when doing this, but when done correctly, no damage occurs. The fascia should be stored safely away from the work area to prevent accidental damage when maneuvering under the hood and/or under the vehicle.

3 The procedural step with the engine involves the removal of the ignition coils. This is accomplished by disconnecting the plug wires from the spark plugs, disconnecting the coils' individual plug harnesses, unbolting the coil brackets from the valve covers, and lifting them out of the engine compartment. The coils are attached to a bracket, avoiding the need to remove them individually.

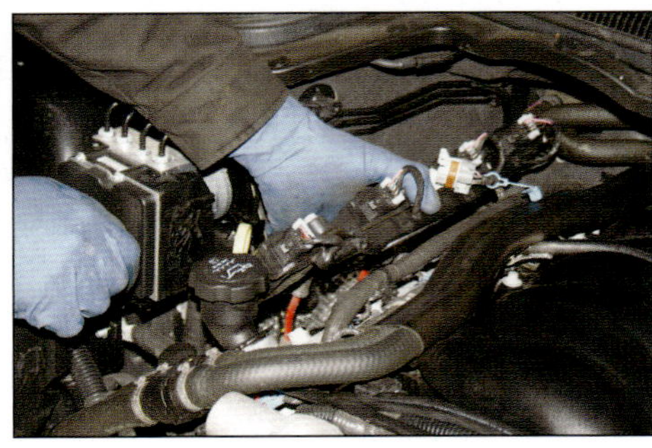

4 After properly relieving the fuel pressure (see chapter 4), the fuel system is disconnected from the fuel rail in preparation for the intake manifold's removal. Fortunately, the Magnuson kit comes with a fuel-line disconnection tool, but you should check the kit's contents for it prior to starting the installation. If the supercharger kit does not include the tool, obtain one before starting the project.

5 The intake manifold on most LS-powered vehicles is easily unbolted, although the comparatively restrictive engine compartments of fourth-generation F-Body cars and the SSR can make access to the rear fasteners more of a challenge. After the disconnection of the fuel system, the air intake tract and a few miscellaneous hoses are pulled off, and the intake manifold should pull relatively easily off the top of the engine. The lightweight nylon construction of the manifold makes removal easy for one person, but that is not true when it comes to installing the supercharger/intake manifold assembly. You should plan to have another person assist with that portion of the project.

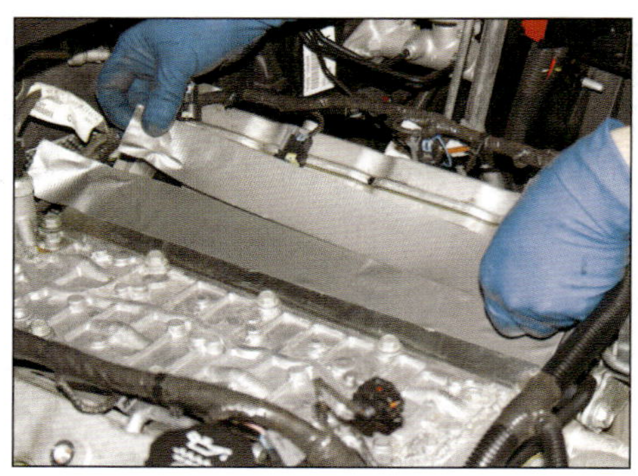

6 To prevent debris from falling into the engine in the time between the intake manifold's removal and the supercharger's installation, duct tape is laid over the cylinder heads' intake ports. A shop vacuum should also be used on the top of the engine to remove any unseen debris. There's no such thing as too much caution in this area.

7 With the intake manifold removed, attention turns to the crankshaft balancer and the steps required to add pins between it and the crankshaft hub to prevent unwanted movement of the press-fit balancer on the crankshaft. The Magnuson kit comes with the pins as well as a bolt-on template to guide the drill bit into the correct positions. (See chapter 4 for a more complete explanation of this procedure.)

8 Many of the installation procedures simply prepare the engine to accept the supercharger. Such is the case with this step. Add a new tensioner/pulley to the front of the engine as the crankshaft-driven supercharger adds a pulley to the accessory drive system. Not seen here is the pulley that bolts to the tensioner bracket after the bracket is secured on the engine.

9 Next, the front of the engine compartment is readied for the charge-cooling system. That process begins with the temporary removal of the electric cooling-fan assembly from the rear of the radiator. It is secured with only a few, easily accessible fasteners. The wiring harness must be disconnected too.

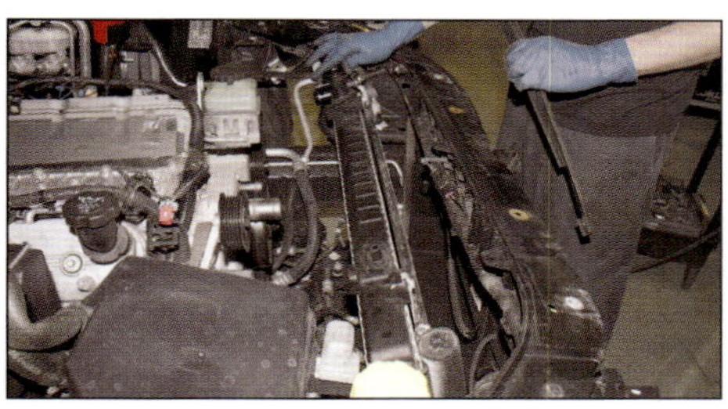

10 Although the installation procedure varies among vehicles, the charge-cooler heat exchanger always mounts in front of the radiator. In the case of this project G8 GT, installation requires disconnecting the radiator (including the removal of the radiator hoses and draining of the coolant) in order to push it back a few inches to slip the heat exchanger in front of it.

11 The heat exchanger for the G8 has brackets that hook on to the top of the radiator to hold it in place. In fact, adhesive-backed rubber pads are used for a tight fit at the top of the radiator and no bolts or other fasteners are used. This isn't the same for all LS vehicles, but holds true for many of them.

12 Here is the heat exchanger nestled in front of the radiator. Because it is essentially a radiator of its own, air freely passes through it and into the engine radiator, so the vehicle needs no further cooling-system upgrades. Some vehicles with compromising radiator positions and/or tight engine compartments (such as the fourth-generation F-Body cars and C5/C6 Corvettes) may benefit from a larger-capacity radiator to ensure cooler overall engine operation, as the supercharger will generate more heat to dissipate.

13 The next step in the installation procedure involves extending the length of the throttle-body wiring harness for vehicles equipped with an electronically controlled throttle. It starts with exposing the harness's individual wires by pulling them out of the protective cover.

Installing a Magna Charger Kit *(Continued)*

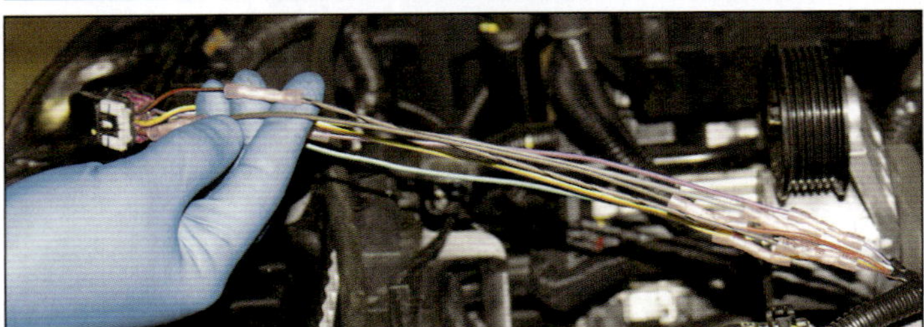

14 After the individual wires for the throttle body harness are exposed, they are cut and extension wires are inserted. The Magnuson kit came with extension wires that matched the colors of the original harness, making the task simpler. To prevent the joints of the extensions from bundling together at the same area in a bulky pack, the original wires should be cut at different points and different lengths. That spaces out the joints for a cleaner finished product that fits more cleanly within the protective loom cover.

15 Here's the extended harness assembly with the wires tucked back inside a longer cover. When done correctly, the modification looks factory with the cleanly spaced extension joints fitting easily within the cover. The extension is required to accommodate the modified mounting position of the throttle body when it is installed on the supercharger, as well the additional reach required for it around the supercharger system's components.

16 This application (along with most similar Roots/ screw-type systems) requires a different cylinder head–coolant crossover vent tube to accommodate the supercharger and new intake manifold. It is easily swapped with the help of a 10-mm socket because the original intake manifold is out of the way. There are O-ring seals on both ends of the vent tube that must be transferred to the new tube.

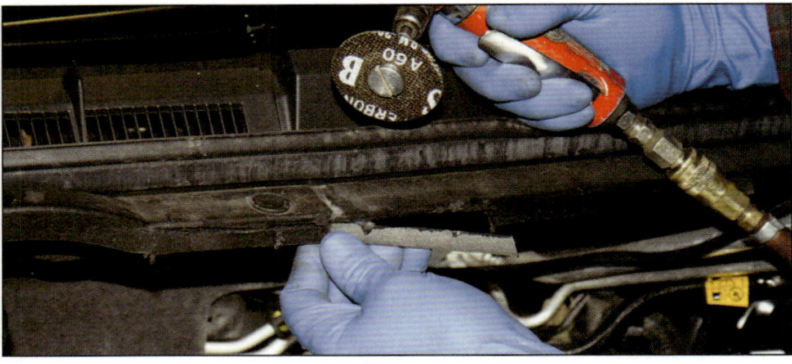

17 Another accommodation for the supercharger on the G8 GT, as well as some other vehicles, is providing adequate clearance around the cowl/firewall area. In the case of the G8 and the Magnuson system, it includes trimming a small piece from the leading edge of the plastic cowl trim. An air-powered cut-off wheel slices easily through the material, leaving a cleaner-looking cut. The edges of the modified sections should be finished or filed slightly to remove "flash" material from the plastic.

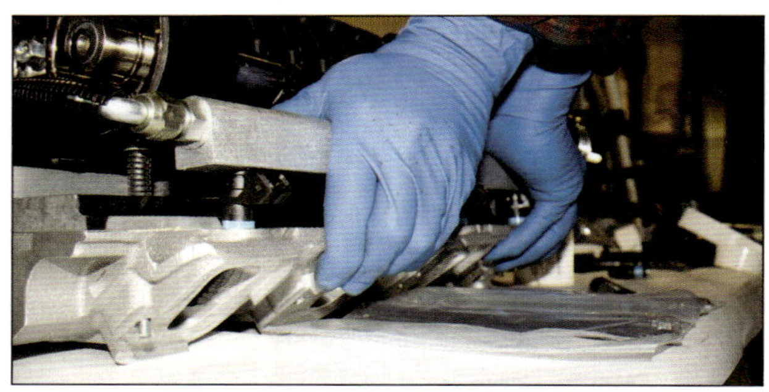

18 With most of the engine and engine-compartment preparations for the supercharger system completed, work turns to prepping the supercharger itself. Here, the new fuel injectors and fuel rails are added to the intake manifold. Be clear about whether the kit includes the injectors or you must obtain them separately. Most supercharger manufacturers offer lower-cost "tuner" kits that do not include injectors, spark plugs, and other parts. Those kits are designed for installation by professional shops that likely stock such parts. Complete kits should include the injectors, plugs, etc.

19 While preparing the supercharger, the installer at Livernois Motorsports noticed the rearmost manifold bolt on the passenger side would be a tight fit during installation, as it was sandwiched directly under the supercharger drive belt. Prechecking for installation issues such as this prevents larger headaches from developing once the assembly is on the engine and in the vehicle. It was determined that hand-threading the bolt would be required until there was sufficient room to get a box-end or open-end wrench on the bolt head. As the mounting position and supercharger design are largely the same for all LS engines, this is a common challenge with a Magnuson installation.

20 The last step before installing the supercharger/manifold assembly on the engine is installing intake manifold gaskets on the intake manifold itself. The Magnuson kit uses convenient, snap-on gaskets that are held in place perfectly until the manifold is fastened to the cylinder heads. Correspondingly, the ports on the cylinder head should be slightly lubricated with a mild soap-and-water solution to ensure a more precise, leak-free fit.

21 At last, the supercharger/manifold assembly is carefully lowered onto the engine. Because of the weight and awkward size of the assembly, it is a two-person task. On some vehicles, a replacement valley cover (including the transfer of the oil pressure sensor) is required and included with the kit, but that was not the case with this G8 application. Also, some vehicles may require the removal or relocation of a factory engine-installation bracket or, on vehicles with an automatic transmission, the relocation of the automatic-transmission fill tube. Again, that was not the case with the G8. Once the assembly is in place, the manifold bolts are tightened to the manufacturer's recommended torque specification.

22 With the supercharger assembly bolted in place, the fuel-injector harnesses are connected to the injectors. It is important to make sure the injectors used with the supercharger are compatible with the harness connectors, as there are primarily two types used with LS engines. Jumper harnesses are available to accommodate nonmatching harnesses and injectors, but check the harness/injector compatibility prior to reaching this stage in the installation.

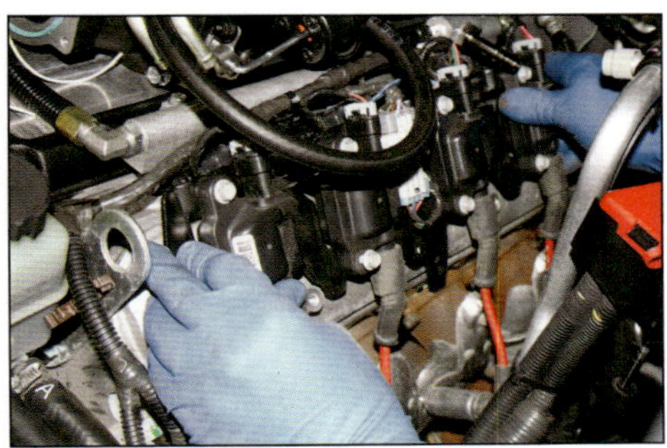

23 Next, the ignition coil brackets are reinstalled. There should be no clearance problems, as none of the supercharger system's hardware affects the location or placement of the brackets, coils, or plug wire routing.

Installing a Magna Charger Kit *(Continued)*

24 After the ignition coils come the spark plugs. Colder-range, NGK TR-6 plugs with a tighter gap are used on this project and recommended for most forced-induction systems. (See chapter 4 for more information on the importance of selecting the right spark plug.)

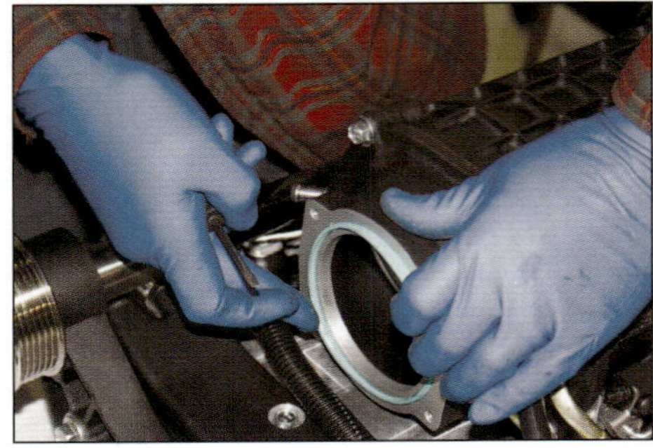

25 All of the small details become increasingly important as the button-up stage of the installation is underway, and that means following the manufacturer's assembly manual closely. Here, the comparatively minor (yet very important) step of installing the O-ring seal for the throttle body is depicted.

26 Next, the new serpentine belt is installed on the engine, including its routing on the supercharger pulley. One of the appreciative features of the Magnuson kit is the integration of the supercharger pulley into the accessory drive system. Some systems may require separate belts and/or a greater modification of the accessory drive components.

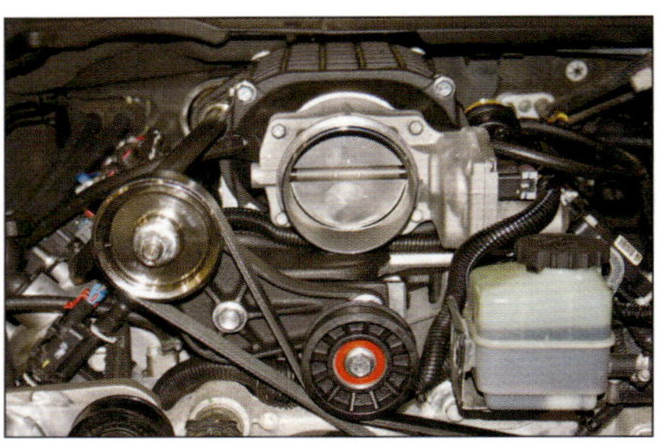

27 This photo shows the throttle body installed on the supercharger, as well as its lengthened wiring harness plugged into it. It also shows the myriad of other hoses, connectors, and fasteners reattached to the engine and/or supercharger/manifold assembly. Despite their common LS-engine architecture, different vehicles have different connections, sensors, and other hardware. Again, the manufacturer's assembly manual should be followed closely to ensure all of the connections have been made. A few items to check for include the Idle Air Temperature (IAT) sensor, EVAP lines (which may require modification or replacement on some vehicles), the purge solenoid, vacuum hoses, and the MAP sensor/wiring harness.

28 Another important reconnection step is the installation of the fuel feed line. Because of the push-lock design of the connector, it simply pushes into place until a positive click indicates it is correctly installed. Unlike the removal process, a special tool isn't required.

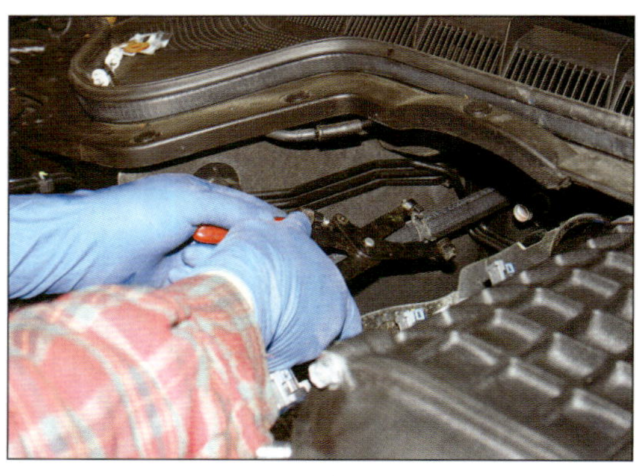

29 Among the plumbing changes brought on by the supercharger system (at least on the G8 GT depicted here) is the need for longer heater hoses. Typically, they're included with the inclusive kits and may not be included with "tuner" kits.

30 A new brake-booster check valve should be included with all supercharger systems to optimize the boost/vacuum pressure created with the supercharged engine.

32 The charge-cooling system also includes a coolant reservoir. Mounting positions vary from vehicle to vehicle, but they are typically mounted higher in the engine compartment, providing easy access to the fill cap.

33 There is also add-on wiring associated with the electric water pump. It simply splices into the factory, underhood fuse box.

31 The brake-booster connection finishes off the connections related to the engine, so the final step is the installation of the charge-cooling system components. On the independently circulated liquid-to-air system with the Magnuson system, begin by mounting the system's electrically driven water pump (arrow).

34 With all of the charge-cooling system's hoses securely connected, the reservoir is filled with a 50-50 mix of coolant and water. Depending on the system, it will take 1 to 2 gallons of mixed coolant. Activating the pump without the engine on helps circulate the coolant to quickly fill the system. This is also the appropriate time to refill the engine radiator with the coolant that was drained previously.

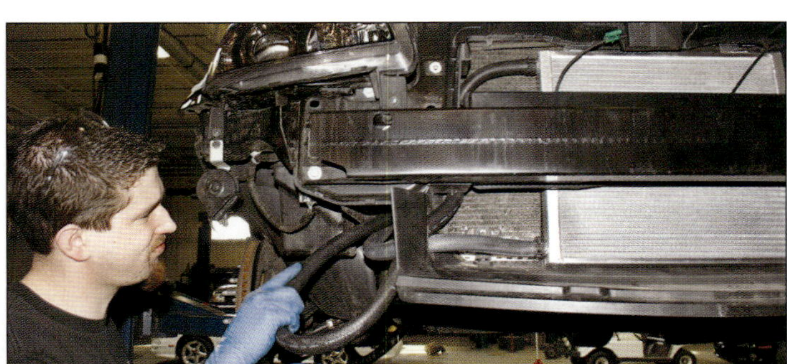

35 Next, the coolant hoses are routed to and from the heat exchanger between it, the water pump, and the reservoir tank. Again, routing and placement of the hoses varies among vehicles; and it typically requires the modification or the removal of components located behind the vehicle's front fascia. In the case of this G8, it required creating a passageway through a plastic "wall" located beneath the bumper.

Here's the finished installation. It looks neat as a pin and, with that black blower case, nearly factory. At this point, refer to the assembly manual to double-check that all the required connections are made. This car also has an aftermarket cold-air induction system that is not part of the Magnuson kit.

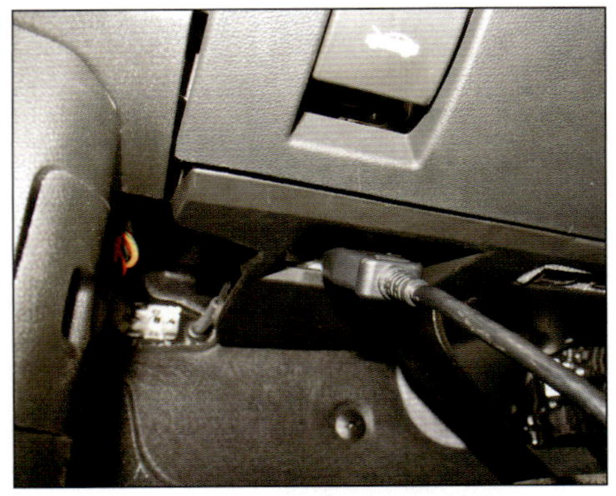

With the super-charger and charge-cooling systems installed, the final stage of the project involves upload-ing the new pro-gramming tune to the engine control module. For most vehicles (whether using the kit's supplied programmer or a custom tune), a connection must be made via the OBD-II port located beneath the dashboard. On other vehicles, add-on and/or supplemental control modules must be spliced into the factory control module. On the G8 GT project vehicle, the tune was simply uploaded through the OBD-II port.

The Magnuson kit comes with its own tuning software and programmer, but Dan Millen uses Livernois Motorsports X-Treme Cal Tuning software. Here, Millen feeds the G8's controller his tune. It is vitally important to never start an engine with nonoriginal fuel injectors until the tune is uploaded, otherwise engine damage will occur almost immediately! Once the engine is started for the first time, it should be turned off after a few seconds to check for any fuel, oil, or coolant leaks; serpen-tine belt alignment; and a general underhood examination. Also, make sure the fuel tank is filled with premium gas, as the tuning is typically dependent on at least 91 octane.

On Livernois Motorsports' dyno, the newly blown G8 put down 423 hp and 401 ft-lbs at the tires. It was a good result but would have been better with a less-restrictive cat-back exhaust system. Neverthe-less, the car made more than 35-percent-greater power than when it entered the shop a few days earlier. Throttle response and overall drivability is excellent too, with the blower's presence only heard and felt on demand.

Project 2: Centrifugal Supercharger Kit

This project covers the basic installation of a centrifugal super-charger. Unlike the Roots/Lysholm-type blower that essentially replaces the intake manifold, a bolt-on cen-trifugal kit typically retains the stock intake manifold but adds the super-charger to the front of the engine, much like other engine-driven acces-sories like the air-conditioning com-pressor or power-steering pump.

Generally speaking, the installa-tion of a centrifugal supercharger is more complex than a Roots/screw-type system but not significantly so. I followed the installation procedures of both the Magnuson system and the centrifugal system and found the Magnuson system was easier to install and took less time to do so. That said, the centrifugal system wasn't necessarily difficult to install, but it required more steps and greater finesse.

The centrifugal blower system outlined here involves an A&A Cor-

General Tools Required

- Metric wrenches and sockets (standard and deep)
- Metric Allen wrenches/sockets
- Torque wrench
- Phillips-head and flathead screwdrivers
- Fuel-line disconnection tool (may be included with the kit)
- Drill (possibly requiring angled head)
- Hose cutters and hose clamp pliers
- Trim removal tool ■

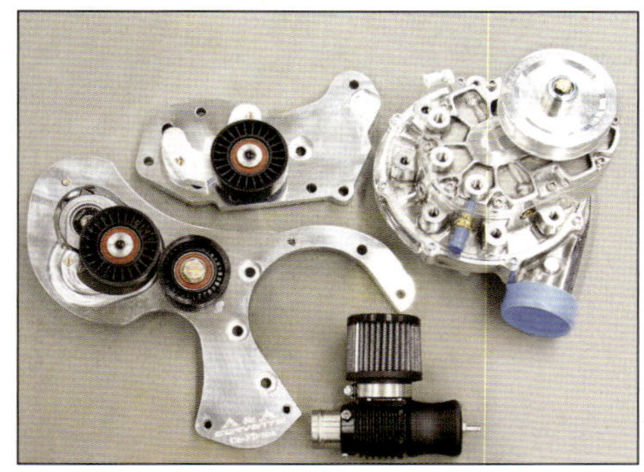

Here are the basic components of a centrifugal system, minus the intercooler hardware. The mounting brackets hang the supercharger on the front of the engine. This kit (from A&A Corvette) includes a large blow-off valve (at bottom of photo), which is a necessary accessory for preventing excessive boost from being forced into the engine after the throttle is closed.

vette kit for a C6 Corvette with an automatic transmission. It uses a Vortech V-2 Si compressor and a custom intercooling system. The blower is fitted with a 3.8-inch-drive pulley that enables approximately 12 pounds of boost. The kit includes a bypass valve, 60-pound fuel injectors, and a Kenne Bell Boost-A-Pump.

The installation was performed by Stenod Performance based out of Troy, Michigan. It took roughly a day and a half to complete the installation, while the Magnuson kit was installed in a single business day. Both installations were handled by professional shops using vehicle lifts and, where necessary, air tools. The accompanying photos should not be considered a how-to guide for installing a blower on a Corvette, but it should be a reference of the basic steps for all centrifugal supercharger systems.

Because the processes for pinning the crankshaft, mounting the intercooler heat exchanger, routing the intercooler coolant tubes, and other details are similar to the Roots-type installation, this project focuses on the aspects of the installation that make it different. That includes mounting the supercharger bracket and compressor. It should be noted that the kit shown here required an oil-feed line tapped into the oil pan. That is not the case with all centrifugal kits (see chapter 4 for more details on that procedure).

Prior to receiving the supercharger, the Corvette used in this project was enhanced with L92 cylinder heads and intake manifold, as well as a blower-spec camshaft (see chapter 9). These modifications increased the airflow capability of the engine to better exploit the capability of the supercharger. The work paid big dividends too, as the Corvette put down 508 hp and 439 ft-lbs of torque to the rear wheels on Stenod Performance's Mustang Dynamometer chassis dyno.

Installing a Centrifugal Supercharger Kit

1 *As with the Roots blower kit, preparation for installation includes the removal of the front fascia to enable mounting of the intercooler system's heat exchanger and related hoses and hardware. The cooling system is also drained and the radiator is removed. Although not necessarily required for every vehicle installation, removing the radiator is quick and easy, and it opens up tremendous working space under the hood while preventing inadvertent damage to the fins.*

2 *After pinning the crankshaft, an oil feed line was routed from the engine in preparation for the supercharger. Some centrifugal superchargers (Vortech blowers, mostly) require this external lubrication. The oiling circuit also includes an oil return line that must be tapped into the oil pan. (See chapter 4).*

Installing a Centrifugal Supercharger Kit *(Continued)*

3 *The next step involves mounting the rear portion of the supercharger support bracket. In most cases, it replaces the factory tensioner or idler pulley, although the location and placement varies among vehicles. The passenger-side location on this Corvette is typical.*

4 *The front part of the bracket is then mounted to the supercharger compressor. The bracket contains a tensioner that replaces the factory unit that was removed to make room for the supercharger.*

5 *Because of the tight fit and/or awkward routing, it may be easier to pre-install the serpentine belt on the supercharger bracket prior to installing the supercharger on the engine. This makes it easier to accurately route the belt on the rest of the engine's accessories.*

6 *The supercharger and front mounting bracket are installed together and loosely threaded onto the rear mounting bracket. None of the fasteners are torqued until the general fitment and clearances around the brackets, blower, and belt are double-checked.*

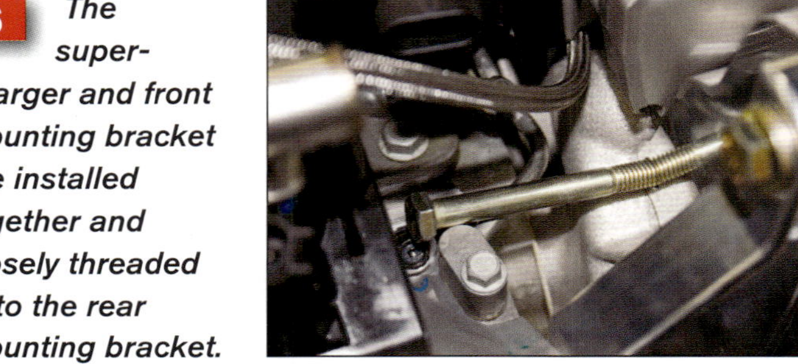

7 *It's vitally important to follow the assembly manual closely. Here, the installer made an assumption about the blower mounting bracket's hardware but didn't take into account the interference of the cylinder heads' coolant crossover tube, which prevented one of the brackets' bolts from sliding into its mounting hole. Rectifying the problem required backtracking, which added unnecessary time to the project.*

8 *With the supercharger and its mounting-bracket components securely tightened, the oil feed line from the engine is connected to the compressor.*

9 *Complementing the oil feed line is an oil return line that is routed from the compressor (left) to the fitting that was added to the oil pan (right).*

10 Next, the intercooler heat exchanger is mounted in front of the radiator. The procedure for the coolant circuit and hose routing for it is similar to the procedures outlined in the Magnuson installation project on page 64.

11 Similar to the Magnuson installation, routing the intercooler's plumbing required modifying some of the vehicle's plastic underbody components to enable pass-through room for the hoses. Note the circular template for the hole, which is easily cut into the soft plastic material of the part.

12 After routing the intercooler plumbing, attention turns to the fuel system. The kit's higher-capacity, 60-lbs/hr injectors were swapped onto the stock fuel rail. Then, the fuel rail was simply pushed back into place on the intake manifold.

Here's the finished installation. There was more fabrication required than the Roots-type supercharger installation outlined on pages 64–69 but some of it is due to the tighter confines of the Corvette's engine compartment. Nevertheless, the installation proved relatively easy and straightforward for a professional shop or an individual who has the necessary experience and tools.

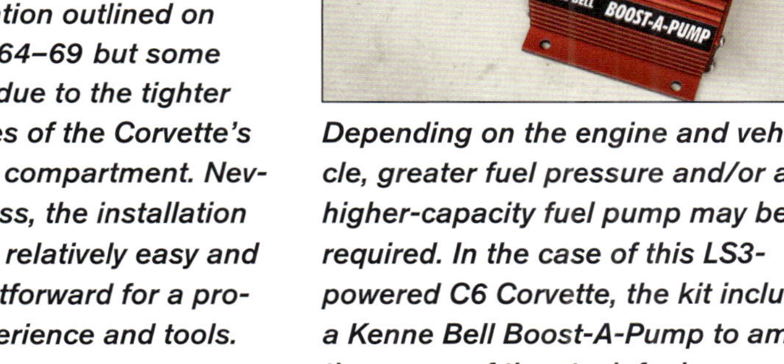

Depending on the engine and vehicle, greater fuel pressure and/or a higher-capacity fuel pump may be required. In the case of this LS3-powered C6 Corvette, the kit included a Kenne Bell Boost-A-Pump to amplify the power of the stock fuel pump. Using it eliminates the most costly and time-consuming need for removing the fuel tank to swap fuel pumps.

Because of the additional modifications, including cylinder heads and a camshaft, the manufacturer's tuning software wasn't sufficient for this project. A custom tune was created at Stenod Performance, and the Corvette delivered 508 hp and 439 ft-lbs of torque at the rear wheels through an automatic transmission. This was on a Mustang dyno that typically isn't as optimistic as comparable chassis dynos from other manufacturers. That's a significant 170-hp/110-ft-lbs jump over the baseline 338-hp/329-ft-lbs numbers.

TURBOCHARGER INSTALLATION PROJECTS

Unlike most bolt-on supercharger systems, which can easily adapt to a variety of vehicles, turbo kits present unique challenges. There is more to contend with in the routing of inlet and outlet tubing between the exhaust manifolds, turbocharger(s), and engine intake. At the minimum, major changes are required of the exhaust system. Of course, all that plumbing changes for different vehicles, whereas adapting a Roots blower, for example, requires comparatively minor revisions to suit mostly the accessory drive and intercooler mounting for different vehicles.

So, while complete turbo kits aren't as plentiful as the range of supercharger systems, they can be created by essentially running enough tubing between the basic elements: turbocharger, wastegate, blow-off valve, and intercooler.

Real-World Project: Lingenfelter System

This project is the installation of the Lingenfelter Performance Engineering's twin-turbo system on a C6 Corvette Z06 (rebodied by Specter Werkes/Sports). Although it is a system Lingenfelter has installed on a number of vehicles, it's not exactly an off-the-shelf kit.

Because of the natural variances between production vehicles, Lingenfelter custom-fits elements such as the water and oil lines after the turbochargers are installed. It's a very precise, well-engineered system, but again it underscores the difficulties in developing a true bolt-on turbo kit. With that in mind, this installation should be seen as representing the components, connections, vehicle modifications, and other details that are common to all turbo systems. The caveat is that the system is specific to Lingenfelter Performance Engineering and the Corvette Z06. In other words, it should be viewed as a general overview of the parts and procedures involved, but by no means is it a definitive blueprint for all LS-powered vehicles. It should also be noted that this installation does not show every procedure; it highlights primary procedures and details.

The Lingenfelter system is designed for use in cars driven primarily on the street, so it works around existing vehicle systems and components. There was no sacrificing of air-conditioning, power amenities, or anything like that. In a nutshell, it uses a pair of medium-size Garrett water-cooled, oil-lubricated ball-bearing turbos and an air-to-air intercooler. Here are the basics:

- A single blow-off valve
- Custom air-to-air charge cooler
- High-capacity fuel injectors
- Kenne Bell Boost-A-Pump
- Upgraded oil cooler
- Custom low-restriction exhaust system
- Custom tuning

Although boost is always tunable, the base system delivers about 10 to 12 pounds of boost to help the 7.0L engine produce 800 hp. More importantly, Lingenfelter's package for the twin-turbo system includes rebuilding the high-compression LS7 engine with stronger internal components, lower-compression (9.0:1) pistons, and a number of other related details. The turbo system isn't installed until the engine is removed, rebuilt, and reinstalled (all the work is performed at Lingenfelter's Decatur, Indiana, shop).

An advantage to having the work performed at Lingenfelter's shop (or

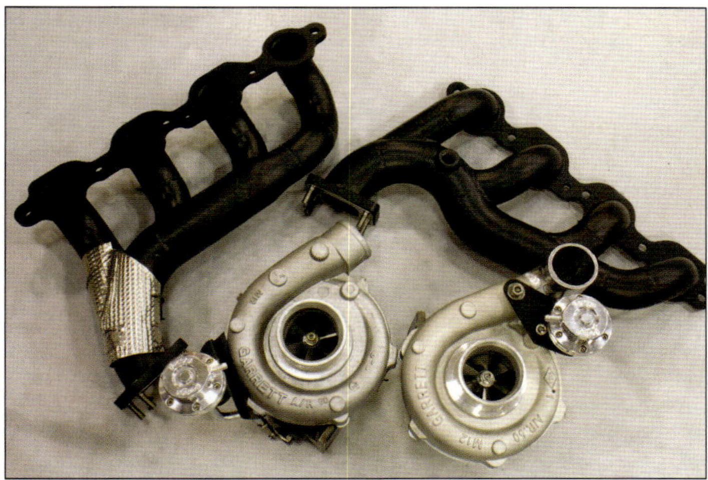

The turbo system is designed to mount the turbochargers directly to custom, heavy-duty exhaust manifolds. In the low-slung Corvette chassis, that still puts them at the bottom of the engine compartment, which helps keep heat farther away from the engine and air-intake system.

Lingenfelter's basic system uses a pair of these mid-size Garrett GT30-series water-cooled, oil-fed ball-bearing turbochargers and Forge wastegates. The medium-size bodies of the turbos make them ideal for easier fitment and quick spool-up. The A/R ratio, as noted on the casting seen here, is 0.50:1.

any reputable shop that does custom turbo systems) is experienced fabricators. The minor, yet important, vehicle-to-vehicle variances between otherwise-identical vehicle models typically requires fabrication work that is not easily accomplished in a home garage.

Whether it's a true bolt-on system or a blend of bolt-on and custom-fabricated, such as the Lingenfelter system, installation takes time, perhaps two or three times as long as a bolt-on supercharger system. Keep that in mind (and its implication on labor costs at the installation shop) as you consider such a modification.

Installing a Lingenfelter Twin-Turbo System

1 *This turbo installation project takes place on a Specter Werkes/Sports GTR built around a Corvette Z06. All of the mechanical work was performed at Lingenfelter Performance Engineering's Indiana facility.*

2 *Prior to installing the turbo system, Lingenfelter removed the Z06's LS7 engine and rebuilt it to suit the demands of turbocharging. That involved rebuilding the short-block with a new, forged-steel crankshaft, forged-steel connecting rods, and lower-compression 9.0:1 pistons. The heads also received high-temperature-resistant Inconel exhaust valves.*

Installing a Lingenfelter Twin-Turbo System *(Continued)*

3 *The first evidence of custom fabrication on the kit is the welded-on elbow added to each turbocharger's air outlet, which is necessary to orient the outlet toward the front of the vehicle.*

6 *One of the other preinstallation procedures is prepping the engine for the oiling requirements of the turbos. That involves swapping the stock oil cooler for an aftermarket model, fitting a scavenge pump to pull returned oil from the low-mounted turbos, and adding a feed line (seen here) to the oil pan that sends the circulated oil back into the pan.*

4 *A thick, 3/4-inch flange is attached to the exhaust manifold, where the turbocharger mounts. This is necessary to prevent warping under the extreme temperatures generated when the system is producing maximum boost. Also note the heat shield attached to the manifold.*

7 *The system's installation started with bolting on the exhaust manifolds. With the hood removed and considerable chassis clearance on the Corvette, it was easy to do from the top of the engine compartment. Other vehicles require careful installation of the manifolds from the bottom of the engine compartment.*

9 *With the exhaust manifolds and their oxygen sensors in place, the first turbocharger is hoisted into position, sliding onto the mounting studs protruding from the exhaust manifold's mounting flange. In this photo, the passenger-side turbo is being installed.*

5 *Turbo systems invariably require custom or modified exhaust systems, so before installation began, the original system was removed and set aside.*

8 *The all-important oxygen sensors are threaded into the exhaust manifolds next, as doing so later would be more difficult with more of the turbo system's components in place. Wideband sensors are installed for more precise part-throttle tuning.*

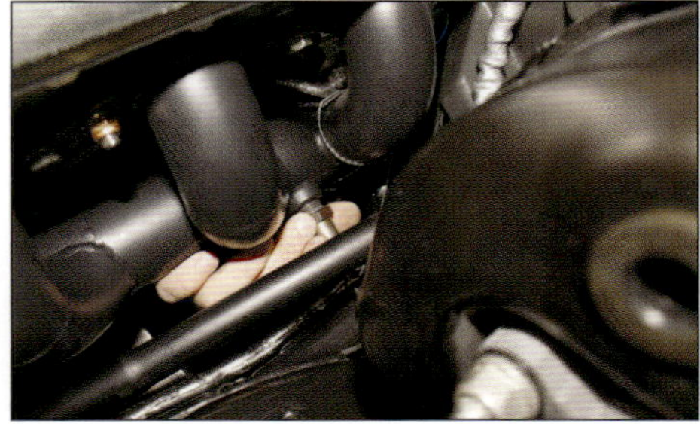

10 *Lingenfelter uses many hard lines in the system, including the oil feed and oil return lines at the turbo, which require custom fitting to account for the slight variances among vehicles. After the first turbocharger was installed, for example, this line was measured and cut to fit the oil feed line to it.*

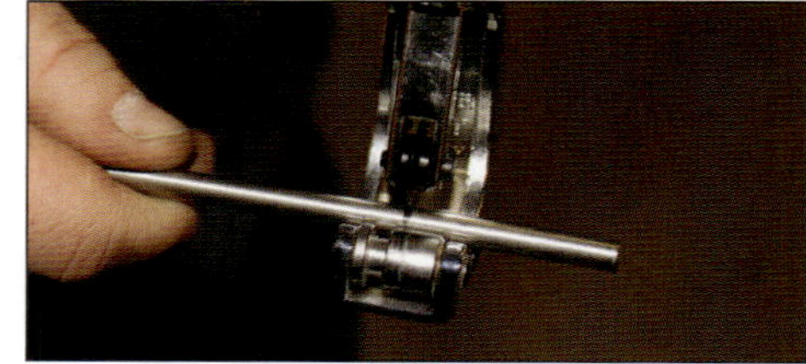

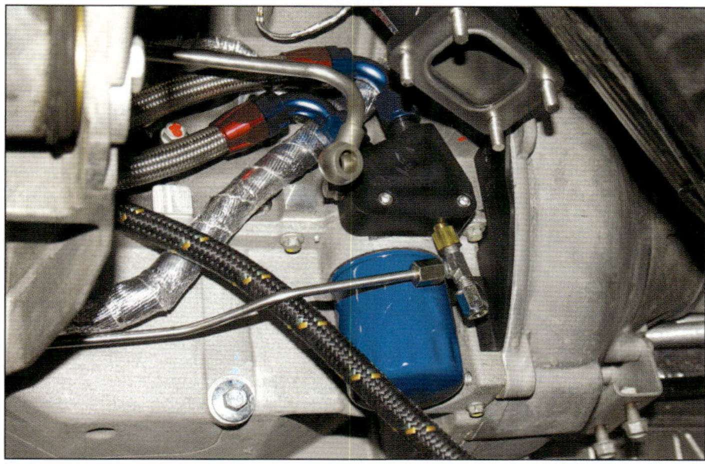

11 *The hard oil feed line wraps under the oil pan and up to a T-junction in an aftermarket oil cooler. The bottom fitting is reserved for the driver-side turbo's oil feed line.*

12 *The installed oil feed line is seen routing away from the turbo and along the oil pan rail. Installing the line at this point in the project is necessary because access to it would be almost impossible after the down tube and other sections of the system are installed.*

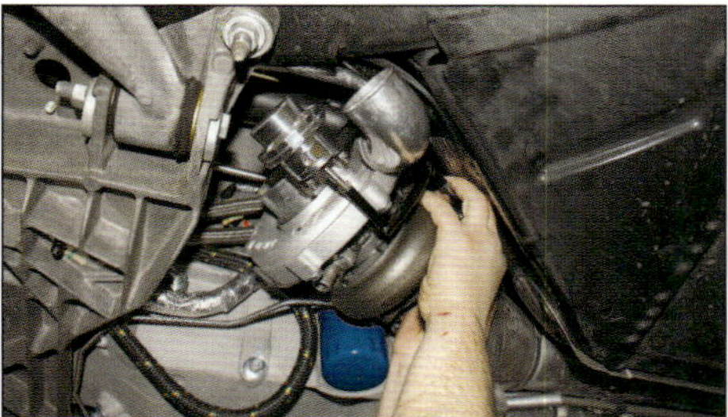

13 *With the passenger-side turbo and its oil feed line in place, the driver-side turbo is installed and its oil feed line attached.*

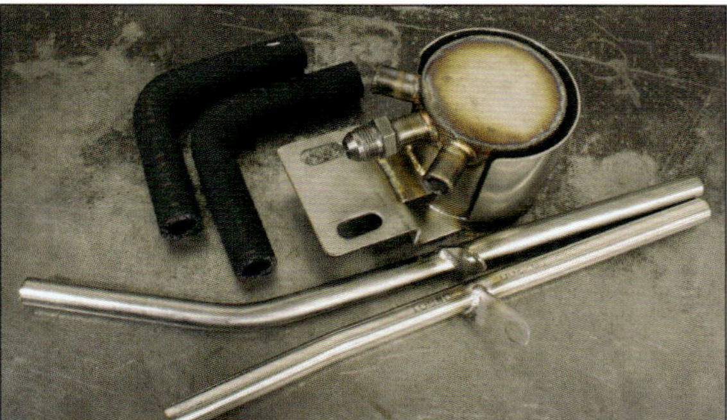

14 *At the other end of the turbos' oiling system is a scavenge system that draws oil cycled through the turbochargers back into the engine's oiling system. Because the turbos are mounted low on the engine, gravity is not sufficient for draining to the oil pan, so Lingenfelter designed a small oil tank that collects the return oil from the turbos and, with the help of an electric pump, draws it out and back into the oil pan.*

15 *The turbochargers are also water cooled, which requires tapping into the vehicle's cooling system for feed and return. Inserting a junction in the heater hoses does the trick. As seen here, it's double clamped on both ends to ensure a leak- and blow-proof seal.*

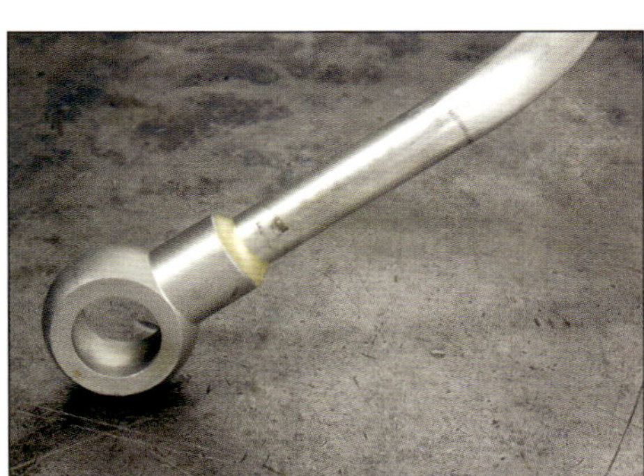

16 *To make installation easier in the tight confines on the bottom side of the engine compartment, banjo-type fittings are used to connect the coolant system to the turbochargers.*

Installing a Lingenfelter Twin-Turbo System *(Continued)*

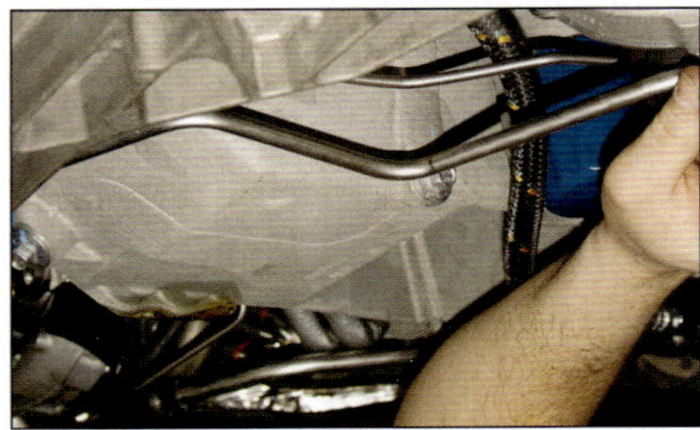

17 *Like the oil lines, the water lines to and from the turbos are hard lines. They're also routed around the oil pan. This configuration is more time intensive to fabricate and install, but if the lines were simply run directly under the pan, they'd be susceptible to damage if the vehicle were to scrape the ground.*

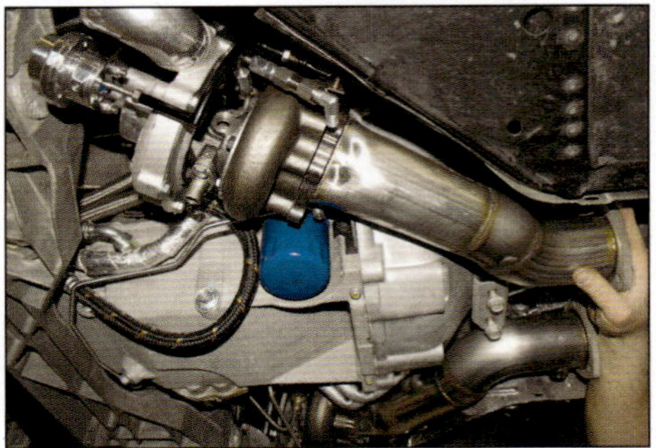

18 *Next, the down tubes (the pipes that connect the exhaust outlet of the turbos to the vehicle's exhaust system) are installed, but not before they're test-fitted to ensure there are no interference issues with any of the other turbo system or chassis components.*

19 *Although a metal gasket was used between the turbochargers and the exhaust manifolds, the down pipes are mated to the turbos with Permatex Ultra Copper high-temperature silicone gasket maker. It is spread liberally on the mounting flange.*

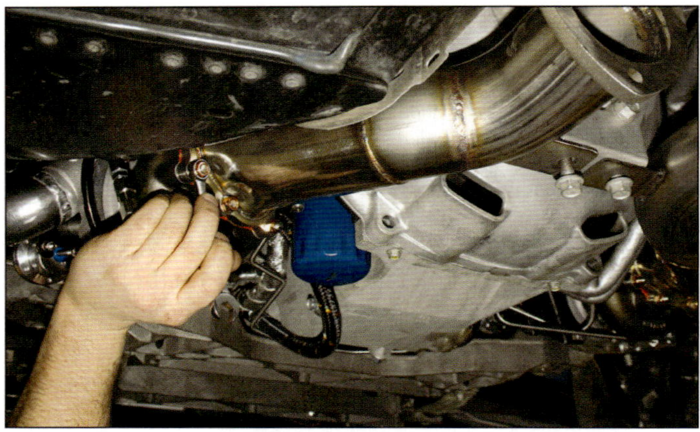

20 *With the copper gasket maker on the flange, one of the down tubes is cinched down against the turbocharger. Note how both down tubes are further supported by mounting tabs that attach to the transmission bellhousing.*

21 *The custom oil-scavenge tank also mounts to the bellhousing. The hard lines feeding the tank carry gravity-fed oil from the turbochargers, while the large flexible hose draws out the oil with vacuum pressure from a pump mounted at the front of the engine. The oil is then reintroduced to the engine oil circuit.*

22 *From under the Corvette, you can see the basic installation and orientation of the twin-turbo setup prior to fitting the air-intake and air-discharge tubes. Look closely and note the careful routing of the hard lines for the oil and water systems, as well as the unique oil-scavenge tank. From here, the installation focuses on the intake tubes, intercooler, and reinstallation of numerous engine/exhaust system components.*

23 The silicone hoses are carefully routed from the turbochargers along the chassis rails. There are numerous checks and inspections to ensure they don't bind or interfere with the suspension and steering systems.

24 Filter-capped intakes are mounted in the front corners of the front fascia. The air-discharge tubes from the turbos feed the intercooling system's heat exchanger that is to be located in front of the radiator.

25 The intercooler's heat exchanger slides down in front of the stock radiator, necessitating the relocation of the oil cooler's heat exchanger. A Y-pipe connects both outlets of the exchanger and feeds the air charge straight into the throttle body. Like other aspects of the installation, the Y-pipe is custom-fitted to each vehicle. After that, the heat exchanger and intake tube are painted black.

26 When the intake tubes are routed and securely attached, the project moves into the final stages of buttoning up a myriad of details. This includes installing the mass air sensor (seen here), adding a 3-bar MAP sensor, reconnecting the fuel system, and performing a number of wiring duties.

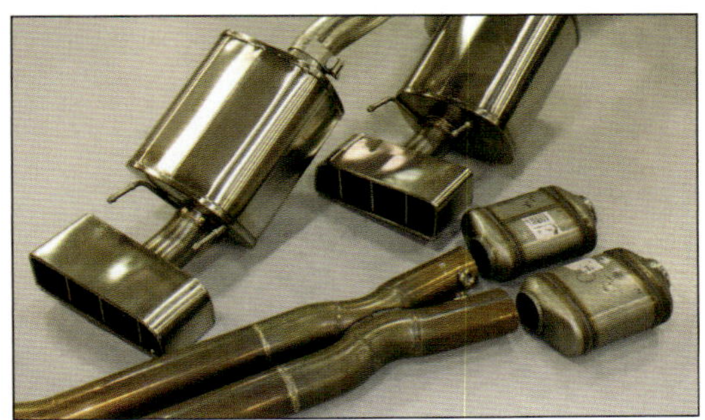

27 The final major task in the installation involves reinstalling the exhaust system. As is the case with most turbo installations, a modified exhaust system is required. In the case of this Z06-based project, it also required reimaging the converter system because the close-coupled, high-mounted catalytic converters on the stock exhaust system were eliminated. Lingenfelter's solution involved using a pair of compact C4 Corvette converters and a lightly modified Corsa C6 Corvette flow tube to fit within the vehicle's underbody tunnel. The rest of the exhaust system was modified to keep the mufflers in the stock location.

Lingenfelter uses flexible silicone hoses for the air-intake tubes and the discharge tubes that feed the boosted air charge to the intercooler. They're custom made a little longer than necessary to enable precise fitment with a little trimming.

An interesting detail on this system is the reuse of the vacuum port that used to actuate the factory's two-stage exhaust system. It now is used to actuate a fuel-pressure regulator mounted at the rear of the vehicle, near the fuel tank.

Custom Turbo System Fabrication

Rather than a system designed for racing, the vehicle's owner, DiabloSport chief Mike Wesley, wanted an integrated system for the street. That meant the system had to work around existing vehicle systems and components. There was no sacrificing of air-conditioning, power amenities, or anything like that. Wesley turned to Stenod Performance to design, fabricate, and install a custom system. It uses a pair of Garrett ball-bearing turbos and an air-to-air intercooler. Initially, because the turbochargers were blowing into a stock LS2 engine, boost was kept to a detonation-avoiding 5 pounds. That was enough to deliver tread-melting performance from all four of the all-wheel-drive TrailBlazer's tires.

Soon, Wesley returned to the Stenod shop for a power boost. The engine was removed and rebuilt with the requisite forged internals and lower-compression pistons, as the wick would be turned up on the turbos to deliver approximately 10 to 12 pounds of boost. The original Garrett turbochargers were retained, but the wastegate actuators were swapped to allow the greater boost (a boost controller was not used).

Basics of the system and supporting hardware include:

- Two Garrett GT28R ball-bearing turbochargers with integral wastegates
- One TiAL 50-mm blow-off valve
- Custom air-to-air charge cooler
- 60-lbs/hour fuel injectors
- Walbro 355-lph in-tank fuel pump
- Stock radiator with fourth-generation F-Body cooling fans and C6 Corvette fan-control unit
- SLP Performance low-restriction exhaust system
- Retention of the stock mass air metering system but with a 3-bar MAP sensor
- Reprogrammed factory controller with HP Tuners tune

On a completely custom build, every inlet, discharge, and intake tube requires fabrication. If you are seeking to have a custom turbo system made for your car, you should do so only through a shop with similar experience. Inspecting other customers' cars and interviewing them about their experience are musts before entrusting your car and money to any shop. The design and fabrication of the TrailBlazer's system required turbocharger mounting brackets, air intake flow tubes, discharge flow tubes, intercooler tubing, and exhaust tubing. Additionally, a number of oil and coolant hoses were routed into and away from the turbochargers, requiring modification of the engine's coolant lines to merge the turbochargers' cooling lines with the engine's water system.

One of the more advantageous aspects of the system's design is the mounting of the turbos out of the engine compartment. They are located down and away from the engine, effectively straddling the transmission. This placement takes the turbos away from the exhaust manifolds, saving the time and money of fabricating custom manifolds while also reducing underhood heat. In fact, factory shielding on the underside of the vehicle, where original exhaust components were located, provides an excellent thermal barrier for the turbochargers.

Upon completion of the upgraded turbo system, the TrailBlazer was tested on an AWD-capable chassis dyno, where it produced more than 600 hp and 550 ft-lbs of torque to all four wheels. It was stunning performance for a vehicle that is driven daily, but performance that is well within the capability of a

Installing a Custom Turbocharger System

1 *Adding a turbo system to the TrailBlazer SS presents the same problem for many LS-powered vehicles: there isn't a bolt-on kit available in the aftermarket (at least not as this book is being written). A custom turbo system was designed, built, and installed by Stenod Performance. Fortunately, there was enough room under the hood and around the chassis to facilitate the installation with minimal impact on the surrounding factory components. As is the case with almost all intercooled forced-induction systems, the project began with the removal of the front fascia, grille, and headlamp components to enable mounting of the intercooler heat exchanger and related plumbing.*

2 *The turbo system includes a pair of Garrett GT28R water-cooled, ball-bearing turbochargers. Seen here is one of the turbochargers mounted to an exhaust extension that bridges between the turbo and exhaust manifold. Because of this arrangement, the turbocharger is located at the bottom of the engine compartment, in the approximate area of the original catalytic converter. The lower mounting position reduces underhood heat, and the thermal barrier for the converter provides heat shielding.*

3 *Here is the passenger-side turbocharger/exhaust extension assembly attached to the exhaust manifold. Note the Y-fitting with large-diameter hoses at the center of the photo. It is part of the scavenge system that draws oil away from the turbochargers and back into the engine-oil circuit. Like the turbos described in the Lingenfelter installation earlier, the turbochargers on this system are water-cooled and externally lubricated. Because of the heat generated by the turbos, very durable, heavy-duty hoses, including braided lines, are used with AN-type fittings.*

4 *The other major component of the turbo system is the intercooler, which includes a custom heat exchanger built by Stenod Performance. It's an air-to-air intercooling system, meaning the pressurized air from the turbo system simply flows through the exchanger and is cooled by air entering through the grille or from the electric cooling fans. There is no liquid coolant circulating in the heat exchanger, as would be the case with a liquid-to-air intercooler. Stenod started with a Bell core and built the inlet/outlet caps to fit the TrailBlazer. It mounts to a removable header that's part of the TrailBlazer's radiator core support, making installation and removal very simple.*

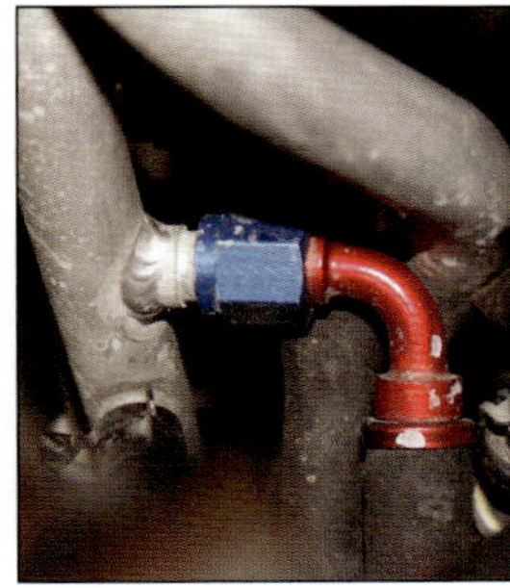

5 *When it came to the coolant lines for the turbochargers, the inlet and outlet hoses were routed from the aluminum hard-line sections of the heater hoses. That required drilling holes and welding fittings to the factory lines. There are other ways to tie into the factory cooling system to provide the same effect, but with one of the hard lines dedicated to inlet and the other a dedicated outlet, this method is foolproof, even if it required careful, labor-intensive aluminum welding.*

Installing a Custom Turbocharger System *(Continued)*

6 With most of the coolant and oil lines routed and connected, the turbos' air intake and discharge tubes are mounted. The relatively large chassis and generous ground clearance of the TrailBlazer SS allowed Stenod Performance to route them easily under the engine K-member, where they feed into the bottom of the intercooler heat exchanger.

7 The air intake filters are mounted as far away from the heat of the turbo system as possible; in this case, at the far corners of the front bumper cover. Note the vacuum hose attached to the intake tube. It's part of a crankcase breather system.

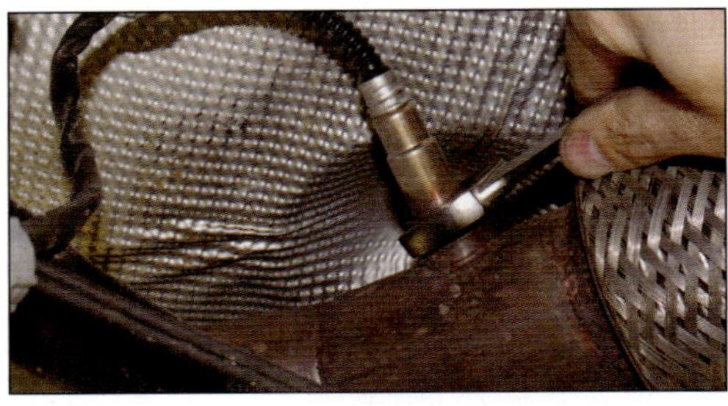

8 The fabricated portions of the exhaust system also included provisions for oxygen sensors: one on each side, after the turbochargers. This system also incorporates oxygen sensors before each turbocharger to satisfy the parameters for wideband tuning.

9 At the top of the engine, the intake tube is sandwiched between the throttle body and the intercooler. It is a large, 4-inch-diameter tube to feed as much air as possible to the engine. The convoluted shape of the tube again demonstrates the careful, custom fitment required of each tube to fit with other factory-installed components. For vehicles that aren't matched with an aftermarket turbo kit, such custom fabrication is the only option. Stenod Performance incorporated a TiAL 50-mm blow-off valve into the intake tube. A blow-off valve should be located in the intake section between the discharge port of the intercooler's heat exchanger and the throttle body, which is right where this one is located.

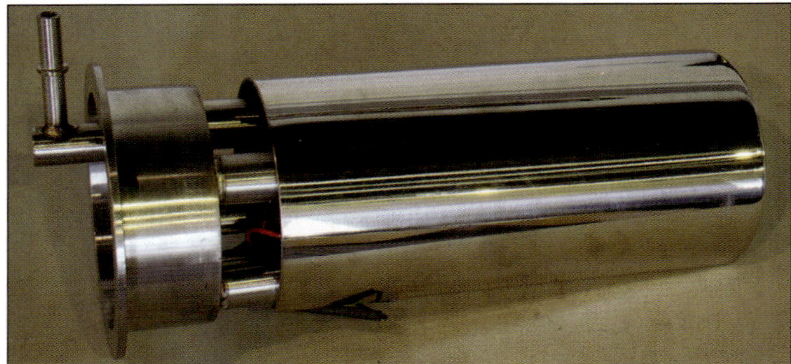

10 The supporting elements of the turbo system are focused mostly on fuel requirements. They include a higher-capacity, 355-lph tank-mounted fuel pump that required the removal of the fuel tank for installation. At the other end of the fuel system, a set of 60-lbs/hr injectors was installed in the intake manifold.

11 The stock radiator was retained, but the cooling fan assembly was swapped with the twin-fan setup from an LS1-powered fourth-generation F-Body car. The fans are driven with the controller from a 2005-and-later Corvette because it offers almost infinite adjustability when tuning the engine, including varying the fan speed to suit different demands. Most other electric fans, such as the fourth-generation F-Body fan, are not adjustable. When they're on, they're on full blast.

carefully designed, installed, and tuned turbo system.

The STS Option

As described in chapter 3, Holley's Squires Turbo Systems (STS) offers a nonconventional method of adding a turbo system to a vehicle. Rather than mounting the turbocharger(s) on the exhaust manifold(s), it is moved far back on the underside of the vehicle, typically near the rear axle. The reasons for this include reduced underhood temperature, lower air-charge temperature, generally lower cost (an STS system eliminates the need for expensive, purpose-built headers or exhaust manifolds) and, perhaps most importantly, comparatively easy installation.

Because the turbo and its plumbing are mounted beneath the car, there is far less need for fabrication and relocation of underhood components. In most cases, installing an STS kit is comparable to a centrifugal supercharger and perhaps slightly easier and less time consuming.

When STS turbo kits first hit the market, skeptics wondered whether a turbo hanging near the rear axle

Here's an STS kit all laid out. Basically, the kit is comprised of tubing, clamps, and the hardware required to install the turbo and its supporting components.

Not seen here is a separate intercooling system that is partnered with many of the kits. Additional components are also required, including higher-capacity fuel injectors and a fuel-pump booster. (Photo Courtesy Squires Turbo Systems)

was the best place for it, citing concerns over its exposure to the elements, rogue road debris, and water ingestion. Generally speaking, those fears have proven to be unfounded, although a measure of turbo lag is common. Largely, the concept has proven to deliver on the promise of lower temperatures, both at the throttle body, overall, and under the hood. It seems the long tubing of the system, running front-to-rear on the vehicle, delivers a passive intercooling effect. Of course, like any turbo system, an STS Turbo system

is adjustable, allowing the builder to adjust boost pressure to make more power.

As noted in chapter 3, STS Turbo no longer offers vehicle-specific kits but universal systems instead, requiring the installing to fabricate exhaust and air-intake tubing and more. The installation procedure outlined here was performed on an LS1-powered Pontiac GTO (similar to the Holden Monaro), using a vehicle-specific kit that is no longer offered. Nevertheless, the overall steps are largely the same for STS Turbo's universal kits with necessary fabricated components required in place of the tubing and some other components shown.

One of the unique aspects of the system is an electric pump that circulates oil between the turbo and engine. This isn't always necessary with a conventional turbo system, but it is definitely required on the STS kit, as there's no way gravity would return oil to the engine.

For the record, the project car produced 480 rear-wheel hp with a Garrett G-67 turbo producing about 8 pounds of boost. The LS1 engine was internally stock but was

This underhood shot of the STS-equipped GTO reveals no clues that there is a turbocharger installed, apart from clearly nonoriginal air intake that snakes down and under the engine compartment. The uncluttered appearance is a hallmark of the STS kit, as it doesn't require tricky fabrication to squeeze the system beneath the hood.

At the top of this photo, the Y-pipe illustrates the merge of the left- and right-hand exhaust outlets and its flow rearward to the turbocharger. The separate tube at the right is the flow tube carrying the boosted air charge to the intercooler and, after that, to the engine. The length of the tubes and their distance from the exhaust manifolds provide a passive intercooling effect.

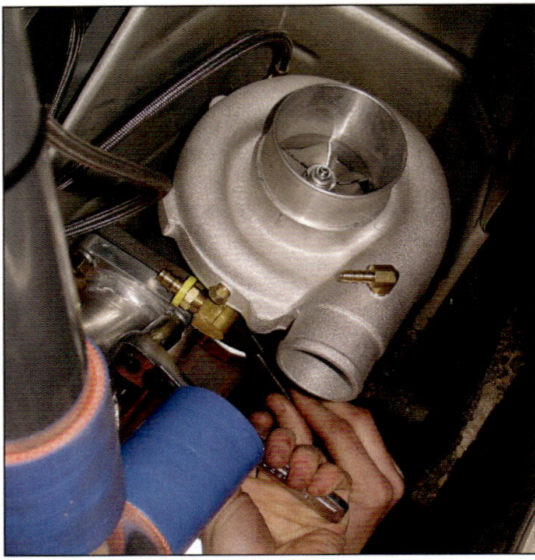

Looking up at the chassis, with the left-rear tire on the right side of the photo, you can see STS' mounting location for the turbocharger. It's the location of the original muffler, which is eliminated with this system (although that is not true for all STS kits). A benefit of this mounting position is the factory heat shield that was originally designed for the muffler.

There's no down pipe or other exhaust system with STS's GTO kit. An exhaust outlet pipe simply mounts where the exhaust or down pipe would attach on a conventional system. The exhaust note with this design is acceptable, and the close-coupled catalytic converters that are mounted right off the exhaust manifolds are retained.

This view looking up at the front of the car shows the inlet pipe from the turbo coming in from the right and the outlet to the engine intake on the left. What's missing in between is the heat exchanger for the intercooler.

An oil-feed line for the turbo is added at the oil filter mounting pad, tapping into an existing unused port. A return line is also required and routes back through the oil fill hole in the valve cover. An electric pump scavenges the oil from the turbo, forcing it back into the engine.

The unconventionally mounted turbo system requires conventional upgrades to the fuel system and ignition system. The LS1-powered GTO sufficed with a set of 42-pound injectors and a Kenne Bell Boost-A-Pump. Also, NGK TR6 spark plugs replaced the originals.

Here's a look at the finished installation. The blow-off valve is visible, but the system doesn't hang much lower than a regular exhaust system. A vehicle with a solid rear axle would benefit from better, over-the-axle tube routing, but the independent rear suspension of GTOs/Monaros, G8s/Commodores, and fifth-generation Camaros demands tubing that runs under the axle.

equipped with an LS6 camshaft and valve springs.

Building a Race Car around a Turbo System

The custom turbo kit on the TrailBlazer SS and the STS turbo kit mentioned earlier represent a system designed to fit within the confines of essentially stock vehicles. For vehicles intended more for the drag strip than the street, accommodating the turbo system is the priority, and the vehicle's bodywork and chassis are modified to support it.

For the popular "street car" and pro-modified-style classes, the engine system typically includes one or two very large turbochargers; a custom intake system; and a large-capacity, liquid-to-air intercooling system (often using an interior-mounted reservoir of ice water). Simply put, these race cars are built around the turbo system, and priority is given to the desired location of the turbo(s).

"We start with where the turbochargers are going to be mounted and go from there," says Stenod's Joe Borschke. "The customer tells us, for example, that the rules for his class allow a 106-mm turbo. That's a big turbo and it's going to take up a lot of room, as is the tubing routed in and out of it."

*Another race car under construction shows a smaller, front-mounted intercooler and more conventional mounting of the turbochargers. While this setup seems tame when compared with the twin-turbo setup outlined in the photo below, it nonetheless involves removing the bumper beam and other underhood accessories to support the system's components. Again, this is **not** a system for the street.*

Although there's not a necessarily perfect location to mount a turbocharger, Borschke typically mounts them at the very front of the bodywork, exposing the air inlet side to the atmosphere.

"For a race car, you want as much exposure to fresh air as possible, as any restriction will affect the maximum boost," he says. "It's for this very reason that you wouldn't duplicate such a system on a street car; you need adequate air filtering on the street."

Another important aspect in race car turbo design is optimal wastegate location and tubing that avoids sharp bends.

"The wastegates have to be priority-fed," says Borschke. "Air must go through the wastegates first [before the turbochargers] to maintain proper boost control."

As for those large intercooler tanks typically seen in the interiors of race cars, there are several reasons for locating them in the cabin. First of all, they are just plain large and don't fit easily in the engine compartment. Also, when filled with ice water, they're quite heavy, so mounting them in the interior helps distribute weight more evenly on the chassis.

Here is a typical turbocharged race car under construction. The turbochargers were mounted up front on a fabricated brace, replacing the original bumper beam. Note how the turbos are fed by reversed, marine-style headers, and the wastegates are located before the turbochargers. The air outlets from the turbos merge into a single, large-diameter tube that is routed on the outside of the engine compartment (underneath the passenger-side front fender) to the passenger compartment, where it is cooled by a large liquid-to-air intercooler. The cooled air charge is then fed through a hole in the firewall to a reverse-facing inlet atop the intake manifold. This is not designed for street use, as all of the typical accessories found on a street car are eliminated to make room for the turbo system's tubing.

Aaron Schoen's 500-rwhp Silverado Homebuilt Turbo System on a Budget

Disproving the conventional wisdom that turbo systems are complicated and expensive, Ohio resident Aaron Schoen built one essentially by himself with used parts from a variety of sources. His 5.3L engine generates 503 hp and 535 ft-lbs of torque to the wheels; and it has sent the heavy Chevy down the drag strip in 12.9 seconds at 114 mph.

In a nutshell, Schoen scratch-built an intercooled turbo system using a single turbo and air-to-air charge cooler along with a methanol-injection system. There are a couple of other things you should know: It was built out of his single-stall, apartment-complex garage, and he spent less than $1,500 on the parts. Here are the highlights of his recipe:

- $300 Stock 5.3L short-block
- $300 6.0-liter (LQ4) cylinder heads
- Free LS1 camshaft (a gift from an uncle who'd swapped the cam in his 2002 Trans Am)
- $25 LS6 valve springs (take-off parts from a 2005 GTO)
- $200 Garrett T61 turbocharger (60-mm inducer/85-mm exducer)
- Free 39-lbs/hr fuel injectors (traded some stuff for them)
- $350 Miscellaneous tubing and hoses
- $90 TrailBlazer torque converter
- Free Corvette servos from a 700R-4-equipped TrailBlazer 4x4
- $30 Electric fan (a Chevy Corsica part from a salvage yard)

Schoen says he was inspired by the unique turbo kits of Utah-based STS. The turbo system flows into and out of the Garrett T61 turbocharger. Because he didn't have the tools to fabricate the necessary tubing, Schoen took his truck and turbocharger to a local exhaust shop. Schoen showed where he wanted the turbo located (on the passenger side of the chassis, under the cab) and had the shop bend the necessary 3-inch tubing to accommodate the design.

Of course, the elements of the turbo system include the flow pipes from the engine's exhaust manifolds, which merge and feed the turbocharger's turbine. From there, more tubing runs to the front of the engine compartment, where the boosted air charge (tuned right now for a maximum of about 11 pounds) flows into an air-to-air heat exchanger that came off a 1989 Toyota Supra. Then, the air is sent into the 5.3L iron-block engine's stock throttle body. An electric pump is required to recirculate oil from the turbo back to the engine; it returns to the crankcase by means of a fitting drilled into the oil fill cap on the valve cover.

One of the additional benefits of this system design is it retains the stock exhaust manifolds, which saves a big chunk of change, as more conventional systems typically require thick, expensive cast-iron manifolds to support the high-heat turbo.

In fact, the entire engine is essentially production-based, although it's not entirely stock for a 5.3L engine. The cast crankshaft, rods, and pistons are used, with Speed Pro rings fitted to the 8.4:1 pistons. Even the intake manifold is stock, although it is equipped with 39-pound fuel injectors. The low-compression pistons help stave off detonation, but so does the methanol-injection system that Schoen rigged up by using a junkyard windshield-washer container and an auto-parts-store electric pump. Methanol injection enables the use of higher-octane fuel and more aggressive tuning to maximize horsepower.

Backing the turbocharged 5.3L engine is a Hydra-Matic 4L60-E electronically controlled automatic transmission that's been beefed up to support the added torque that comes from the turbo system. The torque converter for it is yet another take-off part, coming from a stock TrailBlazer. Additional drivetrain components include a 4.10:1-geared rear axle fitted with an Eaton TrueTrac limited-slip differential.

When it came to tuning his combination, Schoen used tried-and-true HP Tuners software. He went with a speed density air-metering system too.

"There were a lot of reasons I went with speed density," he says. "One of the most important was the fact that, with a 2-bar speed density system, I had more tuning range beyond 6 pounds of boost. The stock, 1-bar mass airflow system is only good to about 10 pounds of boost." (See chapter 7 for more information about 1-bar and 2-bar MAP considerations.)

Pure and simple, Schoen's combination works. It starts, runs, and drives excellent, with no flat spots in the tuning. Turbo lag is minimal and the boost comes on smoothly and progressively. In short, it is a project that proves how excellent forced-induction performance need not break the bank. ∎

Aaron Schoen built an inter-cooled turbo system for his 2004 Chevy Silverado using almost all used parts, but all the basic elements are there and work very well together, including a single turbo, wastegate, blow-off valve, and air-to-air intercooler. There's also a methanol injection system.

The turbo is mounted under the cab on the passenger side. It is a Garrett T61 with a 60-mm inducer and 85-mm exducer. The turbo inlet tube from the engine exhaust is clearly visible at the lower-center of the photo. At the far right is the outlet from the turbo, sending the boosted air charge to the engine. It runs along the perimeter of the frame.

The outlet tubing from the turbo runs up and into an air-to-air charge cooler from a 1989 Toyota Supra. Note the mounting of the blow-off valve on the outlet tubing of the charge cooler. It is the connection between the charge cooler and throttle body. The valve bleeds off the air charge when the throttle closes.

This photo of the entire engine compartment shows the tubing from the intercooler routed to the engine. Also of note is the homemade methanol injection system, which includes a pump and a reservoir located in the upper corner of the passenger side of the engine compartment. The reservoir is a take-off piece from a salvage-yard car.

To enable higher-boost tuning with the 5.3L engine's standard, 1-bar MAP sensor, Schoen converted the engine from mass airflow air metering to a 2-bar speed density system. He uses HP Tuners and a laptop to make adjustments.

Tuned for a maximum of 11 pounds of boost and running on 93-octane pump gas (with 8.4:1 compression), Schoen's truck produces more than 500 hp and 535 ft-lbs of torque to the rear wheels. Turbo lag is minimal and the entire system was hand-built for comparatively little money.

TUNING FOR SUPERCHARGED AND TURBOCHARGED ENGINES

In the most basic terms, electronically controlled engines must be carefully calibrated to take advantage of engine modifications that affect airflow and fuel delivery requirements and do it under positive manifold pressure. That is more imperative for forced-induction engines, which process significantly more air than a comparable, naturally aspirated engine.

The various calibrations, whether adjusting fuel and spark delivery or "telling" the controller about new injectors or sensors, fall under the broad heading of tuning. The importance of accurate, pinpointed tuning changes all boils down to a central goal: optimizing fuel and spark throughout the RPM range and under all load conditions.

All of the other changes and adjustments to the engine controller's programming circles back to maintaining a safe air/fuel ratio. Too little fuel leads to a lean condition that can cause detonation, burned pistons, and worse.

Experienced tuners "sneak up" on a supercharged/turbocharged engine's programming, keeping the fuel mixture rich and spark timing conservative at first. After establishing a safe zone of performance, the air/fuel mixture is refined to maximize horsepower. It can be a painstaking process with many adjustments. Novices are advised not to experiment with their newly force-fed car, as incorrect tuning can quickly lead to expensive problems with an engine under boost.

There is far more to engine tuning and computer programming than found in this single chapter, which covers the basics of what's involved in the procedures and requirements for forced-induction combinations. For a more in-depth look at tuning, I recommend Greg Banish's detailed books *Engine Management: Advanced Tuning* and *Designing and Tuning High-Performance Fuel Injection Systems* as excellent guides.

Custom tuning for a forced-induction system (beyond uploading the preprogrammed tune included with a kit) requires experience and isn't advised for the novice. It is best to seek a knowledgeable tuner who uses an engine chassis dynamometer facility for accurate, safe tuning. WARNING: Do *not* start or drive a newly supercharged or turbocharged engine with higher-capacity fuel injectors if the controller is not programmed for them.

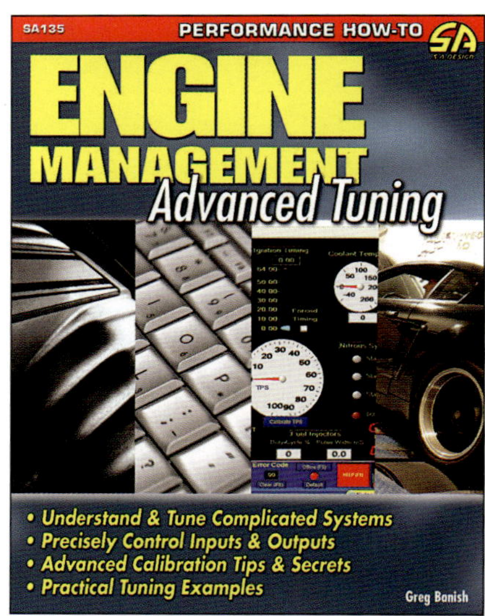

Greg Banish's book Engine Management Advanced Tuning *offers in-depth information on engine tuning theory and application. It should be considered a worthy complement to the information offered in this book, especially the chapter on forced induction.*

Air + Fuel = Horsepower

Of course, the entire reason for adding a supercharger or turbocharger is increasing the airflow through the engine. And with more air, more fuel is required to maintain an optimal air/fuel ratio (AFR) across the RPM band. If sufficient fuel isn't added as RPM and boost increase, the engine runs lean, possibly leading to detonation or worse: burned pistons or catastrophic engine failure.

The factory engine-control systems of LS-powered vehicles ensure optimal combustion based on a programmed set of engine parameters, including displacement, the size of the throttle body, the capacity of the fuel injectors, and even the specifications of the camshaft. Anything done to the engine that significantly alters the engine's parameters, from a simple cam change to 10 pounds of boost, requires updated programming. Otherwise, the controller fights the changes, as it tries to deliver fuel based on its program.

Without question, a supercharger or turbocharger system radically alters the parameters of the engine's airflow and manifold pressure, so the controller's programming must be altered to directly feed the engine more fuel. In a nutshell, that's the goal of tuning. However, a few clicks of the keyboard are not the only way to produce great horsepower in a safe manner; the fuel system must support it. That means the fuel pump and injectors must be matched to deliver fuel at a rate matched with the engine's airflow.

To put it simply, without sufficient fuel to match the boosted air charge from the blower or turbocharger, all the tuning tricks in the world won't produce safe, sustainable performance.

The boosted air charge of a force-inducted engine requires not only a matching increase in fuel but also the engine controller must be programmed with the specifications of the new parts to control the fuel delivery. Inaccurate programming will prevent the engine from performing up to its potential or, even worse, allow an unchecked lean condition that could damage the engine.

Mass Airflow Versus Speed Density

To ensure the engine receives the precise amount of fuel it needs to match the incoming air, the engine controller relies on an air-metering system. There are two basic types: mass airflow and speed density. From the factory, LS-powered vehicles come with a mass airflow system.

In the simplest explanation, mass airflow systems directly measure air, while speed density systems estimate it from a variety of inputs. Mass airflow systems use a sensor to provide a direct reading on airflow through the intake tube, ahead of the throttle body. Basically, the sensor tells the controller how much air is entering the engine and the controller responds by matching that airflow with the appropriate amount of fuel.

With a speed density system, there isn't a direct reading of airflow. Airflow is calculated based on a variety of inputs, including manifold pressure, RPM level, and air temperature.

One of the benefits of a mass airflow system is its ability to roll with certain airflow changes without major tuning alterations. If the increased airflow is within the air meter's sensor range, it simply signals the airflow reading to the controller, prompting increased fuel delivery

(assuming the fuel system is up to the task). That's not the case with a speed density system, which requires tuning updates for all airflow changes. Also, mass airflow systems compensate for engine wear over time.

Generally speaking, the factory mass airflow systems work with low-boost forced-induction systems and has helped make LS-powered vehicles among the easiest to tune for great power increases. Factory mass airflow systems provide excellent performance and optimal air/fuel for up to approximately 15 pounds of boost. In fact, the preprogrammed, uploadable tuning software that comes with most bolt-on blower and turbo kits is designed to work with the factory mass airflow system and provide good drivability and performance.

After 15 pounds of boost, tuning becomes difficult with factory mass airflow systems because the manifold absolute pressure (MAP) sensor cannot provide accurate readings to the controller. Swapping the stock, 1-bar MAP sensor with a 2- or 3-bar sensor alleviates that problem.

Some builders prefer speed density systems with higher-boost combinations because they aren't limited by the range of the mass airflow sensor. They also enable higher boost with 1-bar MAP sensors. However, speed density systems have "fixed" programs, meaning that the controller is programmed to suit the exact parameters of the engine to ensure the AFR. Anything done to the engine that changes the airflow characteristics, or volumetric efficiency, requires a new program for the controller, and that goes for engine wear over time and (sometimes) extreme temperature swings. Also, drivability can suffer somewhat, when compared with a properly tuned mass air system. Generally, however, speed density systems are used more with very-high-boost/racing combinations, where stoplight-to-stoplight smoothness isn't a great concern.

The bottom line is that for most street and street/strip combinations of low to moderate boost, the factory-style mass air system is preferred.

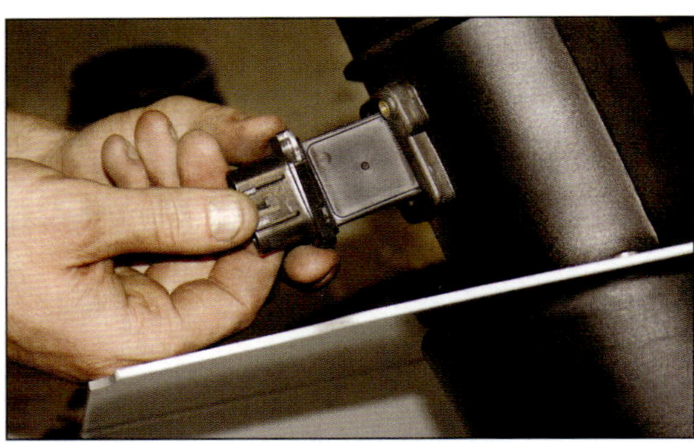

The factory mass airflow meter/sensor assembly is used without modification on most Roots/screw-type supercharger kits. Larger-diameter meters will allow more air but slightly diminish maximum boost. Changes in the meter's diameter or with the sensor must be addressed in the controller's programming.

The bypass valve (lower left) for a centrifugal supercharger system mounted on a C6 Corvette is shown with the front fascia removed. When installed on a vehicle with a factory-style mass airflow system, the bypass valve must be mounted between the intercooler outlet (flowing toward the engine) and before the mass airflow sensor. The intercooled air charge must only pass the mass airflow sensor once, otherwise accurate air metering is impossible. That means bypass air shouldn't be introduced back into the intake stream ahead of the air meter, and bypass air released to the atmosphere shouldn't be vented after the air meter.

The custom intake systems of most centrifugal supercharger and turbocharger systems require swapping the stock mass airflow sensor into port in the intake system. For the most accurate airflow readings, the sensor should be placed in a section of the intake that allows for a straight flow path across the sensor element.

Most modern Eaton superchargers and twin-screw compressors have an integrated bypass valve, negating the need to insert a separate bypass valve in the intake system.

Speed density air metering is the way to go with racing engines because, generally speaking, it can be programmed to handle more power than a mass air-metered engine. It is also necessary on setups like this twin-turbo engine, where air enters the intake plenum in two places and uses multiple throttle bodies.

The MAP sensors for LS engines are interchangeable, with the exception of the LS7 sensor. Here's the factory 2-bar sensor for LS9/LSA engine. Adding a higher-pressure sensor must be accounted for when programming the controller.

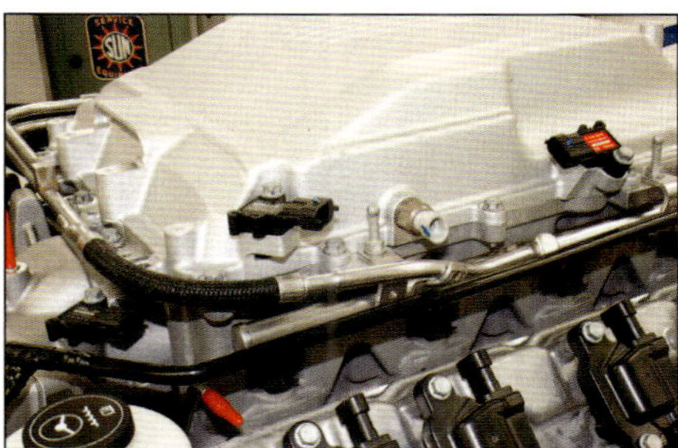

The three factory MAP sensors are visible on this LSA engine. For the most part, aftermarket supercharger systems use only the single MAP sensor from the stock, naturally aspirated engine. If the system is tuned to produced more than 10 pounds of boost, the factory 1-bar sensor should be swapped with at least a 2-bar MAP sensor, and the flash memory for the controller must be updated to accommodate it.

Map Sensors

Whether used with a bolt-on kit on an internally stock engine or on a custom-built engine, a MAP sensor that's capable of reading higher levels of boost must be used. Forced-induction engines making approximately 8 to 10 pounds of boost usually work fine with the 1-bar MAP sensors that are equipped on most naturally aspirated LS production engines.

When the boost level is expected to exceed 10 pounds, at least a 2-bar MAP sensor should be used. The 6.2L LS3 engine uses a 2-bar pressure sensor, while the LSA and LS9 use a trio of sensors: one on the inlet side before the supercharger and two on the outlet side after the supercharger and intercooler. The LS3 sensor, along with the inlet sensors for the LSA and LS9, are the same (GM part number 12591290). The outlet sensor on the factory supercharged engines is a 2.5-bar MAP (GM part number 12592525).

The 2-bar sensors are inter-changeable with 1-bar sensors, but the engine-control module must be modified to reflect the change. For experienced tuners, it is a quick and easy adjustment. The recommended sensor is the more common part number 12591290. The only factory LS-engine MAP sensor that doesn't directly swap out with the others is found on the naturally aspirated LS7. Its sensor has a different-size pin end.

There are aftermarket 2-, 3-, and 4-bar MAP sensors, but for most higher-boost combinations, the GM 2-bar sensor is adequate.

GM Controllers

Generally speaking, all of GM's production LS engine controllers can be tuned to work with supercharged and turbocharged engine combinations. Commercial tuning is available for all of them and each works well with low- and moderate-boost systems.

The later E38 and E67 controllers are the most flexible, offering greater parameter ranges, but the E67 is the most flexible of them all. For high-boost, custom-engine combinations, it is the best option to a certain point (see page 95, "Stand-Alone Control Systems"). It is available from GM Performance Parts under part number 19166569.

Here's a quick look at the most common factory controllers used with LS engines.

LS1A: Used on early LS1 engines equipped with a cable throttle and 24X reluctor wheel. Also features integrated transmission control and a wiring harness with LS1 fuel-injector connectors.

LS1B: Used on later LS1 engines and compatible with electronic throttle control with a separate throttle actuator control (TAC) module and a 24X reluctor wheel. It features integrated transmission control and uses LS1-style injector connectors.

E40: Not as common as the LS1 controllers or the later E38 and E67 controllers, the E40 works with a 24X wheel and electronic throttle control, but the harness uses LS2-style fuel-injector connectors; no integrated transmission control.

E38: Works with a 58X wheel and electronic throttle control; uses LS2-style injector harness and compatible with integrated, automatic 6-speed transmission control.

E67: Same basic capability as the E38 with 58X wheel, electronic throttle, LS2 connectors, and integrated 6-speed automatic transmission control but with a greater range of parameters and increased tuning flexibility. It is the controller used with the factory LSA and LS9 engines, along with several other naturally aspirated LS engines.

It's important to note that the later controllers, including the E38 and E67, were incorporated based on vehicle and system requirements, so different LS-powered vehicles built in the same model year were equipped with different controllers. The 2010 Camaro SS, for example, was equipped with the E38 controller, while the same-year Cadillac CTS-V received an E67. In other words, the next-generation controller didn't necessarily supersede the previous generation in production vehicles; different vehicles received different controllers based on their control system and vehicle electrical architecture.

Prepackaged Programming

The vast majority of supercharger and turbocharger kits include some type of uploadable, preprogrammed tuning system, usually a handheld device that plugs into the vehicle's on-board diagnostics (OBD-II) port beneath the dashboard. When the instructions are followed correctly, the engine controller has all the information it needs to operate the engine safely. For do-it-yourself enthusiasts and those without convenient access to independent tuning shops, it's the only real option for tuning the car.

Because a measure of safety is built into those preprogrammed systems (ensuring adequate fuel delivery and spark control for a number of variables including fuel type, engine load, altitude, and more), it is possible to achieve greater horsepower results with custom tuning. More importantly, the prepackaged tuning cannot be used if other major engine modifications have been made, including a camshaft swap, stroker crankshaft, higher-flow cylinder heads, or even fuel injectors of a different capacity than what was included with the kit. To put it simply, anything beyond the blower kit is not accounted for with a kit's included programming.

Some manufacturers have technical hotlines that allow custom tuning, but the modifications beyond the stock configuration must be conveyed before the kit is shipped. (See page 94, "Livernois Motorsports'

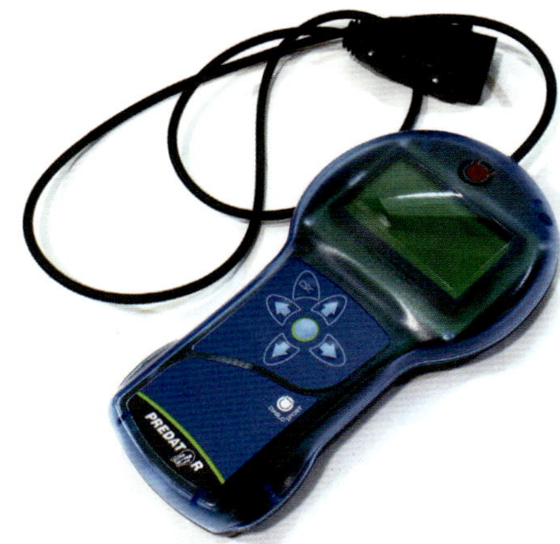

This is a typical plug-in flash tuner for a supercharger kit. There's no need for a laptop computer because, if the directions are followed correctly, reprogramming the factory controller is as easy as pushing a few buttons. What it doesn't allow, however, is tuning for additional engine modifications.

GM's E38 and E67 controllers are the most flexible for tuning of those matched with factory LS powertrain systems. The E67 is the best for forced induction. For higher-boost engine combinations that also incorporate other significant engine modifications, it is the best choice for tuning up to approximately 1,000 hp. It is available through GM Performance Parts (part number 19166569).

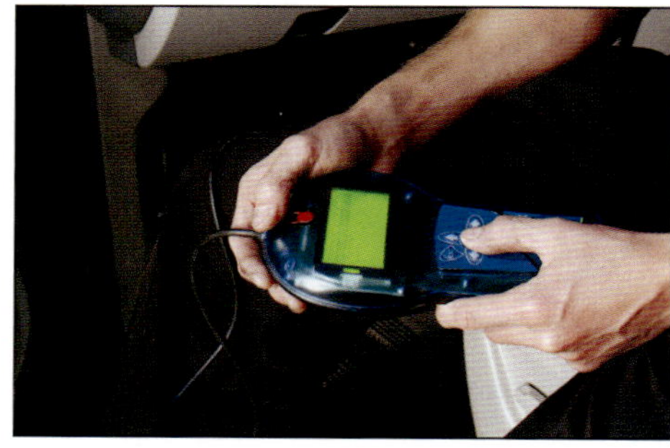

Flash tuners upload their programming to the engine control module or powertrain control module via the OBD-II port located inside the vehicle under the dashboard.

X-Treme Cal Tuning System," for an alternative.)

Aftermarket Flash Software

One of the reasons LS-powered vehicles are so popular among high-performance enthusiasts is the comparative ease with which their controllers can be reprogrammed to accommodate the air/fuel changes that come with engine modifications. Aftermarket software packages enable professional and knowledgeable private tuners to edit and/or alter the operational parameters of the engine-controller program and upload the changes through a flash procedure.

The ability to alter the flash memory of engine controllers is a big change from earlier computer-controlled systems that used control-module chips that required separate ones to be burned for basically every modification. All LS-powered production vehicles use the modern flash-style memory systems that are easily accessed via the OBD-II port under the dashboard.

There have been a number of services offered for LS tuning over the years, but HP Tuners and its VCM Suite of products, including VCM Editor and VCM Scanner, are the leading calibration tools. VCM Editor's flash utility allows not just calibration reflashing and automated recovery but entire VCM/PCM image reflashing. This means the tuner can make any operating system or calibration-level modifications and flash those to the VCM/PCM. VCM Editor also allows for increased vehicle support for tuners, along with access to extra VCM/PCM operating system code modifications.

Like software for a home or business computer, the utilities offered by these companies are licensed either on a singular basis for a specific vehicle or for tuning shops that use the software for multiple vehicles. They are priced accordingly, and single-vehicle systems cost several hundred dollars and multiple-vehicle licenses cost several thousand dollars.

As with HP Tuners, the editing utilities from Carputing LLC (LS1 Edit and LS2 Edit) enable manipulation of the controller's flash memory. The LS2 Edit utility, which covers most later-model LS-powered vehicles, regardless of whether they actually have an LS2 engine, accommodates those vehicles' split powertrain controller system that operates on a controller area network (CAN). That means the engine and transmission controllers perform mostly independently but are linked via the CAN.

Regardless of the utility, you must have a working knowledge of the base fuel, spark, and AFR requirements of the engine, recognizing them in the myriad of tables the flash tuner software is equipped with

and the proper approximate values for tuning the system to accommodate new performance parts.

This is where a book like Greg Banish's book *Engine Management: Advanced Tuning* becomes essential. Both HP Tuners and Carputing offer online assistance for basic tuning issues and troubleshooting. Many popular online enthusiast forums, as well as HP Tuners' website, devote space to flash-memory tuning. If you are contemplating custom tuning for the first time, familiarize yourself with the basics because even a relatively small mistake at the keyboard could result in serious engine damage.

Additionally, HP Tuners and other entities offer beginning and advanced tuning courses specializing in the controllers used with LS engines, as well as the basics for calibrating for forced-induction engine combinations. The few hundred dollars invested in the courses can return bigger dividends when it comes to optimizing the performance of a supercharged or turbocharged engine.

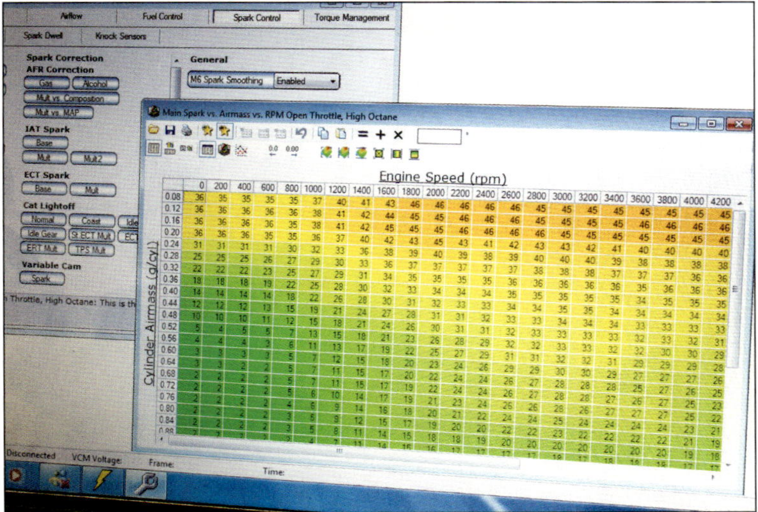

Here is an example of an editable screen of HP Tuners' flash memory utility. When the tables are adjusted and the settings are saved and uploaded to the engine controller, it will direct the engine and/or transmission as programmed. Knowing which values to change and what to change them to is the trick of tuning. An understanding of how the values affect the engine and transmission is necessary before modifying them.

Livernois Motorsports' X-Treme Cal Tuning System

Enthusiasts who perform installations at home or don't have convenient access to a good, reputable tuning shop are challenged when it comes to proper tuning on a combination that exceeds the parameters of a manufacturer's prepackaged programming, such as a cam-and-heads swap in addition to a bolt-on blower kit. As noted earlier, the flash memory upgrade included with most bolt-on systems does not account for additional engine modifications.

Livernois Motorsports' solution is an interface system that allows an easily uploadable, customized flash-memory upgrade based on an individual's specific requirements called the X-Treme Cal Tuning Interface. With this system, the customer receives the interface kit from Livernois Motorsports, which includes a preprogrammed tune based on that customer's specific vehicle equipment (for example, a 2009 Pontiac G8 GT with a Magnuson blower kit, LS3 cylinder heads, and a hotter camshaft). After receiving it, the customer uploads the new tune to the controller, just as he or she would with the prepackaged tune from the supercharger kit.

"It allows us to achieve results equivalent to dyno tuning for simple bolt-ons or more elaborate power adders that normally would require custom tuning at our dyno facility," says Livernois Motorsports' Dan Millen. "The X-Treme Cal Tuning Interface is a single VIN unit with the ability to data log, so it is the customer's to keep. We can send updates to the customer with our tuning files as they become available, or the customer can update his own tune

Lidio Iacobelli from Alternative Auto Performance performs a common test-and-tune procedure, whereby a test drive of a modified vehicle determines the need for further tuning adjustments. With a laptop connected to HP Tuners' interface plugged into the OBD-II port, Iacobelli inputs the value changes he wants and saves them to the controller's flash memory. Then, it's out for another test drive to test whether the changes delivered the desired results.

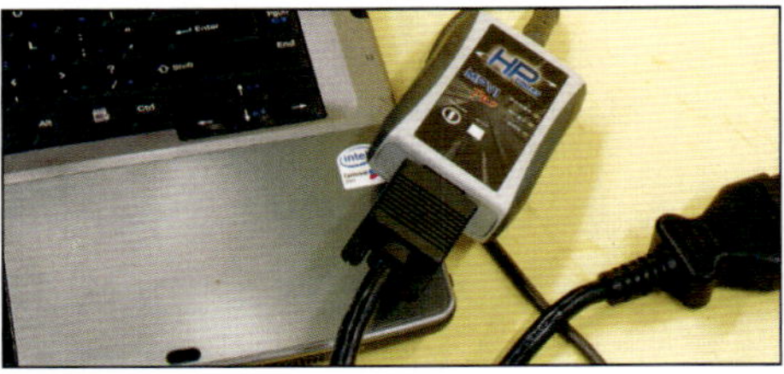

This is an HP Tuners' interface module that connects between a computer and the OBD-II port inside the vehicle. It is what enables modifications in the flash memory to be made, saved, and uploaded. Whether using HP Tuners' system or the LS1 Edit system from Carputing, software is included to facilitate modifications.

Livernois Motorsports' X-Treme Cal Tuning Interface includes a software disk, the interface module, and the cables required to connect between a laptop computer and the OBD-II port.

Among the benefits of Livernois Motorsports' X-Treme Cal Tuning Interface system is how Livernois Motorsports stores each customer's tuning files. This allows them to quickly modify and forward a revised tune if further changes are planned for the particular engine combination.

The ACCEL/DFI Gen 8 engine control module is one of the most advanced engine controllers on the market and is capable of driving a variety of high-performance fuel injectors. It can fire up to eight ignition coils simultaneously. It features three integrated microprocessors capable of supporting engines spinning 15,000 rpm and producing more than 3,000 hp. Additional highlights include the capability to drive low-impedance fuel injectors common to racing engines, programmable inputs to support cooling-fan control, 64-channel internal data logging, and more. Real-time programming software helps dial in combinations very quickly. There are several part numbers of the Gen 8 for different applications; the one compatible with LS engines is part number 75807.

Another popular stand-alone engine controller is FAST's XFI system. Like the ACCEL/DFI Gen 8 controller, it handles high-performance, low-impedance injectors and enables the use of up to 16 injectors (a trait that factory controllers don't have). Another benefit is the XFI system's ability to store four separate engine-mapping programs (tunes), allowing the user to switch fuels (pump gas to racing gas or E85, for example) without having to reflash the memory. The different tunes can be accessed with the simple flip of a switch.

(within reason) to accommodate further modifications."

According to Millen, the X-Treme Cal Tuning Interface reads the factory controller program, which can be saved, to return the vehicle to stock specifications. The system includes software, a USB-to-laptop computer cord, and an OBD-II interface cord.

Stand-Alone Control Systems

Although very adaptable to tuning, the factory controllers on GM vehicles have their limits. In general terms, it's about 1,000 hp. After that, the requirements to fuel the engine demand things the factory controller isn't designed for. Mostly it's injector-driver control because the high-output, aftermarket-performance injectors are known as the "peak and hold" type and GM's controllers aren't designed to operate them.

Joe Alameddine, of ACCEL/DFI provides a more thorough explanation: "Most of the injectors found in the market today that flow significant amounts of fuel for high-horsepower applications are typically low-impedance injectors [less than 12 ohms]. The injector drivers in the stock computer do not support the current levels necessary to drive them properly. Also, the few, specialty high-impedance injectors that are available have a very slow opening rate that causes poor stability at idle and high RPM. The effect is magnified further if the user increases fuel pressure. With an aftermarket computer, such as ACCEL/DFI Gen 8, these issues are not a problem, as each injector driver can handle up to 8 amps. This equates to very finite control at just about any engine speed and compatibility with an injector carrying an impedance rating of 1.5 ohms."

Alameddine further suggests a computer swap in a force-inducted setup with a high-performance camshaft.

"The stock racing-oriented computer cannot compensate for a high level of valve overlap, causing cold-startup issues and general poor-idle quality; and mass airflow sensors typically have a glass ceiling for measurement of airflow, limiting potential power levels," he

says. "While there are many flash programs available to compensate at some level, usually the end user fights some degree of performance to dial in the whole package."

Along with the products from ACCEL/DFI, stand-alone control systems are also available from Fuel Air Spark Technology (FAST) with its XFI electronic fuel-injection system and Big Stuff 3's GEN3 Pro SEFI control system.

Holley's Dominator EFI is one of the latest control systems on the market and has made strong inroads with tuners due to its great comparative intuitiveness and flexibility. Along with the ability to accommodate systems with electronic throttle control, it has dual wideband oxygen sensor capability and integrated electronic transmission control. Holley also offers extensive online product selection and tuning support resources to help ensure the correct supporting hardware and latest software updates are selected.

Chassis Dyno Tuning

Whether a modified vehicle uses a preprogrammed software program or a custom tune, it is highly recommended that the vehicle be tested and fine-tuned with the assistance of a chassis dynamometer. It more closely replicates the real-world performance of the engine by putting a load on the drivetrain. Of course, it also indicates the horsepower and torque levels of the engine. Those numbers are generally referred to as "at the wheels" power numbers, because they're measured at the drive wheels on the dynamometer's inertia drums (the large rollers on which the vehicle is loaded).

Depending on the type of dyno used, the at-the-wheels power numbers can be corrected by a factor of about 15 to 20 percent to indicate the true horsepower and torque output of the engine. The difference between the engine and drive wheels is the result of parasitic losses from the engine turning the transmission, driveshaft, rear axle, etc., before the horsepower and torque get to the pavement.

Most tuning shops use chassis dynos from either Mustang Dynamometer or Dynojet. Generally, the same car tested under the same conditions reveals slightly more at-the-wheels power on a Dynojet dynamometer than a Mustang dyno, although many tuners suggest the Mustang unit imposes a more real-world load on the vehicle that produces a result closer to what the vehicle will deliver on the street.

Confirmation of a newly modified vehicle's power output is certainly important, but ensuring adequate fuel delivery under load is the most important aspect of dyno

A chassis dynamometer is a wonderful tool for gauging the before-and-after results of a supercharger or turbocharger, as well as ensuring the AFR is adequate at WOT. Generally speaking, automatic transmission–equipped vehicles lose more of the engine's power before reaching the drive wheels. Testing automatic vehicles can be difficult on a chassis dyno because their factory lockup-style converters don't always lock up. That means full engine power isn't being transmitted to the drive axle. However, a knowledgeable dyno operator can get the converter to lock and take an accurate measurement. AWD vehicles (such as the TrailBlazer SS) also pose a unique challenge. They require a dyno with both front and rear rolling drums, which can be difficult to find, even in metropolitan areas with numerous tuning shops.

After a "pull" on the chassis dyno, the technician notes the recorded horsepower and torque measurements at the rear wheels and compares them with the baseline numbers that were recorded prior to the installation of the supercharger or turbocharger system. The graphs generated by the dyno pull not only point out the peak power numbers but the graph also displays RPM increments that show where in the rev range the power increases are most effective. If the vehicle is equipped with wideband oxygen sensors, AFR measurements are also compared.

tuning. It is imperative to know that the engine is free from detonation at wide open throttle (WOT) and under full boost. For vehicles undergoing a custom tune, such testing helps determine the precise fuel requirements throughout the RPM range.

Frankly, some tuners are better than others, and a professional shop that's adept at installing parts and fabricating custom systems may not have a staff member who is experienced at the finer points of tuning electronically controlled engines. It is incumbent on the vehicle owner to seek the most qualified tuner to ensure a costly investment in a blower or turbo kit isn't going to end prematurely with burned pistons. The internet makes it relatively easy to probe whether a tuning shop has a good reputation, while old-fashioned asking around at the drag strip or a car show may also help find a knowledgeable local tuner.

Wideband Tuning

As helpful as chassis dyno tuning is, the measurements on the dyno are generated with the engine at wide open throttle. Ensuring a safe AFR and adequate fuel delivery at full throttle is, of course, vitally important, but part-throttle driving makes up the vast majority of conditions for street-driven vehicles. Tuning for those conditions ensures not only the appropriate AFR across the RPM band, but optimizes idle quality, overall drivability, and even fuel economy.

The most accurate way to account for "real world" driving conditions is through what is known as wideband tuning, which requires a wideband oxygen sensor and supporting components. By replacing the original narrowband oxygen sensor with the wideband one, a greater range of AFR detection is enabled. The value of the variation from the ideal, stoichiometric 14.7:1 ratio (when using gasoline) is expressed with the Greek letter Lambda (λ).

With the factory-style narrowband oxygen sensor, its capability is basically limited to determining whether the post-combustion AFR is at the optimal 14.7:1. If not, it triggers the check engine light and registers a code in the computer. A diagnostic check reveals if the difference was because of a rich condition (more fuel than air) or a potentially

Part-throttle performance is more accurately tested on the road, with AFR measurements recorded via a wideband oxygen sensor. Wideband sensors are also used on the chassis dyno during WOT tests, but they are acutely effective at helping fine-tune low-speed drivability and ensuring adequate fuel is available at all RPM and throttle levels.

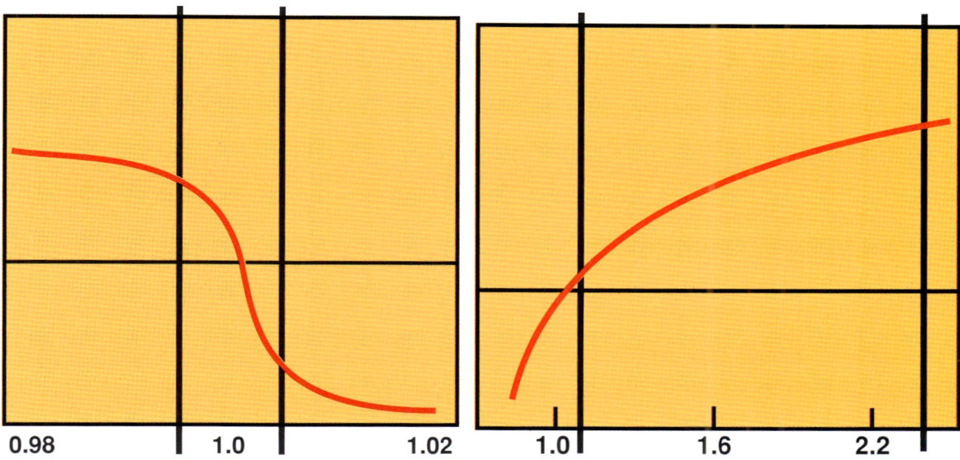

A wideband oxygen sensor simply replaces the standard narrowband sensor in the exhaust system. One should be used in each position originally occupied by a narrowband sensor; most range in price from $50 to $100 each. If you plan to tune the engine yourself, it is a worthy investment. If you use a professional shop for tuning, the shop can usually swap out the standard sensors for wideband sensors during tuning sessions.

These graphs illustrate the difference in AFR measurements recorded by narrowband (left) and wideband (right) sensors. In the narrowband graph, the measurement within the 1.0 value section depicts the limited sensing range of the narrowband sensor, whereas the wider sensing range with the wideband sensor is clear. More importantly for tuners, the wideband sensor tells how lean or rich the mixture is, while the narrowband sensor merely indicates a rich or lean condition.

engine-damaging lean condition (more air than fuel).

Unfortunately for tuners of modified vehicles (especially those with supercharged or turbocharged engines) the narrowband sensor signals rich or lean but cannot indicate the precise AFR that triggered the code. A wideband system has the capability of precise measurements. Typically, a wideband oxygen sensor identifies AFR between 9.65 and 20:1.

Because incorrectly tuned forced-induction systems can quickly lean out the AFR, wideband tuning should be considered a must. In fact, for engine safety's sake, many tuners build in a slightly rich ratio to ensure adequate fuel for any operating or engine-load condition. Typically, such tuning scrubs off a few horsepower, but the tradeoff is often welcomed because it brings with it peace of mind. Without wideband tuning, it would be difficult to accurately measure the AFR and optimize it to ensure a safe tune that doesn't drastically affect the engine's output.

Throttle Body Considerations

The throttle body controls the airflow into the engine; and just as importantly, it dictates the *velocity* of airflow entering the engine. It seems logical that a larger-diameter throttle body will benefit a positive-displacement (draw-through) supercharged engine by enabling more air to be drawn into the engine for compression by the blower. That is generally true, but replacing, say, the stock 90-mm throttle body on an LS3 with a 102-mm aftermarket throttle body may not deliver a dramatic power increase, and that extra power might come at the expense of drivability.

Indeed, the throttle body can restrict airflow to the supercharger if it isn't large enough, meaning it doesn't flow enough air to support the optimal needs of the compressor. That can be measured during dyno tuning by taking air-pressure readings before and after the throttle body. An ideal measurement would see no pressure drop after the throttle body, while a drop in pressure (vacuum) in the intake manifold indicates an airflow restriction. A significant drop in pressure indicates a significant restriction that will affect the maximum boost the compressor can produce.

Generally speaking, upgrading to a larger throttle body should reduce the pressure drop in the manifold and consequently result in greater airflow. Using the LS3 example, increasing from a 90-mm throttle body to a 102-mm throttle body could result in approximately 2 psi more boost and approximately 20 additional horsepower at peak RPM.

A larger-diameter throttle body can enhance the power output with the supercharger or turbocharger, but low-speed and idle performance may suffer. Additionally, there are more throttle body choices for earlier LS engines with cable-operated throttle control. Choices are much more limited on systems with fly-by-wire electronic throttle control.

Nick Williams Performance offers a 102-mm electronic throttle that features a 6-pin connector that's compatible with GM controller harnesses.

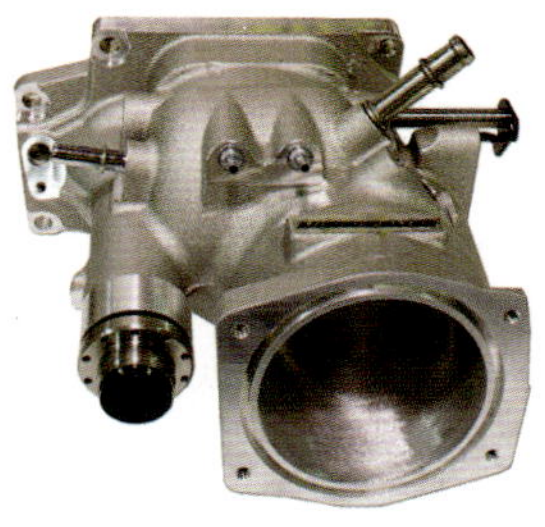

Along with the throttle body, elements of the air inlet tract can also restrict airflow. To alleviate some of the restriction in the factory LS9 engine, for example, Lingenfelter Performance offers a revised inlet between the intake manifold and throttle body. The company claims up to a 30-hp improvement when the inlet is combined with a Lingenfelter pulley kit.

High-boost (more than 20 psi/1.4 bar) turbocharged and centrifugally supercharged engines should have something more substantial than traditional worm clamps to secure the air inlet to the throttle body; V-Band-type fasteners are recommended. This engine features a quick-disconnect aluminum fastener from Accufab, which supports 60 pounds (4 bar) of boost.

In a system designed primarily for street driving, however, a larger throttle body can present idle and drivability issues, especially on an otherwise-stock engine featuring a bolt-on supercharger kit. That's because when the blower isn't producing much or any boost, the engine's airflow needs revert back to the stock parameters that weren't designed for the airflow from a larger throttle body. It's a performance trade-off decision for the builder.

When it comes to the blow-through characteristics of turbocharged and centrifugal-blown engines, the size of the throttle body has less of an effect on maximum performance. That's because the pressurized air is introduced ahead of the throttle body, which artificially increases its max airflow capability. A larger throttle body on a blow-through system can increase the amount of air that flows into the engine, but the trade-off can be a minor reduction in max boost.

Finally, a larger-diameter throttle body is only effective if the intake manifold or supercharger assembly on which it is mounted has a commensurately sized inlet opening. The additional airflow goes nowhere if the manifold's inlet is smaller than the throttle body.

Electronic Throttle Concerns

Some builders have discovered a tuning issue with the electronically controlled throttle body of some LS engines, particularly LS2 engines found in TrailBlazer SS and SSR models. The issue involves the throttle blade being pushed open unintentionally by the supercharger/turbocharger boost pressure.

The condition is usually detected

Most Gen IV LS engines use electronically controlled throttles, but they are not all manufactured with the same internal components. A strong throttle spring is necessary to prevent boost creep that affects tuning and could possibly harm the engine. Higher-boost supercharged and turbocharged engines must all have adequate bypass valves and/or blow-off valves.

through uneven performance, bucking, and even an illuminated check engine warning. It is believed the culprit is a comparatively weak spring within the throttle body and the cure is the installation of another production throttle body with a stronger spring mechanism. Builders who've dealt with this issue report the 2005–2007 Corvette LS2 engine's throttle body has sufficient spring strength to stand up to considerable boost pressure. Another possible culprit may be an insufficiently strong bypass valve.

Another throttle-related issue seems to affect the TrailBlazer SS, Hummer H3, and other AWD vehicles. The comparatively violent acceleration caused by a full-throttle blast with a force-inducted engine can upset the factory stability-control system called StabiliTrak. When this occurs, a warning message may flash on the dashboard and temporarily disable the stability system. It may also cause the stability system to perform in a manner where it believes

it is intervening in a potentially hazardous driving situation. If that happens, the spark may be retarded and the throttle position reduced (even under boost) because that's what the stability system is programmed to do.

Lingenfelter Performance Engineering has a simple module that tricks the stability system with a more appropriate torque signal and it works for most (but not all) LS-powered AWD vehicles. It's called the Delivered Torque Output Limiter (DTOL) and its part number is L460021105.

Methanol Injection

Pushing the edge of the envelope with boosted performance has inherent risks in engine combinations using stock rotating assemblies, not the least of which is detonation. Even with the necessary air-to-air or air-to-liquid intercooling systems, the boundaries of sustainable, pump-gas performance can be easily reached with only moderate boost

A homemade methanol injection system is relatively easy to build. A salvage yard–sourced windshield-washer reservoir makes a perfect storage tank for the methanol solution. Filling up with essentially windshield-washer solution is cheaper and easier than tuning the engine to run on high-octane racing gas too.

levels. One of the ways some tuners expand the pump-gas safe range is with a methanol-injection system.

In a nutshell, an alcohol-based solution (usually a 50-50 mix of methanol and water or even blue windshield washer solution) is injected with the regular fuel supply and delivers a pair of significant advantages: lower inlet temperatures and a greater effective octane rating. Essentially, methanol injection acts as a secondary intercooler. Injection of the solution is done in the intake stream, ahead of the throttle body, much like the nozzle does for a dry nitrous system.

Of course, a methanol-injection system must be accounted for in the tuning, but the lower inlet temperature and higher octane rating enable more aggressive programming. Snow Performance is the aftermarket industry authority on methanol injection systems. It offers installation kits, as well as a premixed methanol solution.

Also required for a methanol injection system is a pump to deliver the solution to the intake system. Unfortunately, the pump for the windshield washer system that pairs with the reservoir isn't strong enough to generate the pressure necessary to provide a finely atomized spray of the alcohol solution in the intake tract. This example is from methanol injection specialist Snow Performance.

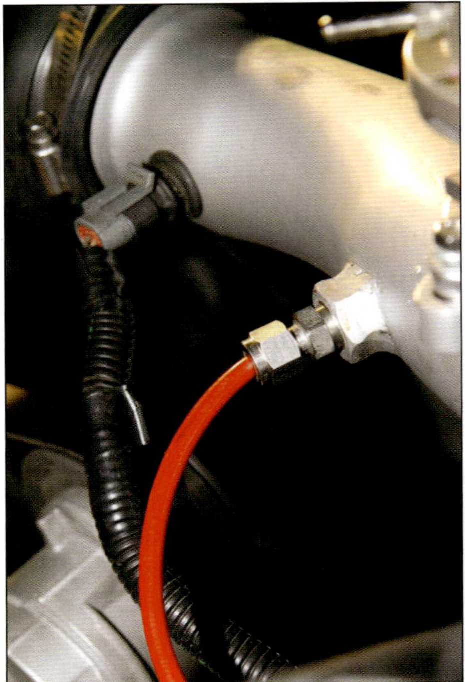

The user must closely gauge the range of the alcohol solution to ensure it matches the gas tank. In other words, if the methanol tank runs dry before the gas tank, a larger methanol tank is needed. In very general terms, a gallon of methanol/water solution should last roughly the range of an average fuel tank. Of course, larger vehicles, such as the G8/Commodore and trucks have larger gas tanks.

E85 Conversion Basics

Adapting a vehicle's fuel system to accommodate E85 fuel is an increasingly popular method of elevating engine output under boost. In fact, there are many advantages to E85 as a performance enhancer, including a higher oxygen content and higher octane rating than gasoline (around 100), evaporative cooling, which helps reduce the air charge temperature, and lower combustion/exhaust temperatures. That helps reduce the chance for or ten-

The intake tract is drilled to accept a nozzle for the methanol injection system, just like it would be for a bolt-on nitrous system. Fortunately, no fuel-system modifications are required for methanol injection, but tuning is necessary to optimize its advantages.

dency toward detonation, which can enable higher boost levels than the equivalent gasoline combination.

With proper tuning, running E85 can produce a 10-percent or greater power output compared to high-octane pump gas. The operative phrase there, of course, is "proper tuning." Because the fuel-burning characteristics of the fuel are significantly different than gasoline (it vaporizes when it enters the engine rather than atomizes like gasoline) it requires a totally different fuel map for optimal engine operation. The AFR with E85 also differs significantly from gasoline (from 14.7:1 with gas to about 9.7:1 with E85), requiring a different stoichiometric AFR table in the engine controller's programming. Gasoline and E85 deliver the best thermal efficiency at about 15-percent rich of stoich, so the equivalent of about 12.78:1 with gasoline would equal around 8.5:1 with E85. When tuning for torque, E85 will generally produce more pound-feet up to about 40-percent rich, or about 7:1.

Converting the fuel system for E85 is a straightforward process that simply builds on the enhancements that are already required to accommodate the turbocharger or supercharger system, including fuel-pump and/or fuel-injector upgrades. In some cases, new fuel rails and/or fuel lines may be required, and it may be necessary to install the next larger-size of injectors or a

The higher octane and inherent cooling effect of E85 fuel enables higher boost levels and more aggressive ignition timing when examined with a comparable gasoline combination to significantly increase horsepower and torque with a boosted engine.

higher-rate fuel pump compared to what was originally suggested for the power adder of choice. Generally speaking, the injectors and fuel pump should be rated 30-percent higher than a comparable gasoline combination.

There are a few drawbacks to E85, chief among them cold starting and significantly greater fuel consumption. E85 simply doesn't ignite as easily as gasoline, particularly in colder temperatures, which can make cold starting problematic. And as for the fuel consumption, anyone supercharging or turbocharging his or her LS-powered vehicle isn't likely concerned about fuel economy. It comes with the territory.

The availability and quality of E85 is not always consistent, which can make it difficult to run a vehicle with a dedicated ethanol tune. Even in areas with readily available supply, the quality of the fuel can vary; and the percentage of ethanol in the blend may not quite equal 85 percent. That can present not only tuning issues but also overall performance problems.

Finally, storing a vehicle that runs primarily on E85, particularly over the winter, can present problems, largely because of its hydroscopic nature. It absorbs moisture, which can result in the formation of mild organic acids if a sufficient amount of water contaminates the fuel. It is generally recommended to drain the fuel tank over the winter or longer periods of storage; and even let the engine idle on gasoline for a few minutes prior to throwing on the car cover for the hibernation period. If draining the tank isn't feasible, an E85-compatible fuel stabilizer should be added to it.

Along with software changes for the tune, converting to E85 requires a number of hardware upgrades, including compatible fuel injectors and a fuel pump rated about 30-percent-greater flow than the comparable gasoline requirements. Fuel line and fuel rail changes may also be required.

BUILDING AN *LS* ENGINE FOR *BOOST:* CYLINDER BLOCK AND ROTATING ASSEMBLY

Builders seeking performance beyond the realm of bolt-on supercharger and turbocharger kits (exceeding about 10 pounds of boost, or so) likely need to consider the construction of a custom engine assembly designed specifically for forced induction. In the simplest terms, that means replacing the factory cast rotating parts with premium, forged components; ensuring greater head-clamping power; and optimizing the compression ratio.

Even vehicles with bolt-on forced-induction systems benefit from a purpose-built engine that supports the power adder, as the engine will likely offer greater durability, resistance to detonation, and more overall power. Although any engine buildup is not regarded as inexpensive by most builders or enthusiasts, there are methods to simplify the process and keep the overall cost to a minimum.

The seemingly easiest and least-expensive option is simply upgrading the vehicle's existing engine with a forged rotating assembly and boost-compatible, lower-compression pistons. Of course, choosing this option or a more extensive engine buildup requires the removal and disassembly of the original engine. In other words, with the heavy lifting required to remove the engine, making the investment in the engine is better justified in the long run.

It's important to keep in mind that while GM's LS engines are commendably robust, durable, and reliable, only the LS9 and LSA versions were designed explicitly for supercharging; the engines were tested and validated to perform within carefully engineered parameters. That means, for example, the rods and pistons of the LS7 engine are designed to deliver the 505 rated horsepower within the stated RPM range with a small buffer, but strong as that engine may be, its components were not validated for forced induction.

Building in strength and durability is paramount in the engine's overall success and longevity. The tremendous power gain delivered by the supercharger or turbocharger lessens the effective differences that lower-mass (lighter) components offer on a naturally aspirated engine. That means the instinct to use, for example, lighter-weight pistons to maximize performance isn't necessarily the correct one, as a heavier forged-alloy piston may slightly increase friction but ultimately prove stronger under maximum boost. And at, say, 20 pounds of boost, the marginal weight difference won't be noticed. In other words, using the strongest rotating parts in addition to a strong cylinder block and premium fasteners is worth the few RPM they may sacrifice in the long run to ensure optimal cylinder pressure.

Cylinder Block

Unless you are planning to use the original engine from your vehicle as the starting point, there is almost an unlimited number of options when it comes to selecting an appropriate cylinder block to use as the new engine's foundation.

Production automotive (and some truck) LS engine blocks are aluminum and reasonably robust for

Factory LS cylinder blocks support moderate levels of boost of less than 15 pounds (1 bar). The LS7 block offers the largest bore at 4.125 inches, while the LS9 block offers greater head-clamping strength with 11-mm cylinder head bolts. No factory block, however, offers the head-clamping strength of six bolts per cylinder, as does Chevrolet's LSX iron block and a number of aftermarket aluminum blocks.

The GM Performance Parts LSX cylinder block was designed with forced induction in mind. Its cast-iron construction is not only strong but it makes it reasonably economical (about $2,800 to $3,300 from most retailers). It is offered in two deck heights: standard 9.240 inches and tall-deck 9.700 inches. Tall-deck versions require spacers for standard intake manifolds because the heads are moved farther apart than with the production-standard, 9.240-inch deck height.

Most significantly, the LSX block includes two additional head-bolt locations per cylinder (for a total of six) that greatly enhance clamping strength to prevent head gasket blowouts under high boost. Street/ strip engines with up to about 15 to 19 pounds of boost will likely survive with conventional, four-bolt blocks, but if the engine is projected to use 20 pounds or more of boost, a six-bolt block is highly recommended. Continual improvements with the LSX block have resulted in a number of part-number changes over the years.

moderate boost pressure. If your plans for the engine exceed the roughly 800-hp range, a high-performance cylinder block is recommended. Although the strength of the block is crucial, the more important factor is the capacity for greater cylinder head clamping through the use of six head bolts per cylinder. Production blocks (including the supercharged LS9) use only four bolts per cylinder; although the LS9 uses larger, 11-mm head bolts versus other LS engines' 10-mm head bolts.

There are a number of high-performance LS blocks on the market, each offering greater structural strength than production LS blocks; most also offer the additional head-clamping strength of six bolts per cylinder instead of the production four-bolt design. They're not exactly inexpensive, however, as the aftermarket aluminum blocks typically cost between $4,000 and $5,000.

One of the overall weaknesses with production LS blocks is their relative flexibility under the extreme cylinder pressures that come with high-boost combinations. That can lead to premature cam and main-bearing wear and even cracking of the block. It's an issue the design of the LSX and other aftermarket blocks alleviate with structural reinforcements.

The final caveat with all aftermarket blocks is careful finish machining. It's a must to ensure assembly accuracy and engine longevity.

Chevrolet Performance LSX Bowtie Block

Introduced in 2007, the LSX block is designed to support extreme high-performance combinations, especially high-boost engines. GM Performance Parts claims the block can support turbocharged engines making more than 2,000 hp and more than 20 pounds of boost. This is due largely to the provision for six bolts per cylinder.

The LSX block has a Siamese-bore design with 3.99-inch bores that must be finished to 4.00 inches with a 4.25-inch recommended maximum bore. The maximum stroke can reach 4.25 inches, but rotating-assembly interference on the cylinder must be taken into account for strokes greater than 4.125 inches. It is offered in a production-style standard deck height (delivered 0.020-inch taller for machining purposes); and a tall-deck version with a 9.70-inch

Another advantage of the LSX block's iron makeup is its capacity for machining. Its thick, Siamese-type bores can be bored to 4.250 inches while retaining a minimum of 0.200-inch wall thickness. And with machining, the standard-deck version can accept a 4.250-inch stroke while the tall-deck version can take a 4.500-inch stroke. Proper machining, including the use of a deck plate as seen here, delivers a more accurate finished product that ensures greater cylinder sealing.

The GM Performance Parts C5R cylinder block (part number 12480030) is very stiff. Its specially machined, 356-T6M-alloy aluminum casting is X-rayed and hipped, which is a reference to the hot isostatic pressure process that pressurizes, heats, and cools the casting to virtually eliminate any chance for porosity. It is a time-consuming procedure that contributes to the block's approximately $8,100 list price. But for all its strength, the C5R was designed for about 750 to 900 naturally aspirated horsepower and, thus, does not include six-bolt head clamping like the LSX block.

height. Fully machined versions are also available.

In the LSX block's favor is its sturdy design, machining flexibility, six-bolt head-clamping strength, the availability of high-flow heads, and a very low retail price. Working against the LSX is the extra weight of an iron casting versus a production aluminum block.

GM Performance Parts Chevrolet C5R Race Block

When the only other choices for engine builders were production blocks, many turned to the unique C5R racing block that General Motors developed for its factory-backed Corvette racing team. It afforded a 427-ci displacement, and the block was considerably stronger than production blocks.

Although it makes a great foundation for moderately powered engines, it's not optimal for higher-boost combinations. That's because the C5R block was designed to support 500 to 600 naturally aspirated horsepower. Most notably, it does not offer six-bolts-per-cylinder clamping. It is also expensive, although prices have come down in recent years.

The C5R is a wonderful piece of engine exotica, but the other cylinder blocks described in this section are better suited to supercharged and turbocharged applications.

Racing Head Service LS Race Block

New in 2009, the LS Race Block from Racing Head Service (RHS) is targeted at maximum-performance combinations, including forced induction. Like the LSX block, it features six-bolt head clamping, including a thick 0.750-inch deck. In fact, the head-bolt pattern is the same as on the GM Performance Parts LSX block, allowing great interchangeability with cylinder heads. Anything that fits the GM block fits the RHS Race Block. However, the LS Race Block is a lightweight, all-aluminum casting.

The block, with outboard priority main oiling, features a Siamese-bore design, but with pressed-in, spun cast-iron cylinder liners. It is available with a minimum 4.125-inch bore diameter and up to 4.165-inch bores. Both production 9.240-inch and tall-deck 9.750-inch versions are available. RHS also touts the LS Race Block as "long-arm friendly"

The RHS LS Race Block is the newest performance cylinder block on the market and features the same six-bolt pattern as the GM LSX block. A raised camshaft position (sized to accept a 60-mm camshaft) and oil galleries that are pushed outward enable a generous 4.600-inch stroke without rod-to-block interference. Various bore sizes are available; the largest allows a 4.165-inch bore. Coupled with the maximum stroke, this aluminum, six-bolt block can offer more than 500 ci.

with a raised camshaft centerline that enables greater rod clearance, allowing for longer-stroke crankshafts with less chance of component interference. A maximum stroke of 4.600 inches is achievable, delivering more than 500 ci with 4.165-inch bores.

Big displacement capability, interchangeability with GM LSX heads, and aluminum construction are the LS Race Block's highlights. A comparatively high price is the only real negative.

Bill Mitchell Products (BMP) LS-Series Chevy Aluminum Block

Made of A357-T6 aluminum, which is stronger than commonly used 356 aluminum, the BMP block is one of the strongest on the market with a number of strategic, strength-enhancing features. Starting at the bottom, the main caps are made of 1045 alloy steel billet and the caps are located by ring dowels and secured with 200,000-psi-tensile-strength ARP main studs. The block also uses a priority main oiling system, which feeds the crankshaft first and the top-end last. And like the GM LSX block, the BMP block has provisions for six-bolt head clamping with the same GM bolt pattern.

The deck height is offered in factory 9.240-inch as well as 9.800-inch with rough bore sizes of 3.990 inches and 4.115 inches, enabling a max bore diameter of 4.165 inches. The cylinder sleeves are centrifugally cast ductile iron with 4.285-inch outside diameters.

With the 9.240-inch version, the BMP block enables a 4.000-inch-stroke crankshaft, while the 9.800-inch tall-deck version supports up to a 4.500-inch stroke. The block weights approximately 130 pounds (59 kg) with the sleeves installed.

Interestingly, the BMP block is designed to accommodate standard LS engine mounts as well as earlier Small-Block Chevy engine mounts, making it easier to use a BMP-based combination in a pre-LS-era vehicle.

Concept Performance LSR Aluminum Block

For about 20 years, Concept Performance has been a behind-the-scenes private-label manufacturer, supporting a number of well-known performance brands. It stepped out on its own with the LSR LS-series aluminum cylinder block to enter the popular world of LS high performance.

Strength and rigidity are the key elements of its design, which incorporates a number of triangulated braces to thwart block flex under high loads and cylinder pressures. It was developed to support more than 1,000 hp.

Like other aftermarket blocks, the LSR is designed to accept Chevrolet's production-based cylinder heads, as well as the six-bolt LSX heads. It is available with a standard 9.240-inch deck height and a 9.750-inch-tall deck version. It also has a seventh transmission bolt built into the rear, making it easier to adapt earlier transmissions, including the stalwart

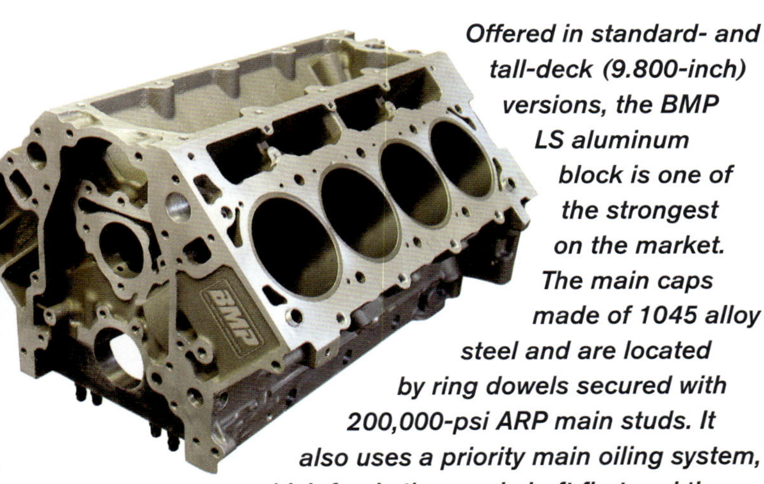

Offered in standard- and tall-deck (9.800-inch) versions, the BMP LS aluminum block is one of the strongest on the market. The main caps made of 1045 alloy steel and are located by ring dowels secured with 200,000-psi ARP main studs. It also uses a priority main oiling system, which feeds the crankshaft first and the top-end last, and the water jackets are redesigned to provide more support around the cylinder, which is a significant consideration for higher-boost applications. It is offered with a maximum bore of 4.165 inches and can accommodate a 4.500-inch stroke with the tall-deck version.

This is what the BMP LS block looks like with the deck sliced off for an inside inspection. Note that the cylinders and head-bolt holes are completely surrounded by a very generous water jacket, yet there is very thick material surrounding the cylinders. The extra-thick material adds strength to the cylinder areas while also serving as a better insulator as the block warms and cools.

Concept Performance's LSR aluminum block is made of 356-T6 heat-treated aluminum and carries a retail price of around $4,200. Reinforcing ribs at the front of the block are among the features designed to reduce flex. Additionally, the block has a priority-main oiling design. Versions with a raised camshaft position are offered, allowing up to a 4.600-inch stroke. The cam bores accept stock-size bearings but can be machined for up to 60-mm roller bearings.

A cross-braced lifter valley is another of the LSR's rigidity-enhancing features. Each valley section has its own oil drainback hole. The block casting also features thicker front and rear valley walls than production LS blocks.

Powerglide. And like the RHS and BMP blocks, it has a priority main oiling circuit.

The block is made of 356-T6 aluminum and the standard-deck version weighs about 113 pounds (51 kg) with billet steel main caps and spun ductile iron cylinder liners installed. It is delivered with 4.120-inch rough bores. It also features eight fasteners per main cap rather than the conventional six-bolt design.

designed to eliminate camshaft and crankshaft flexing that can occur under high loads, which can quickly wipe out bearings. And like a couple of the other aftermarket options, the blocks are offered in standard and tall deck heights, as well as custom camshaft positions. They are also offered in cast iron, cast aluminum, and billet aluminum.

The ultimate LS block in Dart's arsenal is the LS Next MID, which has a unique modular integrated deck design that was developed to essentially eliminate cylinder distortion from block flexing and harmonics. With it, the cylinder liners are seated via compression in the lower-block area, where the maximum amount of the aluminum block material is concentrated. It is offered in standard 9.240-inch and 9.750-inch tall deck heights with bore sizes up to 4.220 inches.

Dart LS and LS Next Aluminum Block

Dart Machinery offers a number of LS-based high-performance cylinder blocks, including the production-style long-skirt design (also known as a Y-block) and the LS Next design, which eliminates the long skirt to open up the bottom end of the engine for reduced windage. In that regard, it's like an LS on top, including the cylinder head mounting provisions, but a traditional small-block Chevy on the bottom end but still designed for all of the LS componentry.

Both of Dart's conventional-design LS block and the LS Next incorporate strength-enhancing features

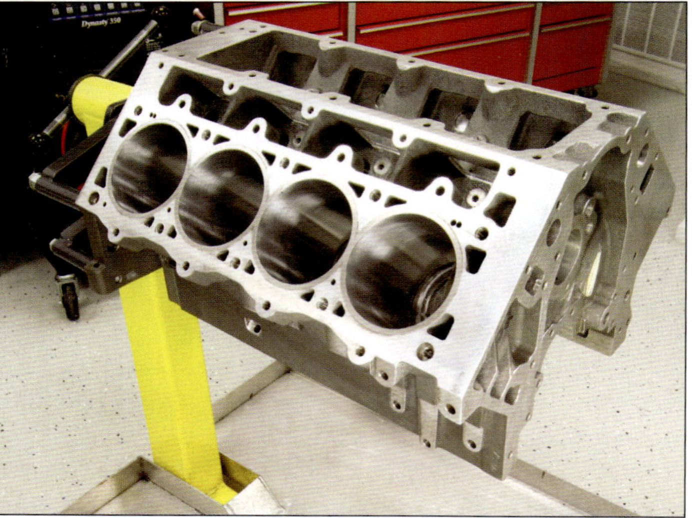

Dart's range of LS blocks is designed for greater strength than factory blocks and features details such as notches at the bottom of the bores that provide clearance for longer-stroke combinations and meatier connecting rods. Versions of the design also include the elimination of the long skirt below the crankshaft centerline, similar to early Chevy small-block engines. That greatly reduces crankcase windage, which can be a challenge in a force-inducted engine.

CFE Racing LS Fusion Aluminum Block

At a glance, the LS Fusion aluminum block looks like an LS design with the Y-block configuration and other details, but that's where the similarities end. Designed as a dedicated racing component, it shares virtually no common dimension with production and aftermarket LS blocks.

Significantly, the bore centers are expanded from the standard 4.400 inches to 4.500 inches to accommodate bore sizes of 4.400 inches. It also has a deck height of 10.2 inches. Those specs negate the use of production and aftermarket heads, intakes, and other components designed for conventional LS applications. The LS Fusion requires custom heads and supporting components, most of which are also produced by CFE Racing, although it is designed to accept LS-style oil pans and front-end accessories.

For builders seeking up to 3,000 hp and perhaps more from a large-displacement foundation, the LS Fusion block is an excellent starting point, as long as cost isn't a factor.

Resleeving the Factory Aluminum Block

Factory LS engines are admirably strong for most serious performance upgrades, including mild- and moderate-boost forced-induction combinations, but they simply weren't designed for high-boost and racing applications.

An LS1 engine, for example, has combustion pressure of about 1,100 psi, although a high-boost engine producing more than 1,300 hp and 1,400 ft-lbs of torque will generate about *three times* that pressure: 3,000

Resleeving a block with ductile iron cylinder liners offers a less-costly alternative than the investment in an aluminum racing block. The process involves cutting the stock, cast-iron liners out of the block (although the design of the LS7 block allows them to be removed intact) and new liners pressed in place. The procedure yields a stronger block that better stands up to the cylinder pressures of forced induction. One drawback is the lack of six-bolt head clamping, as with the LSX and other aftermarket blocks, making this upgrade best-suited to moderate boost levels for street/strip engine combinations and not max-boost racing engines.

psi. In a regular-production, aluminum LS1 engine, it's the cast-iron cylinder liners that take the brunt of the abuse. They crack. It's a similar story for other production LS engines. Even iron-block 5.3L engines, which are growing in popularity among power-adder engine builders, just aren't designed for that level of stress.

A dedicated racing block, such as those outlined in this chapter, provides the added strength necessary to support the cylinder pressures of a high-power engine, but resleeving the factory block with cylinder liners made of ductile iron is another option.

The material, which is infused with nodular graphite, is surprisingly elastic, and that makes it extremely durable. The graphite nodules used in the material are spherical, which inhibits the formation of cracks. In fact, the name ductile iron is derived from its exceptional ductility, or its capacity to deform without fracturing. Its tensile strength is about three times greater than the cast iron used in production LS block cylinder liners.

The ductile iron liners used with most resleeving procedures offer about three times the tensile strength of the stock cast-iron liners. There are two types of liners: dry and wet. Dry liners are installed with a wall of the block material between the liners, and wet liners are designed for direct contact with the circulating engine coolant. For the resleeving procedure described in this chapter, the sleeves are installed dry.

When it comes to cost, resleeving a factory aluminum block is comparable to the cost of a new LSX iron block, which also offers superior strength, but at a significant weight penalty. For the mass- and cost-conscious builder, resleeving is a viable alternative.

Deburring the edges of an engine block is one of the simplest and easiest ways to build strength into it. Knocking down the sharp edges eliminates potential starting places for cracks. It's a procedure that should be carried out before the engine's assembly begins.

Installing Piston Oil Squirters

Piston-cooling oil jets should be considered a must when building an LS engine for forced induction. They douse the bottom of the piston with engine oil, which not only helps minimize friction but also helps keep the pistons cooler under the tremendous combustion temperatures that come with supercharging and turbocharging. The LS9 used them and all of the Gen V (LT family) engines continue to use them.

Typically, the jets are plumbed from the main web to the bottom of the cylinders and builders have used a variety of nozzles for the squirters themselves, including carburetor jets. In 2017, a company called GET'M Garage introduced an oil squirter kit for LS engines that included all the necessary components and fixtures for the project. Although it requires additional time when building the engine, the comparative low cost of the kit makes it a bargain for the additional durability it will offer the engine.

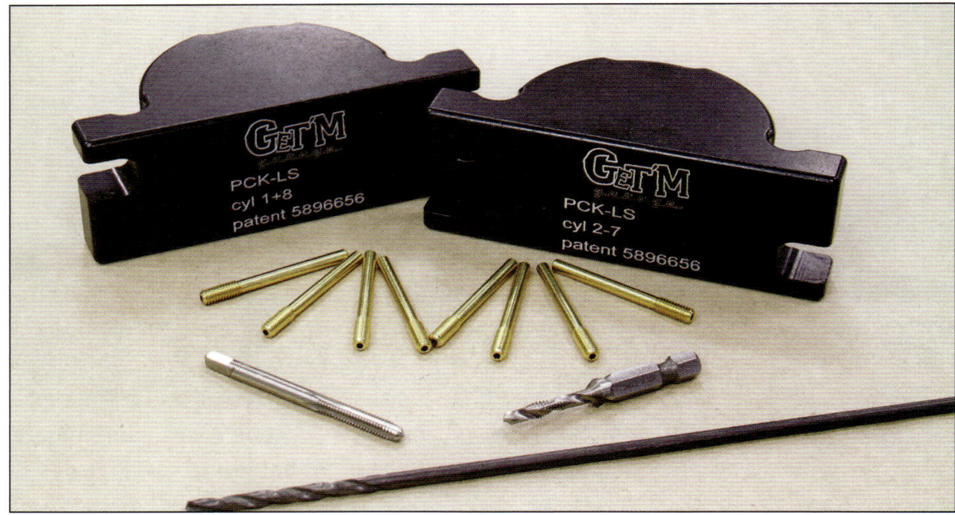

The GET'M Garage oil jet kit includes the fixtures for drilling the oil-supply holes, a drill bit and tap for the procedure, and the squirters themselves.

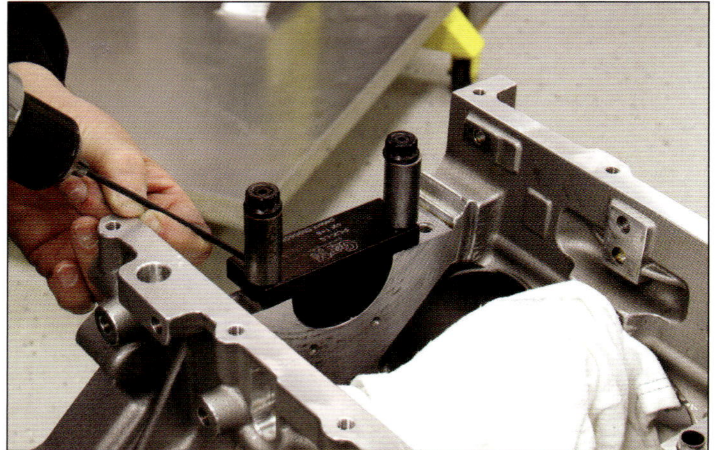

Installing the oil jets starts with securing the GET'M Garage fixture to each main web of the block and drilling down through the oil galleries until the drill bit breaks into the bottom of the cylinders.

After running a tap through the holes, thread the jets into the block with just a touch of blue Loctite thread sealer to secure them. They thread down until they're just below the bearing surface of the main web. And while the jet looks like it's going straight into the main web, it's angled several degrees toward the cylinder.

Here's the installed oil jet (arrow), which has a 0.020-inch outlet. It will shoot engine oil at the bottom of the piston to keep down its temperature. At the extreme cylinder temps that come with supercharging or turbocharging, the pistons and rings can soften without an aid like this.

Rotating Assembly

A forged crankshaft, forged rods, and forged pistons should be the ingredients that comprise the rotating assembly, but there are other factors to consider.

Crankshaft

Assuming a new engine build uses a forged-steel crankshaft, it's important to understand that not all forged crankshafts are created equally. From the factory, only the LS7, LSA, and LS9 engines include a forged crankshaft; all other LS production crankshafts are cast iron.

It is possible to use the LS9 forged crankshaft in other LS engines and brand-new assemblies, but it has a considerably longer snout to support the dry-sump oiling system's larger, gerotor-type oil pump, as well as a unique flywheel bolt pattern. It is possible to modify the crankshaft to work with other oil pumps and front-engine accessory drive systems, but it is easier and less expensive to spec a forged crankshaft from one of the well-known performance crankshaft manufacturers, such as Callies or Eagle.

Even under the banner of "forged steel" there are different levels of forgings that are based on the materials incorporated with the steel to enhance hardness and durability. The most common forgings used in performance engines are 4130 and 4340. Here's what those numbers mean:

- The "4" refers to a steel alloy that is mixed with molybdenum for greater overall strength; the more "moly," the tougher the crankshaft.
- The "1" and "3" numbers refer to other materials mixed in the alloy:

the "1" indicates a steel alloy with chromium added, while the "3" in 4340 indicates nickel and chromium are part of the steel alloy for even greater strength.

- The "30" and "40" numbers refer to the percentage of carbon added to enhance hardness: "30" refers to approximately 30-percent content and "40" indicates an approximate 40-percent content.

While both 4130 and 4340 forged-steel crankshafts are superior to standard cast-iron crankshafts, the 4340 forging is stronger than the 4130 because of its nickel content and higher percentage of carbon. Of course, that greater strength comes with a higher purchase price, but for racing applications, it's worth the investment. A street/strip engine does just fine with a properly prepared 4130 crankshaft.

Proper heat-treating can significantly strengthen the crankshaft, while crankshafts used in engines designed primarily for racing should also be shot-peened for maximum strength. Some builders also have the stress risers on the rod throws removed to improve performance and longevity.

To optimize lubrication, the engine may benefit from slots machined in the crankshaft journals that direct oil at higher RPM. Some racing-engine builders also use full-groove bearings to ensure maximum oiling for the rods. Avoid cross-drilling the crankshaft, however. While it was a common procedure years ago, most professional builders no longer believe it is

The crankshafts of production LS engines have a press-fit damper, and the only one with a crankshaft keyway to prevent slippage is the forged crank of the LS9. When building an engine for supercharged or turbocharged performance, a keyway is a must, and you should spend the time and few extra dollars to have one machined into the nose of the crankshaft. Shown here is a budget supercharged engine build using an LS3's cast crankshaft with a keyway cut into it.

When it comes to installing the crankshaft and main bearing caps, the cap fasteners should be the best you can afford. Rather than using the production-style combination of studs and bolts, all of the main caps should be secured with studs and nuts for more accurate fastening and repeatable removal and installation on an engine that will see moderate to frequent teardowns. ARP's 200,000-psi studs and 12-point bolts (seen here) are the best on the market and should be highly considered.

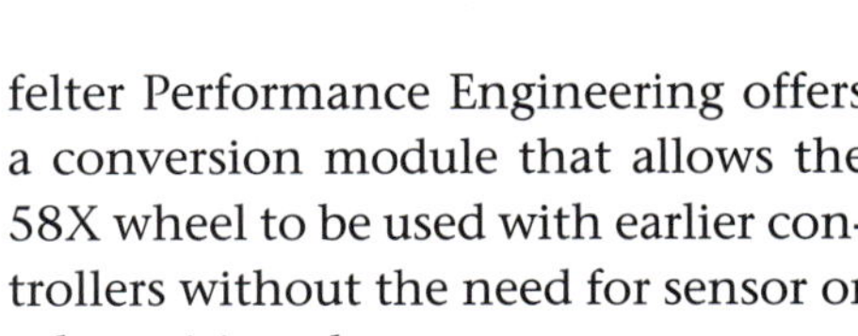

Most of the fasteners on an LS engine feature torque-to-yield specifications. That means rather than a conventional foot-pound or inch-pound torque rating, the fasteners are final-tightened to a specific torque angle, such as 40 degrees or 60 degrees. So, a standard torque wrench is not enough, and you will need to complement it with a torque angle wrench or a modern combination torque wrench (seen here) that includes pound readouts (and Newton meters) as well as angle degrees.

effective. In fact, it may do more harm than good in the long run.

Reluctor Wheel

The crank-triggered ignition system of the LS engine requires a *reluctor* wheel (also known as a *tone* wheel) mounted on the crankshaft. It's a toothed wheel that helps determine crankshaft position to ensure spark-timing accuracy. Early LS production engines came with a 24X (24 tooth), while later engines (including all those equipped with electronic throttle control) used a 58X (58-tooth) wheel.

Generally speaking, either wheel can be used on a custom engine build, but selection depends primarily on the engine controller to be used. The more-common, later-style GM E38 and E67 controllers support the 58X wheel and electronic throttle control, while earlier LS1A and LS1B controllers support the 24X wheel. The 58X wheel can be used with earlier LS engines and later controllers, but revisions to the camshaft-position sensor require an LS2/LS3 front cover on LS1/LS6 and some truck engines.

For example, a 24X wheel should be used if you plan to retain the original engine controller on an engine built for a 2002 Trans Am that was originally equipped with the LS1 engine. If, however, you plan to install an LS7 engine and supercharger, the LS7's 58X wheel must be changed to a 24X wheel if the stock LS1 controller is to be used. Additionally, Lingenfelter Performance Engineering offers a conversion module that allows the 58X wheel to be used with earlier controllers without the need for sensor or other wiring changes.

Aftermarket, stand-alone control systems, such as those from Holley, FAST, and ACCEL-DFI, are compatible with either the 24X or 58X wheel.

At a glance, here's how to tell the different GM reluctor wheels apart. The 24X-style (left) is found on LS1, LS6, and other engines through about 2007. The 58-tooth wheel (right) is used on later engines, although there is some model-year overlap between the reluctor wheel types on LS2 engines. The 2005 Corvette and most 2005 Pontiac GTOs used the LS2 with a 24X wheel. Generally speaking, the 58X wheel is used with Gen IV LS engines that moved the camshaft position sensor from the top rear of the engine block to the front of the engine, near the timing gear. In a custom project that will use a stand-alone control system, there's not a significant reason to use one type of wheel over the other, but when building an engine for a primarily street-driven vehicle that was originally equipped with an LS engine and retains the original controller, it is best to use the original reluctor wheel design to ensure controller compatibility.

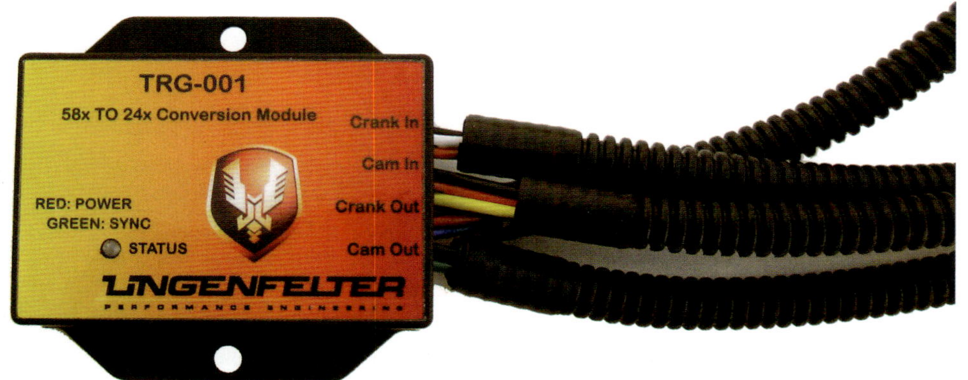

Lingenfelter's TRG-001 conversion module is designed to enable later LS engines with the 58X reluctor wheel to be used in vehicles with earlier, 24X-based control systems without sensor or wiring changes. It plugs into the wiring harness and original sensors, although some early Gen IV engines may need a jumper harness to extend the camshaft position sensor wiring.

Tack-welding the steel reluctor wheel to the crankshaft on a 58X system is a tip some builders have employed since the early LS days when the sheet metal 24-tooth wheels tended to slip on the crankshaft. The later, 58X wheels didn't really demonstrate a comparable problem, but it's a quick and easy measure of insurance to add to a high-boost build.

Pistons

The two most important factors for pistons in a forced-induction engine are cylinder pressure and strength. Simply stated, the cast-aluminum pistons of most production LS engines (only the supercharged LS9 comes with forged pistons) are adequate for low-boost, bolt-on power adders, but builders seeking higher power need stronger, forged-aluminum pistons that deliver a lower static compression ratio.

Although commendably lightweight and durable in naturally aspirated applications, the factory cast piston's high silicon content makes it rather brittle when compared with a forged-aluminum piston. That brittleness doesn't stand up well to the excessive pressure generated by the blower or turbo; and it is especially susceptible to damage if detonation occurs.

Forged pistons are manufactured through a process that forms the part by essentially pounding it into shape rather than the poured metal of a cast piston. They are still comprised of alloys, but the manufacturing process brings greater material density and eliminates the chance for porosity, which greatly enhances strength. They're also more ductile (the opposite of a casting's brittleness), and they typically resist heat better than cast pistons. The best forged-aluminum pistons suitable for boost have less than 1-percent silicon content. (Production pistons are referred to as hypereutectic because of silicon content greater than 12 percent.)

Generally, there are two grades of high-performance forged-aluminum pistons: 4032 and 2618. The 4032 forgings (which contain a small amount of silicon) are less expensive but not as strong as silicon-free 2618-forged pistons. If there's a trade-off with forged pistons, particularly 2618 forgings, it is increased cold-start engine noise due to thermal expansion. The silicon in hypereutectic pistons minimizes the piston's expansion when the engine warms up, allowing for a much tighter piston-to-cylinder-wall tolerance, but the low silicon content of forged pistons means they grow more in the cylinder bore. Consequently, forged pistons need greater piston-to-wall clearance with 2618 pistons needing the most.

In general, a 4032-forged piston needs approximately 0.0025- to 0.0035-inch piston-to-wall clearance, while 2618 pistons need about 0.0035- to 0.0045-inch clearance. That extra clearance means forged pistons typically generate an unsettling knocking noise known as piston slap when the engine is cold. The noise goes away as the cylinders and pistons heat up, causing the pistons to grow and fill up the space. (If the noise doesn't abate after the engine warms up, it may indicate an incorrect engine assembly or other more-serious engine problems.)

Other attributes that contribute to a stronger blower piston include reinforced pin bosses (the areas on either side of the piston skirt where the pin slides in) and a thick piston crown. That's the area between the top ring and the top of the piston. A thicker crown better withstands the

A better piston selection for a supercharged or turbocharged street/strip LS engine is the "D"-shaped dish (seen here) that provides a large, relatively efficient quench area. Quench is described as the squishing effect on the air charge as the piston reaches top dead center. The shape of the piston's dish helps squeeze air through the combustion chamber in a manner that generally helps even out the temperature throughout the chamber and reduces the chance for detonation. The depth of the dish affects the compression ratio.

Here's a look at the production, forged-aluminum LS9 piston. Note that it is dished to minimize the compression ratio, but there is also a slight dome within the dish. It helps reflect the incoming air/fuel charge back toward the spark plug for greater combustion efficiency. It also has a unique ring pack that uses relatively thick top and secondary rings and a very thin, minimal bottom oil-control ring. The specialized machining process of the block enables tighter tolerances that, in turn, allows for the thinner, lower-friction oil-control ring. Also note the friction-reducing Teflon coating on the skirt. In short, the LS9 piston is all about low friction and high RPM. It would make a good choice for low- to moderate-boost engines projected to make about 750 to 800 hp. (Photo Courtesy General Motors)

punishment of detonation, as well as the generally hotter temperature and cylinder pressure that come with a highly boosted engine.

Besides selecting a forged-aluminum design, the pistons for a supercharged or turbocharged engine should be targeted to deliver a compression ratio between 8.5 and 9.5:1. This typically means using a D-shaped head with a dish (also known as an inverted dome) or strictly a dished piston and matching it carefully with the projected combustion-chamber volume. Most LS production engines came from the factory with relatively high compression ratios, including greater than 10.25:1 (the LS7 engine has 11.0:1 compression). That's too much compression for a forced-induction engine, making it difficult to prevent detonation.

One more thing to add is that along with strong, forged pistons, you should also employ heavy-duty piston wrist pins, even at the expense of adding weight to the assembly. As mentioned earlier, the overall weight of a forced-induction engine or its rotating assembly should be secondary to ensuring it is robust enough to withstand the pressure generated by the turbocharger or supercharger. To that end, heavier-yet-stronger wrist pins that are either larger in diameter or have a thicker wall than those typically used in a naturally aspirated engine should be considered.

Piston manufacturers, such as JE Pistons and Diamond, offer a variety of forged applications for LS engines and have excellent technical advisors to guide the builder into selecting the most appropriate parts.

Ceramic-Coated Pistons

The side profile of a piston shows the crown height (the space between the top ring land and the top of the piston). The minimum crown height for a forced-induction LS engine should be 0.200 inch, while 0.300 inch is optimal. Production LS pistons don't have such a thick crown, which (in addition to their cast construction) is why they're not great in supercharged or turbocharged applications.

Ceramic-coated pistons can minimize both heat absorption and friction, but you must be extremely careful to ensure the coating is applied by a knowledgeable, experienced vendor or by the manufacturer itself. Poorly applied coating material or an incorrectly prepped piston can result in the very hard coating flaking or peeling off in the cylinder. This can cause catastrophic damage, as the coating will typically score, scratch, or gouge the cylinder walls, effectively ruining the cylinder block. This risk is typically not worth it on street/strip engines producing less than 1,000 hp and/or less than 15 or so pounds of boost. Use coated pistons on high-power racing engines where engine temperature will be greater.

On engines designed for higher boost and higher power levels, the use of ceramic-coated pistons is an effective way to combat excessive cylinder and combustion heat while also reducing friction. Most piston manufacturers and companies with bearings for high-performance and racing engines offer parts with ceramic coatings. The coatings are generally based on Swain Tech Coatings products.

On a piston, a coating on top reduces the heat absorbed by the piston, helping prevent burning or other damage under high-boost and leaner-fuel conditions. A coating on the skirts of the piston reduces heat-building friction and the same goes for coated main bearings. These coated parts come at a premium cost over noncoated components, but the hedge against the damage caused by excessive heat makes them wise investments.

Some builders use coated main bearings, too, but this is more of a preventative measure against the possibility of oil starvation rather than a performance enhancement.

Piston Ring and Ring Pack

Piston rings service the vital job of sealing the cylinders to prevent combustion gases from entering the crankcase while also controlling oil on the cylinder walls and stabilizing the pistons within the bores. Under the high pressure of supercharger or turbocharger boost, those jobs are all the more important, as maintaining cylinder pressure is essential to performance.

Piston manufacturers that offer blower pistons for forced-induction engines generally optimize the ring-pack location to provide a generous crown for greater overall strength. But LS pistons have a ring pack that is located closer to the crown than, say, old-school small-block engines. The rings are typically thinner than previous-generation engines but bring increased stability with reduced friction.

With the higher ring pack and pressure from forced induction, LS piston rings are subjected to significant heat. For the most part, that means using the strongest, most heat-resistant rings you can afford. That typically means the top ring is moly-coated or similar. Ductile iron has long been the mainstay of rings, but steel is used increasingly for its strength and durability.

Generally speaking, when it comes to ring end gaps, the tighter the gap, the better, as this gener-

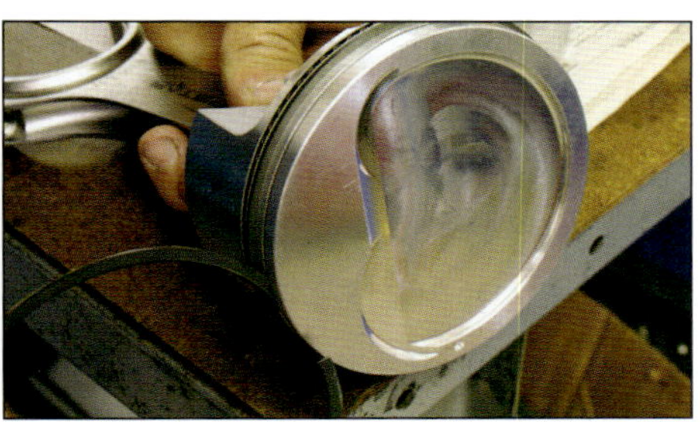

Coated-steel piston rings or nitrided-steel wire rings are the strongest and most resistant to the heat that comes with forced induction, where temperatures can exceed 600°F (315°C). Because blowby is a greater concern with turbocharging and supercharging, a tight ring end gap is necessary, but like other engine components, piston rings grow as the engine heats. That means the end gap is wider when the engine is cold and tightens up as the engine warms. A too-tight end gap when the engine is cold can force the ring ends together with excessive pressure when the boosted engine generates greater heat, leading to failure. A general rule of thumb for forced-induction engines is a top ring gap of 0.006 inch for every inch of bore diameter. That means a 4.125-inch bore should have a top ring end gap of 0.025 inch. Consult the ring manufacturer to select the best parts, specifying the engine's intended duty, operating range, and approximate power and boost levels.

ally maintains cylinder pressure and resists blowby longer. Total Seal offers unique, two-piece gapless top and second rings that offer greater resistance to blowby by preventing a conventional gap from opening between the ring ends.

While production engines' ring sizes vary, most aftermarket LS pistons are manufactured to support 1.5-/1.5-/3.0-mm rings. Thinner rings can be used to reduce friction, but they are made from specialized material that makes them very expensive. They should only be used in a racing engine that will see repeated disassembly, as thinner rings wear out sooner and require more frequent replacement. Stick with thicker rings for street and street/strip combinations.

Make sure piston rings are available for your desired bore size before ordering the pistons or having the cylinder block machined. Assembly plans go right off the tracks when the pistons arrive and there are no rings to fit them.

Gas Porting

The trick to gas porting involves drilling holes strategically in the piston to force the compression ring against the cylinder wall. The idea behind it is that this pressurized ring seal prevents the ring from fluttering at higher RPM while extending the power curve.

Two types of gas porting are typically used: vertical and horizontal. Vertical gas ports are drilled from the piston deck into the top ring groove and behind the ring. This method is employed more by drag racers. Horizontal gas porting involves drilling holes through the bottom side of the top ring land, extending to the back wall of the ring groove. It is used more in circle track/road racing.

Generally, gas porting is best left to dedicated racing applications, where sustained performance at high RPM delivers the greatest benefit. Also, carbon builds up in the ports, so an engine that does primarily street duty (and does not get regular, between-race teardowns) quickly loses the advantage of gas porting when the ports clog. The pressure on the rings also significantly reduces the ring's lifespan, which is another reason to avoid gas porting for street engines.

Connecting Rods

The higher the expected horsepower, the stronger and beefier the connecting rods need to be. Rod failures typically arise from high-RPM strain and/or exhaust-stroke pressure. In general, greater horsepower increases the compressive force on the rods, while greater RPM increases tensile strain. These attributes are amplified considerably with forced induction.

Most LS production engines use powdered-metal rods that, like their corresponding cast-aluminum pistons, are surprisingly robust in an unmodified engine. As mentioned earlier, factory engine components are designed to operate in a performance window within a few percent of the advertised horsepower and torque ratings. Consistently pushing beyond that range puts a strain on the internal components they weren't designed for.

To withstand the strain under boost, high-performance connecting rods need to deliver greater compression strength and tensile strength. The typical upgrade is to a forged-steel material, such as 4340 steel or 300M. Beyond the greater strength that comes with the denser material, these performance rods are typically thicker in key areas to enhance strength.

In most cases, builders choose between I-beam-style and H-beam-style connecting rods. Each is known for delivering strength, but each delivers it slightly differently. The I-beam looks more like a conventional connecting rod but is very thick through the middle, allowing it to handle great compressive loads. H-beam rods have a thin center section but wide, flat outer sides that provide tremendous stiffness and resistance to bending.

Assuming all other attributes are equal, the I-beam and H-beam offer comparable compressive strength, but the thinner center portion of the H-beam typically makes it lower in mass than an I-beam. The lighter H-beam design can make more of a difference with primarily street-driven vehicles, where more low-end power is desired.

Problems with performance rods

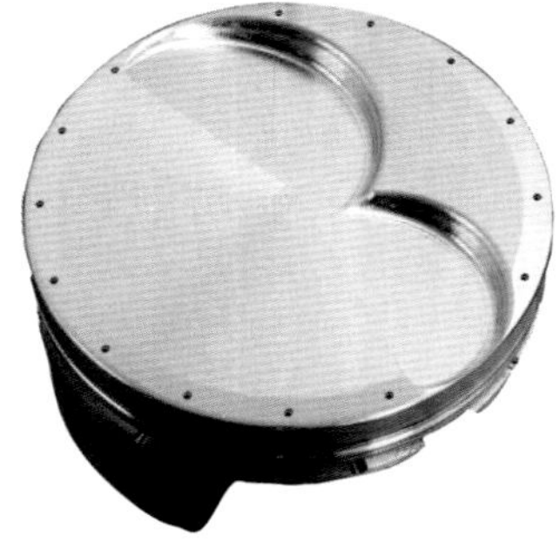

Here's an example of a gas-ported piston intended for racing, you can tell it by the holes drilled through the piston head. Because those tiny holes can get clogged with carbon over even a relatively short period of operating time, gas porting is not an effective idea for street engines. The pressure created on the cylinder rings also wears them out much faster, requiring frequent replacement.

 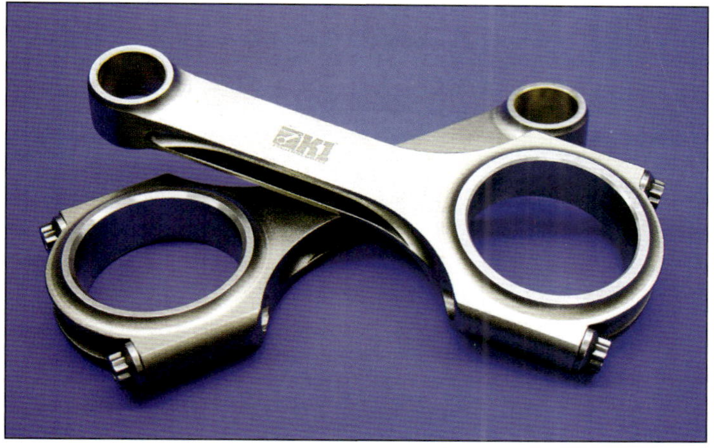

A typical example of I-beam (left) and H-beam (right) are shown here. In terms of strength, they are comparable when made of the same material, offering similar compression strength. The differences, then, are subtler; selecting one design over the other comes down to other engine-assembly factors. Typically, an H-beam rod is lighter than an I-beam, but its big end is generally larger, too, which can mean a greater chance for cylinder block interference on a long-stroke combination. If block interference is not a concern, the extra rev capability enabled by lighter H-beam rods is preferred to offset the other higher-mass, heavy-duty rotating parts. Also, most professional builders insist on using a solid bushing on the small end, rather than the more common and cheaper split bushing.

This is a typical forged-aluminum connecting rod, and at a glance it's easy to see it is physically larger than a comparable forged-steel rod. Aluminum rods tend to stretch the most during the cold-start period and during the compressive loads of varied RPM, which makes them particularly unsuitable for sustained use in a street vehicle. By some estimates, the life span of an aluminum rod is only one-tenth that of a forged-steel rod. They work best in a drag racing engine where the engine is quickly brought up to high RPM and more or less left there during the run. There is an unquestionable impact on RPM capability with aluminum rods, but their fatigue rate makes them best left to racing-only combinations.

A common issue with long-stroked engines and/or those using aluminum or even some forged H-beam-style rods is cylinder block interference. The rotating assembly should be slowly and carefully turned after installation to check for potential interference, as seen here. This LSX-based block will require additional machining to clear bulky forged-aluminum rods.

Note the extra-thick wrist pin being inserted into this piston/rod combination. In high-performance, forced-induction engines, the wrist pin absorbs tremendous bending and radial pressure. To shore up the rotating assembly, it should be large, robust, and made of a strong material, such as a 4130 forging for a street engine. For racing engines, perhaps the ultimate wrist pin is offered from Bill Miller Engineering in the form of its 9310 VAR (vacuum arc remelted) steel pins.

Looking upward at the bottom of the cylinder, here's the machined block, showing the notched areas required for connecting rod clearance. Although time consuming, as it must be accomplished on all of the cylinders, it is a relatively easy procedure to perform on an iron cylinder block. More care is required when dealing with the iron liners in an aluminum block. In fact, the machining requirements simply may not be possible on some aluminum blocks, forcing the use of different, lower-profile rods; a shorter stroke length; or both.

Beefier connecting rods can squeeze the tolerance of the rod ends on the crankshaft journal. The rod side clearance should be between 0.00433 inch and 0.0200 inch.

Bolts stretch. Similar to a spring, they stretch beyond their static length to deliver clamping power. In most cases, a torque wrench does the trick, but when it comes to the connecting rod bolts, measuring their stretch dimension is a more accurate way of ensuring they're torqued accurately. Essentially, the bolts are stretched until they are within the sweet spot of elasticity. That's usually between 0.005 inch and 0.006 inch.

can arise, however, with internal clearance within the cylinder block. Thick, racing-type I-beam rods on larger-stroke combinations (generally, engines greater than 427 ci) can interfere with the bottoms of the cylinders and other walls inside the block. Extreme care must be taken to gently rotate the rod/piston assembly to check for clearance problems. Notching the bottoms of the cylinders, making clearance for other areas within the block, and even machining the small and/or big ends of the rods may be required.

4340 Versus 300M and Forged Versus Billet and Aluminum

The common steel connecting rod forging is made from 4340 steel, which contains up to 2-percent nickel, along with smaller percentages of chromium, silicon, molybdenum, and manganese. It is an extremely durable material for connecting rods, but 300M alloy is gaining favor with many builders. It contains more silicon (approximately 1.5 percent) along with more moly and carbon.

Rods made from 300M can be more expensive, but they are generally stronger than a comparably sized 4340 rod, which enables the manufacturer to downsize the center section by up to 20 percent and still offer the strength of 4340 steel. In a supercharged/turbocharged engine that is already using a number of higher-mass components to reinforce overall strength, the investment in 300M rods can offset a significant source of rotating mass.

Another choice is to choose

billet-steel over forged-steel connecting rods. As the name implies, billet rods are cut from a single piece of steel on a CNC machine. This is generally used for custom applications where a manufacturer may only make a few sets of a particular design that wouldn't be cost effective to set up in a conventional forging operation.

A billet-steel rod can be stronger than a forged-steel rod but only if the steel used is of higher quality than the 4340 or 300M recipes. Because the material does not have to be as malleable as the steel used in forging, it enables the manufacturer to use very strong steel.

As for forged-aluminum connecting rods, they offer very good strength and the obvious benefit of low mass, an attribute that helps offset the weight of heavy-duty piston and wrist pins. But aluminum rods have only about half the tensile strength of a steel rod and are much more susceptible to stretching and fatigue, so they are typically quite chunky in size to maintain their shape longer. This can cause cylinder-bore interference problems, requiring machining that could ultimately reduce overall strength. Aluminum rods are also considerably more expensive than forged-steel rods.

Aluminum rods are not recommended for street and street/strip engines. They are suitable for racing engines that will see frequent inspections and teardowns.

LS7/LS9 Titanium Connecting Rods

The titanium connecting rods of the LS7 and LS9 engines are strong and lightweight, enabling very quick RPM buildup, but they are not necessarily the best option when building a boost-ready engine. That's because

All LS engines employ a windage tray. During assembly, it should be checked for interference with the crankshaft and rods. The process includes bolting down the tray after the rotating assembly has been installed and all the fasteners torqued to specifications. With the tray in place, slowly rotate the crankshaft and check for rod or crankshaft interference. Even if the assembly turns without hitting the tray, check for a too-close relationship that could lead to interference during engine operation.

If a windage tray interference issue is discovered, stacking washers on the main cap studs that also secure the tray is the easiest method of curing the problem. Start with a single washer on each stud and recheck the clearance, adding washers until a satisfactory clearance is achieved.

the rods are designed for the operating parameters of their respective factory engines.

Because the rods are validated to the strength requirements for their respective engines, higher boost and higher horsepower strain their compression-strength resistance. That's not to say these rods are weak by any measure, but they're simply not designed for use in, say, a 700-, 800-, or 1,000-hp forced-induction engine.

Sacrificing low-speed RPM capability for the assurance and longevity of a forged-steel rod is a worthy tradeoff.

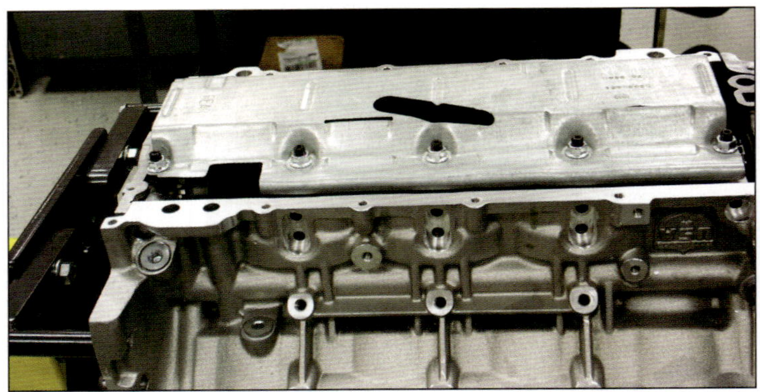

For truly long-stroke combinations, Chevrolet Performance offers a deeper windage tray to clear 4.125-inch strokes (part number 19202609). It also provides clearance for shorter-stroke combinations that use rods with larger, beefier ends.

On supercharged engines, the damper/crankshaft pulley plays an important role in determining the blower's max boost.

The diameter of the pulley must be sized in the correct relation to the supercharger's drive pulley. In this example, the stock 7.43-inch-diameter damper was replaced with an ATI 8.25-inch damper to complement the blower drive pulley.

SPOTLIGHT: Chevrolet Performance's Boost-Ready LSX Crate Engines

GM Performance Parts' LSX376 crate engine is more of a long-block assembly, as it does not come with an intake manifold, oil pan, or other accessories. What it offers, however, is a preassembled engine with a forged crank, 9.0:1 forged pistons, and high-flow LS3 cylinder heads. Its four-bolt head clamping (on the six-bolt-compatible LSX block) and powdered-metal rods aren't ideal for high-boost/high-RPM combinations, but for low- to moderate-boost street/strip engines, it's more than adequate and a comparative value.

Preassembled crate engines offer a time-saving and often cost-effective solution for many builders. Chevrolet Performance's LSX-based crate engine options were designed for forced induction. They include the LSX376-B8 (part number 19260831) and LSX376-B15 (part number 19355575).

Both are based on the LSX standard-deck six-bolt engine block and, importantly, each features low-compression (9.0:1) forged-aluminum pistons designed for boost. The differences between them, however, are based on boost capability. The LSX376-B8 is designed for supercharger and turbo systems producing up to 8 pounds of boost (0.55 bar), using an economical nodular iron crankshaft, production-style LS3 cylinder heads, and an LS3 roller camshaft.

The LSX376-B15 ups the ante to support up to 15 pounds of boost with a stronger forged-steel crankshaft, LSX-LS3 six-bolt cylinder heads, and a hotter camshaft with greater lift and duration that makes the most of the greater airflow enabled by higher boost levels. It also uses forged powder metal connecting rods, while the B8 engine uses conventional powder metal rods.

Both crate engines are technically long-blocks that are delivered assembled but without an induction system, oil pan, and other accessories; and each includes a 58X reluctor wheel. That allows the builder to finish off the engine with the power added of his or her choice.

At the time this edition was published, the retail price for the LSX376-B8 was around $7,200 and the B15 version was about $8,500. It would be difficult to build comparable combinations from scratch for less, making a crate engine a smart choice for enthusiasts seeking ready-built foundations for mild and moderate boost. ■

BUILDING AN *LS* ENGINE: HEADS, CAM, AND INDUCTION

With a stout short-block filled with an all-forged rotating assembly, the remainder of a boost-ready engine assembly includes the cylinder heads and crucially important camshaft. All LS engines benefit from excellent cylinder head airflow (some more than others), but it is the camshaft that is the key not only to optimal power but drivability characteristics.

Cylinder Heads

There isn't sufficient room in this chapter to describe all of the cylinder head choices available to the LS engine builder, and more seem to arrive all the time. The use of heads with six bolts per cylinder isn't an absolute requirement on an engine making less than 1,000 hp or less

than about 15 pounds of boost, but they should be strongly considered for racing applications generating high boost and high horsepower.

The other crucial detail only applies to the installation of supercharger systems that mount the compressor in place of the intake manifold. For these applications, the cylinder head intake ports must be compatible with the intake ports of the supercharger manifold's ports. Mostly, that means the difference between LS1/LS6/LS2-style cathedral-port heads and later-style rectangular-port heads. In fact, even the later heads don't all have matching port shapes; the LS7 head ports have a squarer design, while the LS3/L92-style ports are taller and narrower.

Also, because of the comparatively small bores of LS1 and LS6 engines (3.89 inches), when compared with the later 6.0L and larger engines, they can only use LS1, LS6, and LS2 heads. Using the heads of 6.2L and larger engines causes valve-to-block interference. However, the larger 4.00-inch bore of the

There is an almost endless list of possibilities when it comes to boost-friendly cylinder heads for LS engines. The excellent port design and large-capacity runners allow for easy and efficient cylinder filling. Ensuring intake manifold compatibility with the heads' intake ports is the only major caveat when selecting them for a supercharged or turbocharged combination.

LS2 enables it to use LS1/LS6 heads, as well as L92-style heads (including LS3, LS9, and LSA engines).

The 6.2L engines (LS3, L92, etc.) can use any head except the LS7 and C5R, while the 7.0L LS7 and C5R blocks can use any LS-series head. The C5R head is not recommended, as it is an expensive part with a unique intake-port design that requires a custom intake manifold, as well as a small combustion chamber that promotes a high-compression ratio that's incompatible with forced induction. The LS2, LS3/L92, and LS7 heads use production intakes and offer greater port volume and larger combustion chambers that are desirable with forced induction.

In general terms, higher-flow cylinder heads make the same horsepower with lower-boost pressure than a comparable engine combination with lower-flowing heads. Put another way, the boost of the supercharger or turbocharger overcomes the relative inadequacies of "smaller" heads, as the boost pressure fills the ports and then some. That's not to say the cylinder head isn't important, but for most street/strip applications, the already high-flow characteristics of factory LS heads perform more than adequately with forced induction.

Later-style rectangular-port heads (whether LS7 or LS3/L92 style) are larger and have greater airflow attributes than cathedral-port heads. They are well suited to forced induction, but the ultimate selection may be influenced by bolt-on Roots/Lysholm-type supercharger systems because not all supercharger intakes are currently compatible with all cylinder head port designs.

When it comes to combustion-chamber design, the factory configuration is adequate, and conventional porting/blending provides a modest benefit. More crucial, however, is chamber volume, as it contributes to the engine compression ratio. A larger chamber volume lowers the compression ratio, while a smaller volume raises it. A good rule of thumb is somewhere in the 64- to 68-cc range.

Another consideration for engines projected to generate more than 15 pounds of boost is the use of cylinder heads with six head bolts per cylinder, rather than the factory-style four bolts per cylinder. When used with the appropriate cylinder block (see chapter 8), the additional clamping power (at least 50 percent greater) of the six-bolt heads does much to prevent head gasket failure. Chevrolet Performance offers a six-bolt LSX-LS3, LSX-LS7, LSX-CT (Circle Track), and LSX-DR (Drag Race). Additionally, Trick Flow and a few other aftermarket manufacturers offer six-bolt heads that fit the LSX cylinder block and other aftermarket blocks with the same head-bolt pattern.

Several companies offer modified versions of production GM

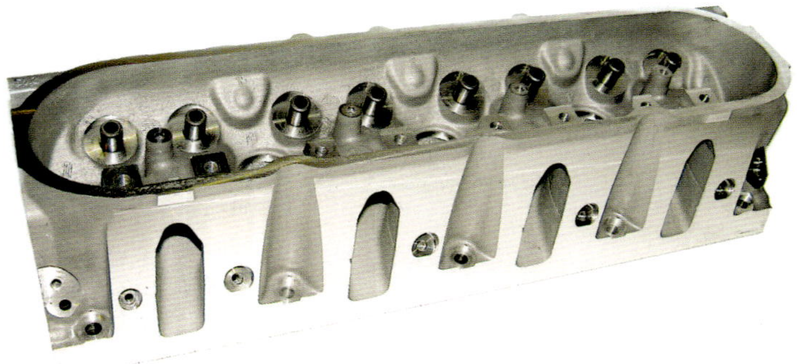

The LS1/LS6/LS2-style cathedral-port cylinder head (seen here) doesn't offer the maximum flow characteristics of later heads that are based on the rectangular-port design of the LS7 engine, but they are adept at generating excellent torque. With minor adaptations, later heads can be swapped on LS1/LS6 engines to maximize the airflow offered by the power adder. Also, 6.0L engines can use 6.2L L92/LS3-style heads to great effect, but again, they must be matched with the correct intake manifold. A 6.0L intake, for example, doesn't fit LS3 heads; and the LS7 intake fits only LS7 heads.

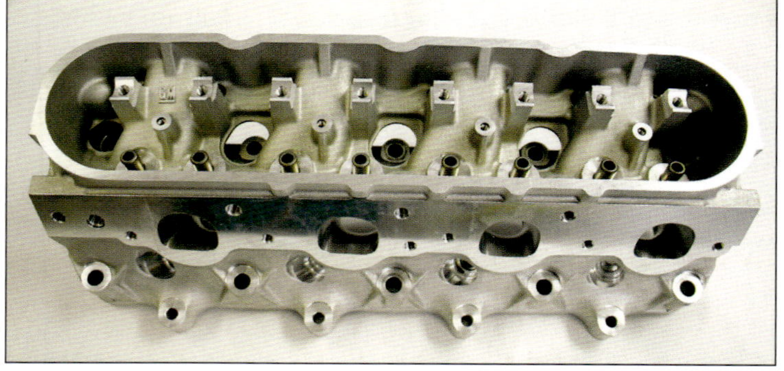

GM Performance Parts offers a range of LSX six-bolt cylinder heads with LS3/L92- and LS7-style rectangular ports, as well as an LSX-DR (drag race) head that offers raised runners, an 11-degree valve angle, and a design the requires shaft-mounted rocker arms. Taking advantage of the six-bolt clamping power, however, requires they be used with LSX or RHS six-bolt cylinder blocks. The standard LSX heads use standard LS intake manifolds, while the LSX-DR requires a unique, carburetor-style manifold (part number 19166954) that can be adapted and used with racing-oriented turbo and centrifugal supercharger systems.

An aftermarket alternative to GM heads is World Products' Warhawk cylinder heads, offered in LS1X and LS7X styles. Each has a six-bolt design that corresponds with World's Warhawk cylinder block but can be bolted to a GM block using the standard four-bolt pattern. The LS1X features cathedral ports, a 15-degree valve angle, 235-cc intake runners, 2.080/1.600-inch valves, and is available with 64-cc or 72-cc combustion chambers. The LS7X head has rectangular ports, a 12-degree valve angle, 285-cc runners, 2.250/1.625-inch valves, and 64-cc or 72-cc chambers. On either head, selecting the smaller chamber volume will promote a higher compression ratio, so it must be matched with an appropriate dished-piston design to keep the compression around 9.0 and 9.5:1 (or lower).

The telltale CNC porting finish on this head reveals a comparatively expensive machining job that won't necessarily pay off with substantially greater performance. The general design of LS heads is very well suited to forced induction with large intake runners and well-designed combustion chambers. It is true that porting and other machine work can achieve flow characteristics that typically can't be matched with an as-cast head, but the effect of that work is marginalized because the supercharger or turbocharger is cramming as much air into the chambers as they can take. The author's recommendation: unless the heads are offered in a CNC-ported design out of the box, leave porting for naturally aspirated engines.

heads that typically include CNC port work. These ported heads offer notable flow increases that are helpful on cathedral-port heads, but their relative expense doesn't provide as much of a return on investment on the high-flowing rectangular-port heads. As-cast rectangular-port heads flow very well for supercharged and turbocharged engines.

In short, there are countless choices for LS cylinder heads when building an engine for supercharging or turbocharging.

Valves

Superchargers and turbochargers, especially turbochargers,

Perhaps the ultimate in strength and durability for a forced-induction engine is the factory head for the supercharged LS9 engine. Based on the 6.2L LS3/L92 head's port and chamber design, it is made of a premium alloy and manufactured with a unique roto-cast process that spins the mold as the molten aluminum is poured to provide a more even, denser casting that all but eliminates porosity. They are available over the counter under part number 12621774. The LS9 heads, however, do not have a six-bolt design; they use larger 12-mm head bolts to increase clamping strength (other LS engines use a mix of 11- and 8-mm bolts). Adapting them on other LS engines requires resizing the head bolt holes in the block to accommodate them. (Photo Courtesy General Motors)

GM Cylinder Head Comparison Chart (Production and Chevrolet Performance Parts)					
Cylinder Head	Port Shape	Port Size (cc)	Chamber Volume (cc)	Valve Sizes (intake/exhaust in inches)	Notes
LS1	Cathedral	200	67	2.00/1.55	Introduced basic 15-degree valve angle and bolt-down rocker configuration. Use only on 5.7L engines.
LS6 (production)	Cathedral	210	64.5	2.00/1.55	Originally equipped with hollow-stem/sodium-filled valves. Use only on 5.7L engines.
LS6 CNC-ported *	Cathedral	250	61.9 or 65	2.00/1.55	Offered in two part numbers: 88958622 (small chamber) and 88958665 (low compression); use lower compression for forced induction.
LS2 (production)	Cathedral	210	64.5	2.00/1.55	Can be used on 5.7L (LS1/LS6); originally equipped with solid-stem valves.
LS2 CNC-ported *	Cathedral	250	64.5	2.00/1.55	Comparable to CNC-ported LS6, but less expensive; recommended upgrade to LS6 hollow/sodium valves.
L92 (production)	Rectangular	260	70	2.165/1.59	Can be used on 6.0L and larger engines with 4.00-inch bores; originally equipped with solid-stem valves.
L92 CNC-ported *	Rectangular	279	68	2.165/1.59	Similar to production L92, but with approximately 8-percent greater intake port volume.
LS3 (production)	Rectangular	260	70	2.165/1.59	Can be used on 6.0L and larger engines with 4.00-inch bores; originally equipped with solid-stem valves.
LS7	Rectangular (varied from LS3/L92)	270	70	2.20/1.61	Requires LS7-specific intake manifold; titanium intake valves and sodium-filled exhaust valves; requires minimum of 4.100-inch bores.
LS9	Rectangular	260	70	2.165/1.59	Special roto-cast manufacturing method and unique alloy material; titanium and sodium valves.
LSX-LS3 *	Rectangular	260	70	2.160/1.59	Six-bolt head clamping design.
LSX-L92 small-bore	Rectangular	260	70	2.00/1.55	Six-bolt configuration; designed for smaller-bore engines, including LS1 and LS6, but with production-style L92 port design. Uses LS3/L92-style intake manifolds.
LSX-LS7	Rectangular (varied from LS3/L92)	270	70	2.20/1.61	Six-bolt configuration; production-style titanium and sodium valves.
LSX-LS9	Rectangular	260	70	2.165/1.59	Six-bolt configuration; production-style titanium and sodium valves. Not manufactured with production roto-cast method.
LSX-DR	Rectangular	313	50	2.25/1.60	Unique design requires specific intake manifold; small combustion chamber promotes high compression (may not be suitable for forced induction without modifications).

* Chevrolet Performance Parts

generate more heat than a normally aspirated combination. Valves with the strength to withstand that heat are critical to the engine assembly. The factory-supercharged LS9 engine of the Corvette ZR1, for example, uses titanium intake valves and sodium-filled exhaust valves.

The titanium valves are extremely durable and low in mass, but comparable performance and heat resistance can be found with stainless steel intake valves, although they don't have the weight advantage of titanium. As for the exhaust side, the use of sodium-filled valves has long been an effective way to combat exhaust heat, but like titanium intake valves, inconel-material exhaust valves offer a less-expensive yet heavier alternative. Also, some builders shy away from sodium valves because of their multi-piece construction and the resulting damage that could occur if the pieces separate at high RPM, but contemporary products have proven very durable.

Valvetrain Components

Stronger, higher-rate valve springs typically go hand in hand with higher-lift camshafts, but even if the camshaft profile remains relatively close to the stock cam, the boost pressure of a forced-induction engine generally demands stronger springs. That's because the increased pressure in the cylinders wants to push the valves open or, at the very least, make it more difficult for them to close; the greater the boost, the stronger the springs need to be.

Lifter type plays a role here too, as a roller-type lifter can withstand about twice the valve spring pressure of a flat-tappet type. High spring pressure and high boost can affect the longevity of the camshaft as greater pressure is transferred to it. So, a roller lifter is strongly recommended.

Production LS engines use non-roller rocker arms with, generally, a 1.5 or 1.6:1 ratio. Using roller-tip rocker arms reduces friction, and a higher-ratio arm (typically 1.7 or 1.8:1) delivers the effect of a mild increase in cam lift. But because of the intake-side pushrod position on LS7/LS3/L76/L92 heads, the rocker arms are offset. There are few choices currently for roller-tip rockers for these offset-style arms, but SLP Performance has a set that fits LS3, L76, and L92 engines (part number 50189). The rockers have a 1.85:1 ratio.

Stainless steel intake valves are hard to beat when it comes to strength and heat resistance. High-boost supercharged and turbocharged engines should employ a thermally active exhaust valve, such as sodium-filled or Inconel material, to withstand severe heat. The largest valves used in production LS engines are the LS7's 2.20-inch intake and 1.61-inch exhaust valves.

Surprisingly, no production LS engines use roller-tip rocker arms; they're all stamped steel, flat-tip rockers. Later, rectangular-port heads use offset intake-side rocker arms (as seen here) that accommodate the valve position for both the large valve heads and the large ports within the head. Beehive-style tapered valve springs are LS-standard, too, but they don't stand up well to the increased pressure from a higher-lift cam or the cylinder pressure of high boost.

Shaft-mount rocker arms, such as the Jesel Pro J2K 1.8-ratio rockers (seen here), offer exceptional stability and virtually eliminate problems with valve lash as the engine quickly revs to the upper-RPM band. However, valve cover clearance is an issue when using shaft-mounted rockers, requiring machining of the valve cover rails on the heads and/or a valve cover spacer to prevent interference. Some aftermarket heads, such as World Products' Warhawk heads and GM Performance Parts' LSX heads, are cast with taller rails to accommodate taller rocker-arm assemblies.

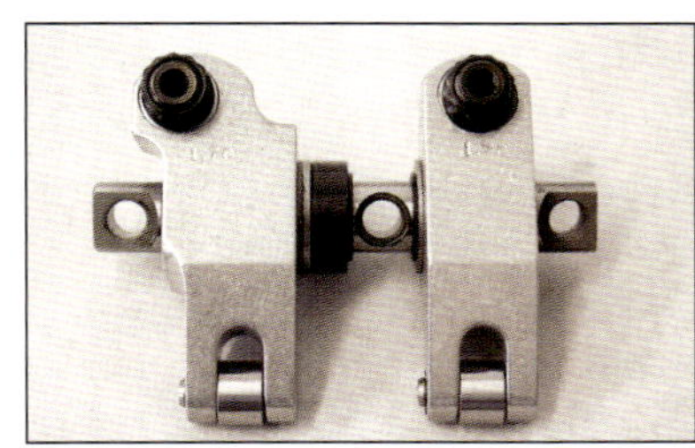

Although there are several choices for roller-tip rocker arms for the conventional rocker arms of LS cathedral-port heads, there are only a couple of options when it comes to upgrading rectangular-port heads with offset rockers. T&D Machine Products offers these 1.70:1-ratio, shaft-mount roller-tip rockers for rectangular-port heads.

Higher-rate valve springs are a must on a purpose-built forced-induction LS engine, especially if the combination includes a camshaft that exceeds about 0.510-inch lift. Shown here are the components of COMP Cams' 1.30-inch dual-coil valve spring, which withstands up to 0.600-inch lift without binding. The dual-coil design is heavier than the production-style beehive design, but it offers exceptional strength and resistance to boost pressure. Using titanium retainers with the springs helps offset their additional weight over the stock springs.

Stronger-than-stock valve springs are recommended with increased-ratio rockers.

Cylinder Head Gaskets

Because cylinder head sealing is crucial for forced-induction LS engines, the head gasket is a vital component in building a durable engine that stands up to great pressure. The factory-style gasket is a multi-layer steel (MLS) design that has proven very strong and reliable in naturally aspirated conditions and lower-boost engines of up to about 700 to 750 hp. However, the pressure of a supercharger or turbocharger, particularly when used with production-style four-bolt cylinder heads, often makes the head gasket one of the primary failure points on otherwise-stock engines.

The MLS head gaskets from Ohio-based Cometic Gasket have proven to be very strong and durable in forced-induction engines. Most importantly, they're available in a variety of bore sizes for the six-bolt pattern of the GM LSX block and the RHS LS Race Block. They are constructed of two embossed, Viton-coated, stainless steel outer layers sandwiched around a variable stainless inner layer.

Also, Fel-Pro's four-layer gaskets have proven to be very durable at higher horsepower. Copper gaskets or O-ring-style gaskets are suggested for racing engines producing more than 2,000 hp.

Camshaft

The camshaft needs for forced-induction engines are different from those for naturally aspirated engines. While supercharged and turbo-

A premium, multilayer steel head gasket is an absolute must when building a force-inducted LS engine, particularly on higher-boost engines that don't have the benefit of six-bolt head clamping. Fel-Pro and Cometic Gasket manufacture what have become the preferred gaskets for professional builders.

The factory LS9 cylinder head gasket is comprised of a whopping seven layers of specially treated steel. It will fit other 6.2L engines (part number 12622033), but its added thickness when compared with standard four-layer gaskets will slightly reduce the compression ratio. That's perfectly acceptable on a supercharged or turbocharged engine. (Photo Courtesy General Motors)

charged engines both feed pressurized air to the combustion chambers, there are differences that can affect the optimal camshaft profile, particularly the exhaust duration.

Before getting into the specifics of camshaft selection, here's a quick primer on common cam terms.

Lift: The distance the valve head is raised off its seat when the camshaft lobe is at its highest position (and in combination with the rocker arm). Lift is measured in fractions of an inch or millimeters. In theory, greater lift enhances performance by creating a wider opening to the combustion chamber and allowing a larger air/fuel charge to be packed in it.

Duration: The amount of time a valve is held open, measured for both the intake and exhaust valves in degrees of crankshaft rotation (i.e., 250 degrees on the intake valve and 255 degrees on the exhaust side). In general terms, longer duration enhances performance at higher

RPM or helps extend the RPM range of the engine.

Lobe/Lobe Ramp: The part of the camshaft that interfaces with the lifter (with the ramp section being the part that initiates the lifting and descending of the lifter). The profile of the lobe determines the speed or rate at which the valve opens and closes.

Symmetrical/Asymmetrical Lobe Ramps: A camshaft with symmetrical lobes has matching opening and closing ramps on both the intake and exhaust. An asymmetrical cam has different opening and closing ramp profiles on each lobe.

Base Circle: The lowest point of the camshaft lobe and the place in the camshaft's rotation when the valve is completely closed.

Lobe-Separation Angle (LSA): The distance in camshaft degrees between the maximum lift points of both the intake and exhaust valves. It affects performance by affecting valve overlap to impact the overall performance range of the engine. In a nutshell, a narrow angle promotes a steep, immediate power curve and a wider angle spreads the power out across the RPM band.

Valve Overlap: Measured in degrees of crankshaft rotation, it's the amount of time both the intake and exhaust valves are opened in a combustion chamber. It takes place as the exhaust stroke ends and the intake stroke begins. In general terms, greater overlap builds power at higher RPM by helping pull the fresh air/fuel charge into the chamber. Great lift and duration increases overlap, as does reducing the lobe-separation angle.

Intake Centerline: The point of greatest lift on an intake lobe, measured in crankshaft degrees after top dead center. In an assembled engine, it is measured by the crankshaft degrees between top dead center and the point of maximum valve lift.

Hydraulic Flat Tappet versus Hydraulic Roller: All production LS engines feature hydraulic lifters, but not hydraulic roller lifters, which are the friction-reducing rollers that interface with the cam's lobe ramps.

In general, a camshaft for a supercharged or turbocharged engine should have a wider LSA than a naturally aspirated engine to spread the power across the RPM band and deal with the increased cylinder heat that comes with forced induction. The rule of thumb for the LSA is 112 to about 114 degrees, although several LS engines' stock cams feature a 112-degree LSA, and the LS2 cam's LSA spec is a wide 116 degrees, for example, while the factory supercharged LS9's LSA is an extra-wide 122.5 degrees.

The optimal LSA must be matched with the appropriate

Camshaft selection is very important when it comes to maximizing the performance of a force-inducted engine. In general terms, both supercharged and turbocharged engines respond the best with a camshaft that has a lobe-separation angle of around 114 degrees, but the nature of how boost is produced and processed (including the role of overlap) requires markedly different approaches to the duration specifications.

A longtime debate for high-power street/strip and racing-oriented engines is whether to use a hydraulic roller camshaft or a solid-roller cam. As with normally aspirated engines, a hydraulic roller cam is suitable for high-power street and street/strip engines. It's not until the engine is expected to turn extremely high RPM and the cam's lift specs reach the 0.750-inch range (and higher) that the more positive valvetrain actuation offered by a solid roller is required.

exhaust duration to better handle exhaust pressure. Again, in general terms, a supercharged engine needs more exhaust duration than a naturally aspirated engine, while a turbocharged engine needs less duration.

Turbocharger Camshaft

Generally speaking, a turbocharged engine benefits from a milder cam (one with lower duration) to make the most of the exhaust-gas pressure that drives the turbocharger's turbine. In a nutshell, the camshaft should be used to keep heat out of the cylinders.

Ideally, the boost pressure of a turbo engine should be greater than the exhaust pressure at the low end of the power band as the engine nears its peak torque. The boost pressure and exhaust-gas pressure are nearly equal when the engine approaches its peak horsepower. However, at peak horsepower, there is typically greater exhaust back pressure than boost.

For optimal efficiency and maximum effectiveness of the turbo sys-

tem, the boost should exceed (or at least be equal to) the exhaust back pressure over the RPM range. When this doesn't occur, the culprit can be a turbocharger that is too small.

The original LS7 engine's cam had 0.591/0.591-inch lift, 211/230 degrees duration, and 121-degree LSA specs. Katech Performance used a camshaft with greater lift (0.615/0.613-inch) to maximize airflow, slightly more intake valve duration (220 degrees), and less exhaust valve duration (229 degrees). The cam's LSA was also dialed back to a more appropriate 116 degrees.

The reason a turbo engine needs less duration than the supercharger cam is because the turbocharger itself is an exhaust restriction that increases exhaust gas pressure; it's the exhaust gas pressure that spins the turbo. Therefore, a milder cam with lower duration helps exploit boost-enhancing exhaust gas pressure.

A supercharged engine's boost is generated at the front of the engine's air stream, so a cam with greater duration than what would be used

The LSX iron cylinder block can be machined for a Jesel belt-drive timing-belt system.

with a turbo engine helps expel exhaust gases more completely, clearing the chamber and promoting unrestricted airflow. But as COMP Cams' Billy Godbold pointed out, the camshaft for any forced-induction engine should have less overlap to prevent boost from escaping through the exhaust port.

An important note about the samples given: They are meant to provide an illustrated comparison and shouldn't be considered recommendations for any LS forced-induction engines. Factors determining the

LS Engine Factory Camshaft Specifications			
Camshaft	Lift Intake/ Exhaust (inches)	Duration (at 0.050 degrees)	Lobe-Separation Angle
LS1 (1998–2000)	0.497/0.498	202/210	116
LS1 (2001–2002)	0.467/0.479	197/208	116
LS6 (2001)	0.525/0.525	207/218	116
LS6 (2002–2004)	0.551/0.547	207/217	117
LS2	0.525/0.525	207/217	116
LS3	0.551/0.522	204/211	116
LS7	0.591/0.591	211/230	121
LS9	0.562/0.558	211/230	122.5
LSA	0.480/0.480	198/216	122.5
LQ9 (truck engine)	0.479/0.467	207/196	116
L92 (truck engine)	0.500/0.492	195/201	116
LS Hot Cam (GM Performance Parts)	0.525/0.525	219/228	112

A carefully selected camshaft will complement the airflow attributes of the supercharger or turbocharger system to maximize efficiency and build more power. The camshaft, however, shouldn't be selected blindly. It should be discussed with a specialist who understands the engine displacement, cylinder head selection, and power adder capacity, as well as the primary use of the engine.

I spoke with COMP Cams' Billy Godbold about selecting the right camshaft for a supercharged or turbocharged LS engine. And while he points out that every combination is unique, there are guidelines to get you started in the right direction. Here's what he had to say:

How should a builder approach camshaft selection for a forced-induction LS engine?

The more complete a picture the builder has of the project and its intended use, the better the component selection will be. That includes details such as the true RPM range the engine will perform. For example, is it primarily a street car

or a race car? Answering that question is why good cam guys ask so many questions about gear ratios, transmission type, tire size, vehicle weight, and converters.

Many people have a hard time setting out a good plan. They want the 10,000-rpm Pro Stock cam but also want to cruise coast-to-coast down the interstate at 1,800 rpm. You generally can't have it both ways. The engine needs to be built around a given RPM range and application; that's what separates the really great combinations from the merely good and not-so-good engines.

The second part is as simple as the first: Go to people you trust and take their advice. I'll pick a camshaft for myself, but not the ignition, transmission, converter, induction system, pistons, rods, rings, or radiator. I go to the experts in those fields for advice. Even the best builders in the world rely on others for parts selection, but often it's the novice or inexperienced builder who fails to seek advice. Don't worry about sounding like you don't know everything about building an engine. Few people do. That's why we (and other companies) have a staff of professionals to help.

Cam Talk *(Continued)*

Generally speaking, how do LS engines respond with superchargers and turbochargers?

A typical LS1 combination will run well to about 6,000 to 6,500 rpm with very similar intake and exhaust duration. With a blower, you'll typically want to add 4 to 12 degrees of duration to the exhaust. With the rectangular-port heads (even with normal aspiration), the LS3 and L92 engines want more than 8 degrees added to the exhaust. Both the cathedral [LS1/LS6-style] and rectangular heads will respond very well to camshaft changes, but they should be "cammed" carefully to match the airflow characteristics of the cylinder heads.

Does a camshaft swap make a meaningful difference on an otherwise-stock engine that has a bolt-on supercharger or turbo kit?

Yes. LS heads flow great when compared with older overhead-valve V-8 heads. Including a modern camshaft design tailored to the application's intended use makes the combination that much better. A great cam selection will not match a blower in terms of power improvement, but it is common to see as great a gain in changing the cam with a supercharged engine as it is changing the cam in a normally aspirated engine.

How does the camshaft affect the performance of a supercharged or turbocharged engine?
And how does the addition of a blower or turbo affect performance relative to the camshaft?

Essentially, boost is the resistance to flow. It is common in blown applications to go to a better head and see a drop in boost (even with the same pulleys) but see a substantial increase in horsepower. Basically, the head change made it easier for the engine to breathe.

On turbocharged and supercharged engines, we see similar improvements when the proper camshaft is selected. Clearly, if you force air into the engine, you make more power and operate at a higher RPM. However, if you tune the valve events for the forced-induction system and the correct RPM, everything is just that much better; both power and airflow will increase.

Generally speaking, you need more duration in a normally aspirated application than a supercharged or turbocharged engine operating at the same RPM if you are selecting the cam for peak power or a specific, smaller operating window.

What are the attributes that make a good blower cam (i.e., overlap, lobe separation, etc.)?

A blower grind does not need overlap to provide a signal from the exhaust to the intake, so these cams typically have less overlap. However, as soon as you open the intake, air will start flowing into the combustion chambers. While it might not always be the case in a normally aspirated engine, blowers would love an infinitely fast camshaft profile if it were stable. Going to the most aggressive profile that is stable in the intended RPM window will make the best power.

Because charge is lost through the exhaust when both valves are open, blower cams typically have a few degrees of wider lobe separation. This is most important when the blower is operating near the airflow limit. If you have extra blower capacity, a little extra overlap is less of an issue. With centrifugal superchargers, we tend to run smaller intake profiles to maximize low-speed torque but couple them with larger exhaust profiles to reduce exhaust-pumping loss at higher RPM.

With positive displacement camshafts [Roots-type, Lysholm-type, etc.], low-speed torque is generally not a problem. With those applications, we can run larger camshafts that do not need to "cheat" the exhaust side as much.

So generally speaking, with centrifugal blowers we try to make torque with the camshaft and power with the blower. And with the positive-displacement blowers, we let the blower give us the torque and we make sure we give it enough camshaft to run at high engine speed.

What about lift and duration?

It's hard to make a general statement because each application is different, but we jokingly like to say, "As much duration as you need and all the lift the engine will take without throwing parts through the valve covers."

Seriously, the guidelines discussed above will serve you well with street blowers. With LS engines, keep in mind that a positive-displacement blower tends to make the camshaft act smaller at idle, due to reversion not making [its way] backward through the blower. So, you get less of a negative effect of the camshaft in the mid-240 range [degrees of duration]. Also, with a good centrifugal system, you can make surprising power with a "small" performance grind that may only be in the low 230s at 0.050 inch on the intake side.

The most important thing is speaking with a technical representative from your cam company to make sure he understands your engine specifications and performance goals. You don't want to guess. Make sure the cam is tailored to your engine.

Does COMP Cams have a standard blower cam?

It has a number of blower grinds for various applications. Its LS-R cam series has several that are appropriate for supercharged engines. It's best, however, to speak with someone before ordering a camshaft.

How does a camshaft for a turbocharged engine differ from a supercharged engine?

They are very different. The pressure drop across the combustion chamber (comparing intake manifold pressure to the pressure in the exhaust headers) is very great, but it can be all over the board with a turbocharged engine. Some of the newer turbo systems have mild backpressure, but some may have three times the amount of backpressure than boost. In some ways, turbo systems are like normally aspirated engines with great cylinder heads. Regardless, there are very different things going on with the valve timing points in a turbo engine. Again, speak to your camshaft rep and spell out all of the turbo system's specs to select the best grind.

How important is the cylinder head with a camshaft and forced induction?

Of course, airflow absolutely matters, but it's true that a blower or turbo will make just about any cylinder head perform better. That said, matching the cam means knowing how the heads flow, as you can use less duration with a better-flowing head. ∎

"perfect" camshaft grind include the size of the supercharger or turbo compressor, the displacement of the engine, cylinder-head changes over stock, and even the type of performance expected (i.e., street, street/strip, or dedicated racing).

Ignition and the Crank Trigger Conversion

The production-style coil-near-plug ignition system is surprisingly good for even moderately high boost pressure (up to about 12 to 15 pounds) and horsepower levels up to about 1,000. As boost pressure increases, a higher-energy spark system is required because the higher pressure can effectively blow out the spark before it can jump the gap on the spark plug (much like trying to light a match in the wind). A few aftermarket companies, including MSD Ignition and ACCEL, offer replacement coil packs that provide greater energy than GM's factory units. That greater energy helps light the mixture under pressure while also ensuring a more complete burn.

The production-style individual-coil system works very well for even heavily modified engines making up to 1,000 hp or more. Aftermarket coils, such as these from MSD Ignition, provide more energy that is helpful on engines with higher boost levels.

ACCEL is another source for hotter-than-stock ignition coils. The greater energy helps the flame of the spark withstand boost pressure that wants to blow it out, much like blowing out a match.

When the individual coil system reaches its limit, the only alternative is a conventional distributor-driven ignition system. GM Performance Parts offers the conversion kit, which mounts to the front of the engine (part number 88958679). A conventional distributor, such as the front-mount type for a Ford Windsor small-block, is used with it.

On racing engines, where high boost and high RPM define the engine's primary operating parameters (those making approximately 1,500 hp and more) the sequentially triggered individual-coil system has neither the energy nor speed to deliver adequate and dependable ignition control, even when using hotter aftermarket coils. The alternative is converting the engine from the production-style crank-triggered system to a conventional distributor-based system that is also linked to a high-energy coil.

Fortunately, the tools for the conversion are already on the market, thanks to circle track series that require distributor-driven ignition systems. To support them, GM Performance Parts offers a conversion kit (part number 88958679) that happens to be perfect for force-inducted racing engines. The kit provides the distributor-mounting fixture for the front of the engine, as well as the distributor drive gear that is attached to the camshaft. From there, a standard distributor and coil are used.

"It's the only way to ensure adequate spark energy with the cylinder pressure and speed that the engine achieves so quickly," says experienced LS engine builder Brian Thomson. "The factory coil system is very good for even 1,000-hp combinations, but at this level, something stronger is needed."

Intake Manifold

In a general sense, the intake manifold doesn't have as great of an impact on the output of a forced-induction engine because the boost pressure largely overrides a manifold's plenum volume and runner design. That said, the intake should offer low restriction and a straight path to the combustion chambers.

For vehicles used primarily on the street, a production-style intake manifold with greater plenum volume helps maintain low-end torque for greater low-speed drivability on the street when the engine isn't under boost. Bolt-on centrifugal supercharger and turbo kits (even those used on modified, purpose-built short-block assemblies) perform very well on the street and drag strip with production intake manifolds, including factory-style intakes from aftermarket companies, such as FAST.

Systems employing a Roots-type or twin-screw supercharger will feature a dedicated manifold on which the compressor is installed, eliminating the need for adapting a factory or aftermarket manifold. Some of these systems also incorporate a charge cooler within the manifold, augmenting an external heat exchanger, much like the factory systems from General Motors, to optimize air-charge cooling.

Vehicles designed primarily for drag racing, where the engine will spend most of its time at higher RPM, benefit from a carbureted-type "spider" aluminum manifold that has shorter, direct, and straight intake runners. These manifolds are readily available from several aftermarket companies, as well as GM Performance Parts. Using one with a high-boost turbo or supercharger system requires an adapter and/or elbow on top of the manifold, as well as an intake tube, to feed the manifold.

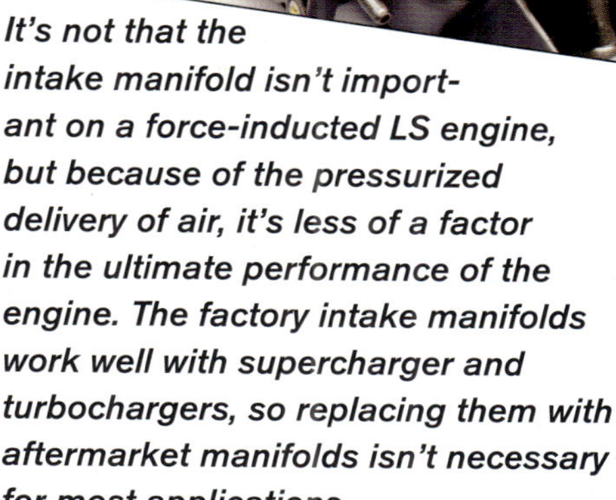

It's not that the intake manifold isn't important on a force-inducted LS engine, but because of the pressurized delivery of air, it's less of a factor in the ultimate performance of the engine. The factory intake manifolds work well with supercharger and turbochargers, so replacing them with aftermarket manifolds isn't necessary for most applications.

The use of a carbureted-style aluminum intake manifold comes with racing applications that will see very high boost pressure and require custom plumbing to route large-diameter tubing through the engine compartment.

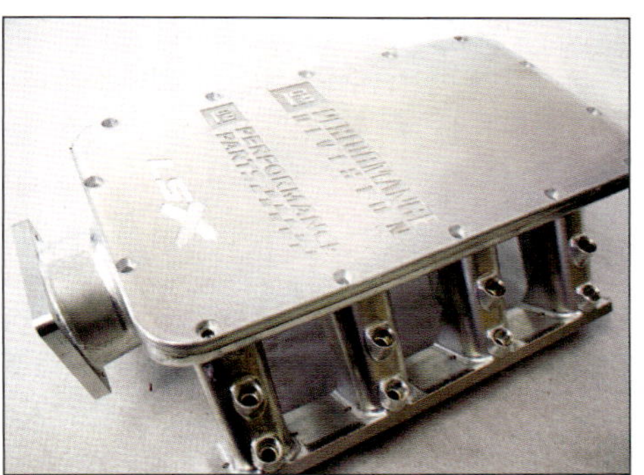

This impressive-looking tunnel ram–style intake has a fatal flaw for high-boost forced induction: as air rushes through the front of the manifold under pressure, it packs into the rear intake runners, leaving the front runners relatively starved. A better solution would be to introduce the air at the top of the manifold, where the airflow would be better spread among the runners.

These are generally custom-built parts, as the engines that employ such induction systems are typically custom built.

When selecting a spider-type intake manifold, be sure to match it with the cylinder head intake-port design. The manifolds are designed to match the cathedral-port and different rectangular-port configurations of LS heads. Also, adapter plates are needed (perhaps requiring cus-

The intake manifold for positive-displacement supercharger systems is the foundation for the compressor, and the latest kits (such as this Harrop system with Eaton 2650 rotors) incorporate the charge cooler.

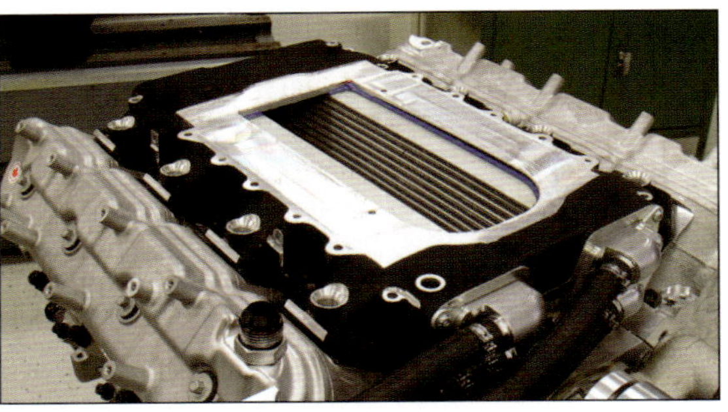

With the compressor housing removed, the charge cooler within the Harrop manifold is visible. The compressed air generated by the supercharger is forced through the cooling bricks before flowing into the cylinder heads. The charge cooling is necessary to stave off detonation, but it's a restriction that ultimately reduces max boost.

This photo shows a typical racing setup that uses a carbureted-style intake with an elbow designed to accept the injection system's throttle body. The aluminum intake also provides a measure of safety for high-boost engines, as the cast aluminum is less likely to shatter than the brittle nylon material of a production intake.

This cutaway look at a Magnuson positive-displacement supercharger housing shows charge-cooling bricks mounted above the rotors, which is the design employed on GM's factory-supercharged engines such as the LS9.

Turbocharged and centrifugally supercharged engines are blow-through systems, where the pressurized and intercooled air charge is forced into the intake manifold rather than the draw-through design of positive-displacement supercharger systems.

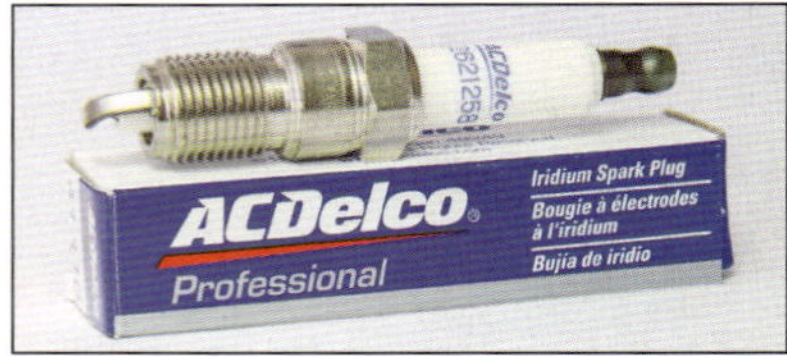

Spark plugs with a colder heat range are essential in a force-inducted engine build to help prevent detonation. There's not a universal rating for heat ranges, so the builder must compare the heat ranges for each manufacturer's plugs.

tom fabrication in some cases) when using any intake manifold with a tall-deck cylinder block, as the heads are pushed out farther than on an engine with a standard-deck block.

For safety reasons, an aluminum or sheet metal intake should also be considered for racing-oriented engine combinations that will see 20 pounds of boost or more. Rather than being cast as a single part, the nylon/plastic production-style intake manifolds are generally comprised of multiple pieces that are assembled with adhesive bonding agents. They weren't designed for the extreme pressure that comes with high boost and inadvertently discovering the pressure point at which the components separate or the brittle nylon material shatters is not something a racer wants to discover on the starting line.

Throttle Body

The throttle body must be compatible with the engine control module, particularly when using a GM controller that is calibrated for either a cable-operated or electronic throttle. For most street/strip combinations of up to 1,000 hp or so, a production GM throttle body (such as LS7's large, 90-mm unit) works

and flows just fine.

Aftermarket throttle bodies of 100 mm and larger are available but must be port-matched with the intake manifold or intake elbow for optimal performance. These large throttle bodies can present some low-speed drivability challenges in street vehicles as well, even with excellent tuning. It can be a trade-off in the quest for maximum horsepower.

It is possible to adapt an electronically controlled throttle to a vehicle originally equipped with a conventional cable throttle and vice versa, but modifications are required, including changing the engine controller and pedal assembly, and is generally not worth the time. If the vehicle was originally equipped with a cable throttle, use a larger, cable-actuated throttle body if necessary; and if the vehicle came with an electronic throttle, continue using the same type.

Fortunately, GM cable-operated and electronic throttle bodies are generally interchangeable on intake manifolds, so a cable throttle body can be used on an LS7 intake manifold, allowing for example, this high-flow intake to be used in a fourth-generation F-Body with a cable-operated throttle system.

Dedicated race cars should use a

cable throttle for maximum driver control. In fact, for safety reasons, many sanctioning bodies require it. Also, the airflow requirements of a 1,500- to 2,000-hp engine can't be met with current production-based electronic throttle bodies. See chapter 7 for more information on throttle-body considerations.

Electronic Throttle Bodies and Blow-Off Valves

Some builders have reported a condition with supercharged LS engines that use electronically controlled throttle bodies where excessive boost pressure pushes on the throttle blade after it is closed (such as when the driver takes his or her foot off the gas), forcing unwanted air into the engine. At the least, it can cause stumbling and other drivability issues, but it could also lead to engine damage if the excessive airflow causes a lean condition.

The problem can be due to an inadequate supercharger blow-off valve (in many cases, the issue has been reported with Eaton-type Roots superchargers) that doesn't bleed off enough boost pressure when the throttle closes. It can also be due to a throttle body with a throttle blade spring that doesn't have sufficient strength to keep the blade closed. Or

Cable-operated throttle bodies are manufactured in a number of very large sizes to suit high-power racing engines, but options for engines with electronically controlled throttles are limited. Some companies offered ported and modified versions of production throttle bodies, but their effectiveness is limited, as they simply don't offer a significantly larger flow path for the air charge.

The 90-mm electronic throttle body found on LS7 and LS9 engines (they are of similar diameters but not the same part) is sufficient for 6.2L-and-smaller engines making up to approximately 1,000 hp. With larger-displacement engines, the airflow requirements are greater and the 90-mm unit runs out of breath around the 750- to 800-hp level.

it could be a combination of both issues.

Some enthusiasts have had success swapping the throttle body with a strong factory unit, such as the LS3 unit from the C6 Corvette; however, it requires additional tuning to match the throttle body with the engine controller. A stronger or larger bypass valve is another solution.

Fuel Injectors

In a turbocharged or supercharged combination, matching the engine with fuel injectors tailored for the projected power output is just as important as a set of forged pistons. They are typically sized in pounds-per-hour measurements, such as 24 pounds, 36 pounds, etc. The sizes are based on a general operating fuel-pressure rating of 43.5 psi for the LS-type port-injection system.

The appropriate size, or flow rate, is based on a number of factors, starting with the estimated horsepower output of the engine under maximum boost. Here's the formula:

Horsepower x brake specific fuel consumption (BSFC) / the number of injectors x the duty cycle

BSFC is the amount of fuel an

Building in adequate crankcase ventilation is important for a force-inducted LS engine, as excessive blowby can be an issue. Here, the breather port in a production rocker cover has been enlarged to accept a −12 fitting for a large-capacity breather.

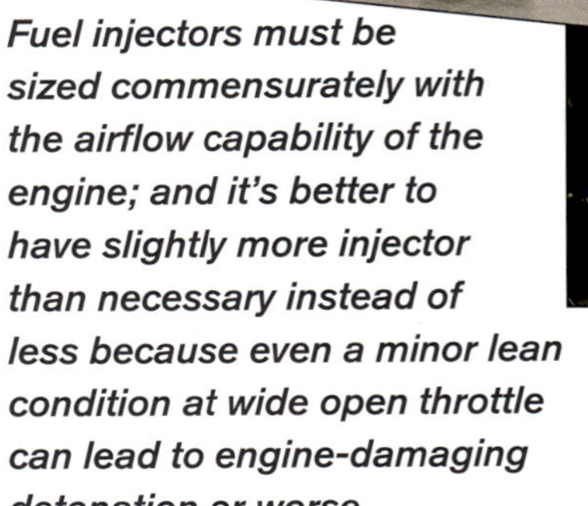

Fuel injectors must be sized commensurately with the airflow capability of the engine; and it's better to have slightly more injector than necessary instead of less because even a minor lean condition at wide open throttle can lead to engine-damaging detonation or worse.

engine needs to make 1 hp for 1 hour. Generally speaking, that's between 0.40- and 0.60-pound per hour, with forced-induction applications at the high end of the range. A 0.55 BSFC rate is used for the following calculations. The duty cycle is the approximate load on the engine. Most injector calculations use a duty cycle between 80 and 85 percent. In other words, the injectors are delivering fuel 80 to 85 percent of the time. An 0.85-percent duty cycle is cited in the following calculations.

The equation for an estimated 500-hp (at the flywheel) engine with eight fuel injectors would look like this:

$$500 \times 0.55 / 8 \times 0.85 = 40.44$$

Rounding up to the nearest standard injector rating is 42 lbs/hr.

Larger injectors work in the application, and if additional engine modifications are expected, installing 60-pound injectors or slightly larger injectors would be fine.

Generally speaking, 60-pound injectors are suitable for engines up to about 700 to 750 hp. After that, 72- to 83-pound injectors work up to about 900 hp. As power approaches 1,000

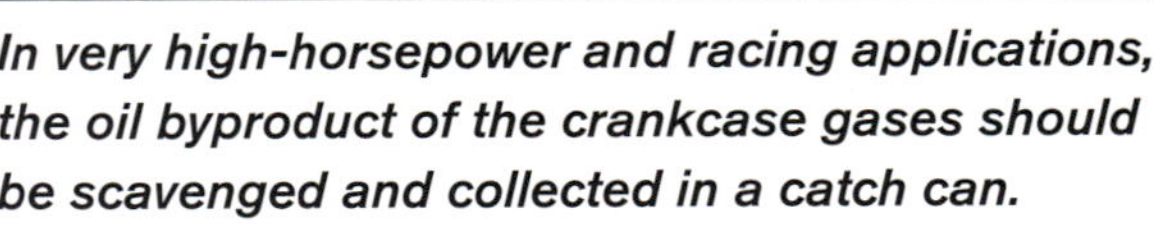

In very high-horsepower and racing applications, the oil byproduct of the crankcase gases should be scavenged and collected in a catch can.

hp and beyond, even-larger-capacity injectors are required.

A Word About LS Injectors

From the factory, LS engines have used three injector types:

- LS1 and LS6 engines used tall injectors with a Minitimer type of harness connector
- LS2 and some other 6.0L engines used tall injectors with the newer-style USCAR harness connector
- LS3/LS7/L92 engines used a short injector with the USCAR connector

The injector types are interchangeable among all engines, but those included with a blower or turbo kit may not match the engine's wiring harness. If that is the case, adapter kits are available from FAST. They include jumper harnesses with a Minitimer connector on one end and a USCAR connector on the other.

IMPORTANT! Do not attempt to start an engine with upgraded fuel injectors until the engine-control computer has been flashed with new tuning data that includes the new injectors' specifications. Doing so almost immediately fouls the spark plugs and could lead to other problems or engine damage. Start the engine only after new injector data has been programmed into the controller.

ENGINE BUILD PROJECTS

A look at a couple of real-world engine builds (supercharged and turbocharged) wrap up this book's look at boosting the versatile and capable LS engine platform. Both of the engines outlined in this chapter were developed primarily for street use but with the capability for drag racing. To that end, they were designed with lower compression ratios and fuel systems intended for high-octane pump gas.

Each of the combinations uses primarily off-the-shelf components with designs and power ratings that are easily repeatable, and each demonstrates the capability builders can expect with attention to detail in the engine build and careful tuning on the dyno. Both engines were assembled and tested by LS engine guru Brian Thomson.

Pictured is the LS7-based 7.0L engine with the LS9 Roots-type supercharger with TVS 2300 rotors.

The standard cylinder block for the 7.0L LS7 is the foundation for Thomson's LS7/LS9 hybrid engine and is available through Chevrolet Performance (part number 19213580). It's aluminum with pressed-in steel bore liners and forged-steel main-bearing caps; the bores measure 4.125 inches in diameter.

Machine work prior to assembly included deck plate honing of the cylinders and line boring of the crankshaft mains. They're common high-performance engine-building procedures with the line boring supporting the addition of ARP main studs.

To reduce piston temperatures (especially under boost), Thomson Automotive machined the cylinder block to accept oil squirters, similar to what's standard in the production LS9 engine. See chapter 8 for more details on installing oil squirters.

Supercharged Engine Build

Engine Build Basics	
Displacement	427 ci (7.0L)
Cylinder block	LS7 aluminum
Cylinder heads	LS9 roto-cast aluminum
Compression ratio	9.0:1
Power adder	LS9 supercharger (TVS 2300 rotors)
Horsepower (hp)	769 at 5,800 rpm
Torque (ft-lbs)	844 at 4,000 rpm

LS engine builder Brian Thomson has spent the better part of a decade refining the ultimate factory-based hybrid engine combination: marrying the blower from the C6 Corvette ZR1's LS9 engine with the larger-displacement LS7 found in the C6 Z06 and Gen V Camaro Z28.

In fact, Thomson has built so many of this dynamic combination, it's basically a crate engine package for his customers. There's much to like with it, starting with the 13-percent increase in displacement the 7.0L foundation delivers over the factory LS9's 6.2L. With a couple of tweaks, including a smaller blower pulley to increase boost, the engine is good for around 770 hp on pump gas.

"It's a sweetheart of a street engine," says Thomson. "It starts, idles, and has the low-speed drivability of a stock engine, but when you tap into it, it's amazing. With more than 800 ft-lbs and the instant power delivery of the blower, it's an engine with two distinct personalities."

The version depicted here officially made 769 hp and 844 ft-lbs, with a safe AFR of about 11.4:1 under full boost. Thomson says that more-aggressive tuning will easily yield significantly more horsepower, but he tends toward the conserva-tive side of things for customers who will use the engine primarily for the street and only a few annual trips to the drag strip.

"The 20 or so horsepower we give up with a richer mixture are hardly missed when you've got 840 ft-lbs to deal with and instant boost," says Thomson. "It's a no-brainer setup for pump gas, but you can certainly tweak it."

The Bottom End

While the LS7 is the source of the engine's short-block, Thomson only uses the block and crankshaft, and even the crankshaft is replaced if the customer doesn't plan to use the factory dry-sump-styling oiling system. That's the case here; the engine received a conventional wet-sump system, so Thomson installed a Callies forged crank. After that, the rods and pistons were replaced and the camshaft was swapped for one with Thomson's own specifications.

There are a couple of good reasons why Thomson replaces the stock rods and pistons. For one, the featherweight titanium connecting rods of the LS7 simply aren't designed for the load, stress, and horsepower range of the supercharged engine. They're strong but relatively brittle. Instead, a set of Oliver Racing Parts forged I-beam rods is used.

As for the stock pistons, their hypereutectic (cast) material causes concern in a supercharged application (the LS9 is the only LS engine with factory forged pistons), but they also deliver too much squeeze in the cylinders. The LS7 has a high 11.0:1 compression ratio, which is way too much for a street-driven blower engine. In their place, a set of Diamond forged-aluminum pistons were used, each with a sizable dish to help lower the compression to a more manageable 9.0:1.

Airflow

Thomson uses LS9 heads on the engine rather than the higher-flow LS7 heads because the intake ports on the LS9 supercharger don't match the LS7 ports. That's not a detriment, however, because when the boost level is up, the blower is supplying all the airflow the heads can manage. And fortunately, the LS9 heads are based on the admirable L92 design but feature swirl-inducing wings cast into the intake ports for better mixture motion.

Another thing going for the LS9 heads is their superior construction. They're manufactured with a roto-cast method that spins the mold while the aluminum is poured, resulting in more even material flow and almost no chance of porosity. They're also made from a stronger, A356T6 alloy than other LS heads that should help them withstand warping and other heat-related issues.

Straddling the heads, of course, is that big Eaton Twin-Vortices blower with four-lobe rotors. Because it was developed for the factory LS9's 6.2-liter displacement, it wouldn't provide the same maximum boost on the 13-percent-larger 7.0L engine. So, Thomson made a new, smaller-diameter blower pulley and uses a stock-diameter ATI balancer/pulley. This allows the blower to spin faster and deliver about 14 pounds of maximum boost.

Dyno Notes

As we mentioned above, the engine produced 769 peak horse-

Although it was originally designed for a naturally aspirated engine, the LS7 camshaft works surprisingly well as a blower cam, thanks to its wide, 121-degree lobe-separation angle. Lift and duration specs include 0.558/0.558-inch lift and 211/230 degrees of duration.

power at 5,800 rpm and 844 ft-lbs of torque at 4,000 rpm. Those numbers were achieved with the engine directed by a GM E67 controller and blowing through stock LS7 exhaust manifolds, which Thomson prefers to headers in most cases.

"They have great flow attributes," he says. "GM did its homework designing them."

A broader look at the numbers reveals a great, broad torque curve. The engine made more than 800 ft-lbs by 3,000 rpm and held above that mark through 4,700 rpm. Similarly, the horsepower came on strong at lower RPM and carried through the entire RPM band. It made 500 hp at 3,200 rpm, 600 hp by only 3,800 rpm, and zoomed past 700 hp by 4,500 rpm. It kept rising from there all the way through 6,000 rpm.

According to Thomson, there's more horsepower on the table, too, because the electronic throttle body is restrictive on this engine combination. Using a GM 90-mm unit, the air pressure drop after the throttle body is about 12 kPa (about 1.7 psi). That indicates the engine isn't drawing enough air for maximum power.

"There are larger aftermarket throttle bodies out there, but the factory unit delivers great drivability," he says. "We give up perhaps 20 horsepower or so with the 90-mm throttle body, but the trade-off in daily drivability is worth it for most people."

More than a builder, Thomson is his own customer for this basic engine combo. He uses a larger-displacement version in his own 1972 Chevelle SS, where it makes 930 hp. The unique elements with it include a Concept Performance cylinder block (see chapter 8) with 4.130-inch bores and a longer 4.125-inch stroke, which takes displacement to 442 ci (8.0L). It also uses Chevrolet Performance LSX-LS7 six-bolt cylinder heads and a unique blower pulley combo to pump up boost to about 15 pounds (1.03 bar).

Displacement notwithstanding, it's a proven combination that makes excellent power across the RPM band and is as docile on the street as an airport rental car. When it comes to supercharged performance, it's a hard combo to beat.

A Callies forged-steel crankshaft is used, delivering a 4.000-inch stroke that combines with the 4.125-inch bores to give the engine its 427-inch displacement. It's used with an LSA oil pump, which is a high-volume unit for a conventional wet-sump oiling system but doesn't require the longer-snout crankshaft of the dry-sump LS9 or LS7.

Stock LS engines (except LS9 and LSA) have press-fit dampers and consequently no keyway on the crankshaft. To prevent slippage at the boost and power levels this engine will be capable of, Thomson insists the crank is fitted with one.

Supercharged Dyno Results		
RPM	Ft-lbs	Horsepower (STP Correction)
3,000	807	461
3,100	814	480
3,200	822	501
3,300	826	519
3,400	829	537
3,500	831	554
3,600	833	571
3,700	837	590
3,800	839	607
3,900	842	625
4,000	**844**	643
4,100	843	658
4,200	841	672
4,300	839	687
4,400	834	699
4,500	826	708
4,600	817	716
4,700	807	722
4,800	796	727
4,900	786	733
5,000	771	734
5,100	759	737
5,200	749	742
5,300	740	747
5,400	731	752
5,500	723	757
5,600	717	765
5,700	707	768
5,800	697	**769**
5,900	683	768
6,000	672	768

Peak numbers in **bold**.

The LS7's cast-aluminum pistons were replaced to enhance strength under high cylinder pressure and reduce compression. Forged-aluminum, coated pistons from Diamond are used. They are dished to lower the compression ratio to a detonation-avoiding 9.0:1. The blower-specific pistons also have a thick crown and reinforced pin bosses.

The pistons' gold-colored top coating is a ceramic material that reduces heat absorbed by the pistons, which is a notable concern with a high-horsepower, supercharged engine. Also, the skirts of the pistons are Teflon-coated to reduce friction.

Forged I-beam rods (in the stock 6.067-inch length) are used in place of the LS7's titanium rods. The lightweight titanium rods simply aren't designed for the load and power levels of this engine. The effect of greater mass on the rotating assembly with heavier I-beams will be quickly offset with the rise in boost pressure under load.

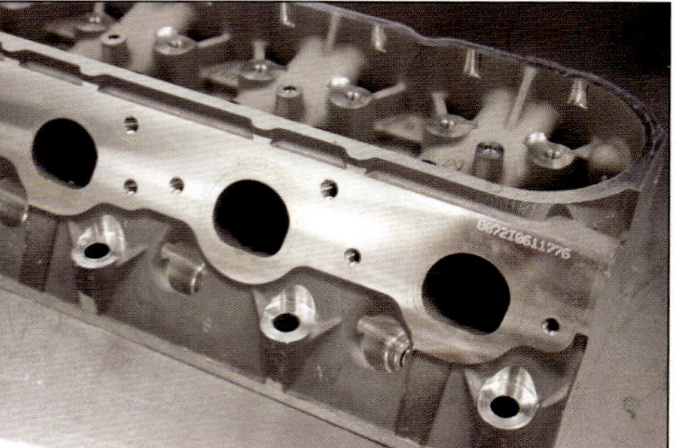

Interestingly, the larger-capacity LS7 cylinder heads aren't used but only because their intake ports didn't match those of the supercharger manifold. That made the factory LS9 heads the only real choice, which is fine because they're based on the high-flow L92 head and manufactured with a stronger alloy that helps them withstand the extra heat that comes with forced induction.

Valvetrain details read essentially like those for a stock LS9, including the stamped, non-roller 1.7:1-ratio rocker arms. The valve springs are matched to the camshaft specs.

Stock 2.16-inch titanium intake valves and aftermarket (but stock-size) 1.59-inch Inconel exhaust valves are used. The thermal properties of the Inconel valves better suit the higher combustion temperatures of a force-inducted engine.

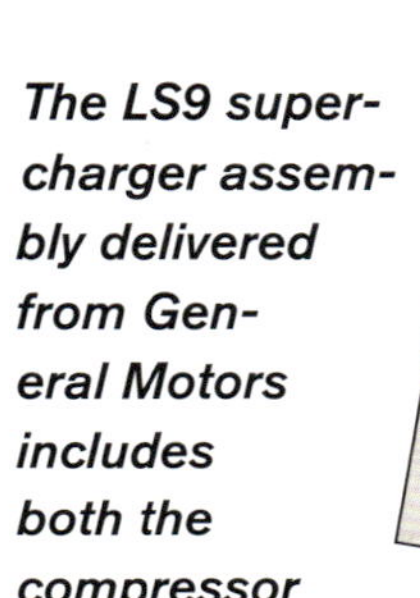

The LS9 supercharger assembly delivered from General Motors includes both the compressor

To align with the LS9 supercharger pulley, Thomson uses a complete LS9 front dress assembly, including the water pump, brackets, accessories (alternator, power steering), and pulleys. Even the LS9 valve covers must be used because the alternator and power-steering pump won't fit otherwise.

and an integrated liquid-to-air charge cooler mounted on top, along with the fuel rails, injectors, and throttle body already installed. The sixth-generation, TVS positive-displacement blower comes from Eaton and is its largest-ever Roots-type compressor, displacing a significant 2.3 liters per revolution.

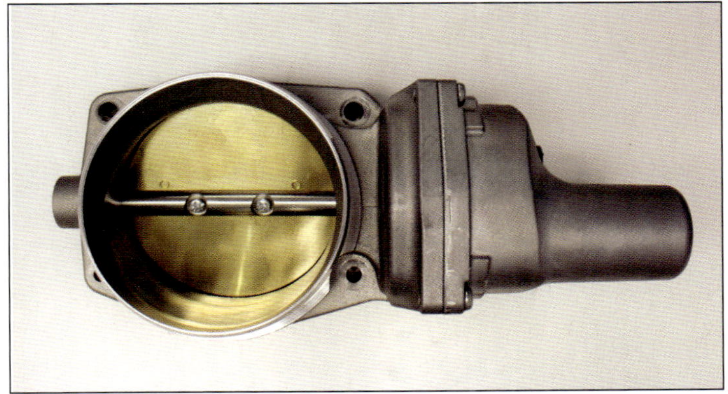

On the 6.2L LS9, the blower generates about 10.5 pounds of boost, but only about half of that with the 7.0L displacement, so Thomson machined a new, smaller-diameter pulley to spin the blower faster and bring the boost up to about 14 psi.

Despite larger aftermarket throttle bodies being available, Thomson sticks with the 90-mm GM unit for drivability and tuning reasons, although he admits the 90-mm throttle body is an airflow restriction for the engine. A 100-mm, or larger, throttle body would add about 20 hp.

The LS9 supercharger assembly comes with 48-lbs/hr fuel injectors. Thomson swaps them for higher-capacity, 65-lbs/hr injectors.

No detail is too small. The use of cold-range spark plugs is necessary to help stave off detonation. For this engine, it was a set of Autolite Racing 3933 plugs.

Here, the supercharger assembly is bolted in place. The factory 2.5-bar MAP sensor (seen at the rear of the intercooler cover) is used to ensure accurate air-pressure readings when the blower is making more than 10 pounds of boost. Engine mapping is controlled by a GM E67 controller from GM Performance Parts (part number 19201861).

Another pulley change involves the damper, which is sourced from ATI. Thomson machines a custom hub for it to mount on the crankshaft. Look closely and you'll see the pulley is divided; the wider section is connected to the blower and power-steering pump, while the narrower section is for a separate belt that drives the alternator and air-conditioning system. This engine won't use air-conditioning, so a custom idler pulley will be created.

With base timing of 27 degrees and 18 degrees under boost, along with 93-octane pump gas, the engine produced a best of 769 hp and 844 ft-lbs of torque with 13 pounds of boost. Under maximum boost, the AFR goes to about 11.4:1; plenty safe without sacrificing performance.

On the dyno, the engine was tested with factory LS7 exhaust manifolds. They make more power than headers but give up a few ft-lbs to headers, but with more than 840 of them on tap, they're not missed. Unfortunately, they only fit the C6 Corvette chassis.

The finished engine assembly includes a custom-painted intercooler lid and matching valve covers. Note, too, the original "LS9" designation on the lid is replaced with a custom displacement insignia.

Turbocharged Engine Build

Turbocharged Build Basics	
Displacement	427 ci (7.0L)
Cylinder block	LSX cast iron (standard deck)
Cylinder heads	LSX-LS7 aluminum
Compression ratio	9.0:1
Power adder	Twin 72-mm turbochargers
Horsepower (hp)	1,225 at 6,500 rpm
Torque (ft-lbs)	989 at 6,500 rpm

On the dyno, this 7.0L twin-turbocharged creation fires to life and idles at a docile, glass-smooth 650 rpm. No spurts, no sputters, and no hunting. After a few minutes, the oil gets up to temperature and the first serious pull is made. It kicks out 1,000 hp as if it were just waking up, yawning while stretching its arms. Builder Brian Thomson is nonplussed.

"It'll do more," he says, matter-of-factly. He was right. With a few more taps on the laptop, a fuel trim adjustment was made via the Holley Dominator EFI controller and the engine was ready for another pull. The 7.0L pump-gas engine (a mix of the very best custom aftermarket parts, such as ceramic-coated Diamond pistons and surprising off-the-shelf GM components, including AC Delco ignition coils) pulls harder than before, nearly

burying the big analog torque output dial on the dyno console. In fact, it swings past 900 ft-lbs so quickly, it would be easy to assume it was the tachometer.

"That's better," says Thomson. He was right again. The engine zoomed past the 1,200-hp threshold, still exhibiting the easy-going attributes you'd expect of a stock engine making only a quarter of the power. And while the best numbers of the day (1,225 hp and 989 ft-lbs of torque) are unquestionably impressive, the engine's performance was more notable for how *unimpressive* it was while achieving it. No drama whatsoever.

Sure, Thomson's twin-turbo 427 hardly holds the record for peak output from an LS engine, but it is nonetheless a testament to today's threshold of high performance. It's a strong example of what's possible for an entirely streetable turbo combination.

Simple Combination

At its core, the twin-turbo engine's combination is deceptively simple: an LSX block, LSX-LS7 heads, a not-so-radical camshaft grind, and a whole lot of boost via a pair of 72-mm Nelson Turbo Engines–supplied turbochargers. Of course, there's more to the assembly than the sum of its parts, and tolerances for every component were fastidi-

This twin-turbocharged LSX-based 7.0L engine produces more than 1,200 hp with a comparatively mild 12 pounds of boost.

The starting point for the engine is Chevy Performance's standard-deck LSX block (part number 19260093). Its iron construction makes it strong and affordable. It can also be generously overbored, which is something that can't be done with production aluminum blocks. More importantly, it has priority oiling and features provisions for six-bolt head clamping, which is essential for high-boost combinations.

ously measured with an eye on more than 1,000-hp capability. Thomson also installed a custom oil-squirter system for the pistons to ensure the pistons are cooler and well-lubricated under the intense cylinder pressure generated by 12 pounds of boost.

Along with six-bolt clamping, the LSX block also offers priority main oiling, which is a key safety

Align-honing was also performed on the block to get the main bearing journals sized just right for optimal clearance (and consequently optimal oiling for the bearings).

The 6.125-inch forged rods are hung on the crankshaft. They're fastened via the stretch method, which is a more accurate way of ensuring the proper preload and clamping force on the ARP bolts. Essentially, the bolt is stretched until it is within its sweet spot of elasticity, usually between 0.005 inch and 0.006 inch.

The LSX block comes with 3.880-inch semi-finished bores. Thomson finished them off to 4.125 inches. Deck plates are used during the procedure to simulate the slight but important distortion the block sees when the heads are bolted on. The block was also machined for piston oil squirters. See chapter 8 for more details on installing them.

A forged Callies DragonSlayer crankshaft is anchored in the block, delivering a 4.000-inch stroke, which combines with the 4.125-inch bores to give the engine its 427-ci displacement. A keyway was machined into the crankshaft nose because production LS engines don't have one; it's a must to prevent slippage on the damper with the high loads and quick engine spin up that will come under boost.

Forged-aluminum Diamond dished pistons are used with a heat-resistant ceramic coating on the heads and a friction-reducing Teflon coating on the skirts. The pistons are designed with thicker crowns for greater strength under boost and resistance to the effects of detonation. The dish in the piston is required to keep down the compression ratio to a boost-friendly 9.0:1.

factor in an engine that generates so much cylinder pressure and heat. As the term implies, it feeds the main bearings first in the oiling circuit, followed by the camshaft, lifters, etc., ensuring those critically important bearings receive adequate lubrication, particularly at high RPM.

The installation destination was a radical Camaro built by HS Customs in Logan, Utah. The shop mocked up the turbo system's layout in the car, so there wouldn't be any trial-and-error fitment after the engine was assembled. HS Customs then shipped the turbochargers, modified Stainless Works headers, and related plumbing to Thomson for assembly and dyno testing.

"We try lots of parts and fall back on the parts that have been proven to work the best for us," says Thomson. "It's hard to beat many of the GM parts for the money, and the ACDelco coils are better than the aftermarket parts we've tried."

He admits the boost and the 1,200-hp level are crowding the edge for a coil-on-plug ignition system.

"Those coils will handle the power capability, but it's the boost you have to be careful about at that level," says Thomson. "When you get to 15 pounds and beyond, the boost can blow out the spark like a candle. We're at a good place right now with the 12 pounds of boost, but if we were taking it much beyond that, we'd have to look at changing over to a distributor."

Holley Dominator Details

Tuning with a factory E67 controller has its limits, too, especially when it comes to high-power turbo combinations that rely on a boost controller and other accessories for optimal performance. So, Thomson gave up the mass-air-metered GM control system and went with Holley's self-learning Dominator EFI speed density system.

There's a lot to like with the Dominator system, and it starts with its relative simplicity. You can pretty much get the engine running as soon as you peck in the basics of the engine's displacement and injector size. There are also a number of basic fuel maps to use as a starting point.

"We've been using it for more than a year now and have had good success with it," says Thomson. "The self-learning capability is very helpful because it will make mapping adjustments automatically in certain situations, which can really save time."

The Dominator ECU will also control up to 24 injectors, multiple stages of nitrous, and the all-important boost controller on Thomson's twin-turbo build. It's also compatible with dual-channel wideband oxygen sensors.

"It's a good system for novice tuners, too," says Thomson. "There's a lot in there to help someone with little tuning experience to get a more basic engine combination up and running."

More on the Table

To be honest, the pair of 72-mm turbos used for this buildup is way more than the engine needs to make 1,200 hp, but they leave plenty of room to grow should the car's owner build up a tolerance to his Camaro's force-inducted thrust.

"With these turbochargers and the boost they're capable of, 1,600 hp is doable—and even more—but this is an engine for a street car with

The high-volume wet-sump oil pump (part number 12612289) used is for the LSA 6.2L supercharged engine. It was selected because it's a heavy-duty, high-volume pump and, as with Thomson's engine, it supports a piston oil-squirting system. It's thicker than a standard LS pump found on, say, an LS3, but it fits behind a stock front cover.

excellent drivability," says Thomson. "It idles smoothly and runs great on pump gas. We didn't observe any spark knock at the 12 pounds of boost we dialed in and still exceeded the horsepower target by 25 percent."

This is one of those engines that if you have to ask how much it cost to build, you can't afford it, but the civility of it on the street offers incalculable value. And when the time and opportunity comes to call up the boost, there are more than 1,200 horses raring to run.

Turbocharged Dyno Results		
RPM	**Ft-lbs**	**Horsepower (STP Correction)**
3,000	597	341
3,100	604	356
3,200	612	373
3,300	621	390
3,400	630	408
3,500	639	426
3,600	646	443
3,700	652	459
3,800	660	477
3,900	671	498
4,000	688	524
4,100	708	552
4,200	728	582
4,300	756	619
4,400	780	653
4,500	800	686
4,600	820	718
4,700	837	749
4,800	856	782
4,900	871	812
5,000	882	840
5,100	893	867
5,200	904	896
5,300	917	925
5,400	931	957
5,500	946	991
5,600	959	1023
5,700	969	1052
5,800	973	1074
5,900	971	1098
6,000	967	1105
6,100	966	1122
6,200	967	1142
6,300	972	1166
6,400	980	1195
6,500	**989**	**1225**
Peak numbers in **bold.**		

One of the attributes that makes the engine a sweetheart on the street is its moderate camshaft. It's a hydraulic roller from COMP Cams with 0.629/0.656-inch lift and 215/247 degrees duration at 0.050. It also has a wide lobe-separation angle of 121 degrees, which reduces overlap for better idle characteristics when the engine isn't making boost. It also helps reduce the chance for knock, which is much-appreciated when the engine is making boost.

Valvetrain details include PAC Racing dual-coil valve springs, titanium retainers, and production LS7 rocker arms with COMP Cams trunnions. The 580-pound springs (part number 1530) are rated for up to 0.750-inch lift and have a 1.284-inch outer diameter. The seat load is 160 pounds at 2.000-inch installed height. The LS7 rocker arms have a 1.7:1 ratio. A set of Trend 7.900-inch pushrods is also installed.

HS Customs scratch-built the plumbing, which includes Stainless Works headers that were sliced, diced, and put back together to mount the turbos in front of the engine. The 4-inch-diameter intake tubes funnel the pressurized air charge into a custom intake manifold. Because of the header routing, Thomson relocated some of the coil packs and insulated the plug wires to protect them from heat.

A pair of Nelson Racing Engines 72-mm water-cooled mirror-image turbochargers feeds a moderate 12 pounds of boost into the engine. The mirror-image design means one of the turbos spins counterclockwise, which enables a more-symmetrical installation under the hood.

The cylinder heads are Chevrolet Performance's LSX-LS7 six-bolt design. Like the production parts, they have the high-flow, 270-cc intake runners; 70-cc combustion chambers; and 2.200-inch titanium exhaust valves. The additional two head bolts per cylinder provides exceptional head clamping strength for forced-induction engines.

Complementing turbo-system components include a TiAL bypass on the intake tube. There are also a couple of TiAL 42-mm wastegates incorporated.

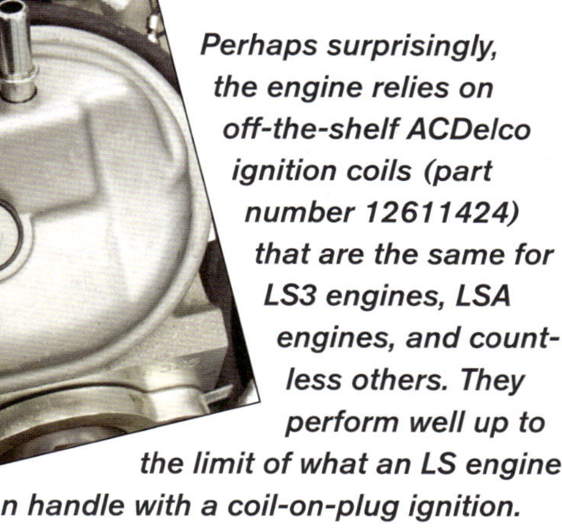

Perhaps surprisingly, the engine relies on off-the-shelf ACDelco ignition coils (part number 12611424) that are the same for LS3 engines, LSA engines, and countless others. They perform well up to the limit of what an LS engine can handle with a coil-on-plug ignition.

Complementing fuel-system components include a Holley Dominator 12-800 inline twin fuel pump, which supports up to 1,800 hp. It allows one pump to be used primarily for low-RPM driving and highway cruising with the second stage kicking in when the boost comes up. And by staging the second pump, recirculation and unnecessary heating of extra fuel is eliminated.

A custom intake manifold was fabricated for the engine. It is matched with an LS7 90-mm throttle body. It's also fitted with a set of 85-lbs/hr injectors to feed the force-fed 427 all the fuel it can take.

Engine management is controlled by the self-learning, speed-density Holley Dominator EFI system, which has the ability to run up to 24 fuel injectors, progressive nitrous control, and dual-channel wideband oxygen sensor compatibility. It also offers an integrated data-acquisition system.

There was no dyno drama with the twin-turbo engine. It idled smoothly at 650 rpm and ran easily up to 6,500 rpm, where it made 1,225 hp and 989 ft-lbs of torque. It crossed the 1,000-hp mark at 5,600 rpm and 800 ft-lbs at only 4,500 rpm, where the boost really started to come on strong.

SOURCE GUIDE

ACCEL
accel-ignition.com

ACCEL/DFI
accel-dfi.com

AiResearch Industrial Division
airflowreasearch.com

Alternative Auto Performance
alternativeauto.com

A'PEXi
apexi-usa.com

APS Performance
airpowersystems.com

Big Stuff 3's
bigstuff3.com

Bill Miller Engineering
bmeltd.com

Blower Drive Service
blowerdriveservice.com

BMR Fabrication
bmrfabrication.com

Callies DragonSlayer
callies.com

Carputing LLC
carputing.com

Cometic Gasket
cometic.com

COMP Cams
compcams.com

Diamond
diamondracing.net

Dynojet
dynojet.com

Edelbrock
edelbrock.com

Exedy
exedyusa.com

FAST
fuelairspark.com

Fastlane, Inc.
fastlaneincorporated.com

GM Performance Parts
gmperformanceparts.com

Harold Martin
haroldmartin.com

Harrop Engineering
harrop.com.au

HP Tuners
hptuners.com

JE Pistons
jepistons.com

Katech Performance
katechengines.com
katecheng.com

Kenne Bell
kennebell.net

Lingenfelter Performance Engineering
lingenfelter.com

Livernois Motorsports
livernoismotorsports.com

Magna Charger
magnacharger.com

Magnuson
magnusonproducts.com

Martin Motorsports
haroldmartin.com

MSD Ignition
msdignition.com

Mustang Dynamometer
mustangdyne.com

Northern Tool and Equipment
northerntool.com

Oliver
oliverconnectingrods.com

Powerdyne
powerdyne.com

Pratt & Miller
prattmiller.com

ProCharger
procharger.com

Pro-Filer
profilerperformance.com

Quaife
quaife.co.uk

Racing Head Service
rhsheads.com

RPM Transmissions
rpmtransmissions.com

SLP Performance
slponline.com

Snow Performance
snowperformance.net

Specter Werkes Sports
spectergtr.com

Squires Turbo Systems
ststurbo.com

Stenod Performance
stenodperformance.com

Strange Engineering
strangeengineering.net

Swain Tech Coatings
swaintech.com

T&D Machine Products
tdmach.com

Thomson Automotive
thomsonautomotive.com

TiAL
tialsport.com

Total Seal
totalseal.com

Trick Flow
trickflow.com

Turbonetics
turboneticsinc.com

Turbo Technology
turbotechnologyinc.com

Ultimate Performance and Racing
upandracing.com

Vortech
vortechsuperchargers.com

Whipple Industries
whipplesuperchargers.com

World Products
worldcastings.com

Yank Performance Converters
converters.cc